IMAGES
*of America*

# Lower Brazos River Canals

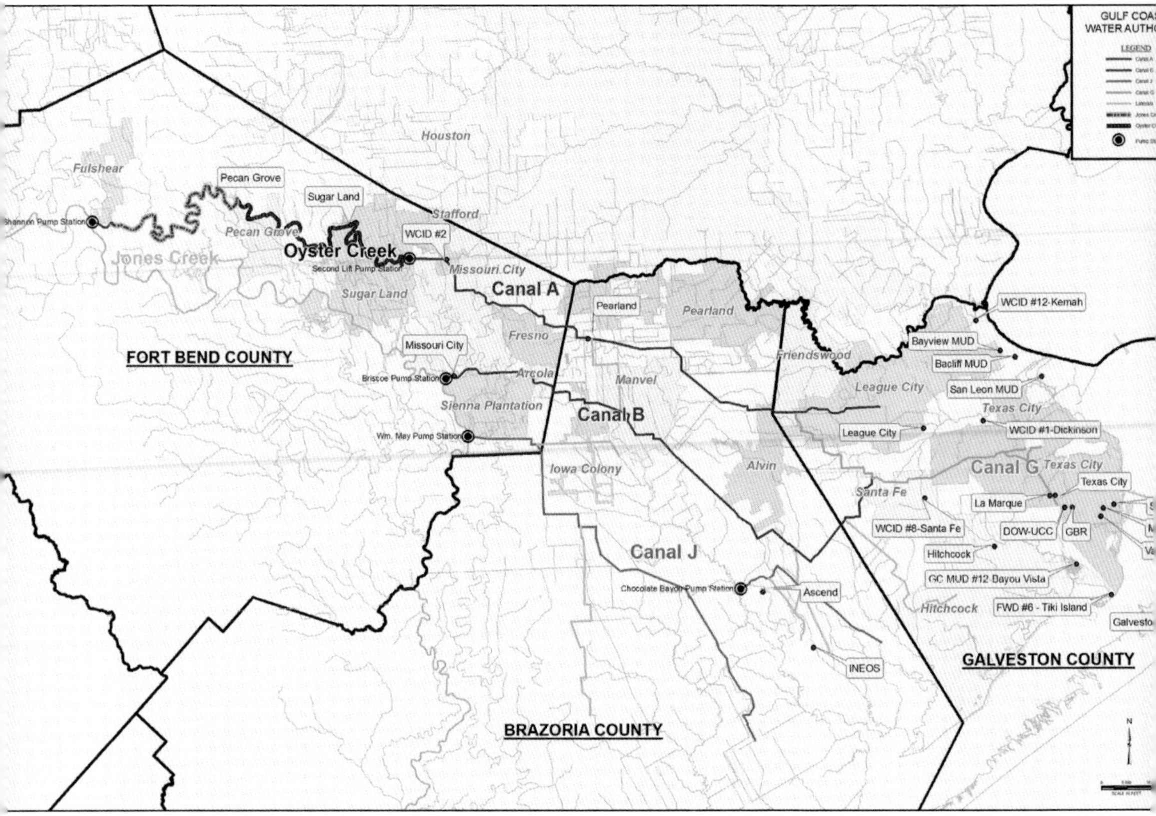


This map shows the Gulf Coast Water Authority Canal System, which takes water from the Brazos River and uses it to supply water to municipalities, industry, and agriculture throughout the southeast Houston region. (Courtesy of Gulf Coast Water Authority.)

ON THE COVER: The Brazos River is pictured at the turn of the 20th century in Sugar Land. (Courtesy of Fort Bend Museum.)

IMAGES
*of America*

# LOWER BRAZOS RIVER CANALS

Lora-Marie Bernard

ARCADIA
PUBLISHING

ISBN 978-1-4671-3224-4

Published by Arcadia Publishing
Charleston, South Carolina

Printed in the United States of America

Library of Congress Control Number: 2014933720

For all general information, please contact Arcadia Publishing:
Telephone 843-853-2070
Fax 843-853-0044
E-mail sales@arcadiapublishing.com
For customer service and orders:
Toll-Free 1-888-313-2665

Visit us on the Internet at www.arcadiapublishing.com

*In honor of my parents, Minchen and Paul;*
*my brother, Robbie;*
*but mostly just Bobby Gervais,*
*for making everything in my life mean something.*

# Contents


Acknowledgments 6

Introduction 7

1. Wrestling the Brazos 9
2. The Farm Crops and Ranch Cattle 21
3. The Sugar Bowl Plantations 31
4. Imperial Sugar 51
5. The Rice Belt 65
6. The River with Two Mouths 119

Bibliography 127

# ACKNOWLEDGMENTS

I made new friends and reconnected with old ones as a result of this book. It has been an immense pleasure to work with Michael Bailey, curator of Brazoria County Historical Museum and the staff, Jackie Haynes, Jamie Murray, George Easterling, Neal McLain, and Zach Stebbins. They swung their doors open and became my friends. What a great team at Gulf Coast Water Authority! Thanks so much to Ivan Langford, David Sauer, Juan Hernandez, Matt Chapman, Hank Adickes, and Joe Crow for their support. Just love you guys. My Arcadia publisher Jeff Ruetsche and editors Laura Bruns and Jared Nelson believed in me when I wasn't sure I could do this. Thank you for the confidence. I have to applaud the kind supportive assistance from Chris Godbold, curator of collections for the Fort Bend Museum and George Ranch Historical Park. I can never forget my sweet fan, Manvel mayor Delores Martin. Of course, Linda Turner, Texas City Museum curator, and her assistant Billie must be mentioned. Linda's friendship over the years is rock solid. The unconditional support and immense friendship from Tim Baker, Jay Carnes, and Lori Carnes must be heralded. Without their accommodations, I could not have done the book at all. Finally, I have to always thank Bobby Gervais for just being Bobby. Nothing ever matters without him. Unless otherwise noted, all images appear courtesy of the Brazoria County Historical Museum.

# Introduction

Oil fuels Texas, but water is its lifeblood. Without Texas's rivers, streams, bayous, and gulf coast, the Texas economy we know today would not exist. Fifteen major rivers create the foundation for Texas's water network. The Brazos River is the birthplace of Texas, the heart of the Sugar Bowl, and the center of the Rice Belt. The river is an engineering marvel since it has two mouths. The Brazos captures imaginations as it meanders 1,280 miles from its source to the gulf.

Texas's wettest river collects between 17 and 34 inches of rainfall per year. This abundant rainfall once caused massive flooding, but it also led to the creation of an important network of reservoirs, dams, lakes, and other water management systems that help to support the Texas economy.

The Brazos's lower basin's mighty presence and vast width make it a commanding community centerpiece. It's mentioned in many songs, such as Lyle Lovett's "Walk Through the Bottomland," "Texas River Song," and "Front Porch Song" and is also mentioned in Bruce Springsteen's "Across the Border." The 2010 Census reported its Houston–Woodlands–Sugar Land region to be the second fastest growing metropolitan area in the nation. This distinction is not necessarily unexpected, however. Texas was birthed on the lower Brazos River, and it has always attracted people looking for better lives.

The Karankawa Indians were the first to make the river's lower deltas their home. As they roamed the coastal prairies between Galveston and Corpus Christi, they would often travel the Brazos River. They would wander from Oyster Creek to the river mouth on the Gulf of Mexico as they searched for food, harvesting pecans, persimmons, and freshwater clams. Spanish explorer Alvar Nunez Cabeza de Vaca came upon the Karankawa at Oyster Creek in 1528, and lived among the tribe for six years while observing and noting their customs.

In 1543, a notable year in Texas oil history, the Karankawa came upon the survivors of DeSoto's ill-fated expedition near Galveston's Sabine Pass. The Karankawa knew that the coastal prairies harbored oil, as they often found it seeping up through the soil. They even used the oil that they found as medicine. But Luis de Moscoso, who led the Spanish expedition after DeSoto's death, had found oil floating in the water, and used it to caulk his boats. There are some reports that claim Moscoso and his men may have even reached the Brazos River, but if he did, none state where. Regardless, most reports agree that the Karankawa lived along the river and the coast without further Spanish or French interference until the late 1600s.

By 1690, documentation of the Brazos River had become confusing, resulting in the longest river in Texas being called by many names. According to the French explorer La Salle, the Indians called the Brazos by the name Tokohono, but in 1685, he was calling it the Maligne. Further problems arose when explorers confused the Brazos with the Colorado River, and vice versa. This issue became an important part of Texas history.

At the turn of the 18th century, explorers and settlers found a low point on Oyster Creek, which they used to travel between the coast and San Antonio de Bexar, the Spanish capital of Texas. The Spanish used the river so much that they named it the Brazos de Dios, or "Arms of God." By 1721, the Spanish navigated the Brazos more frequently than any other river in Texas. During this period, the Karankawa fought to defend their Tokohono River and coastal homelands. They battled French and Spanish explorers as they wound their way through the water routes. The Tonkawa and the Comanche peoples—allies of the Europeans—also warred against the Karankawa in this period.

In 1820, failed mining magnate Moses Austin saw in Texas an opportunity to rebuild his family's lost fortune. He trekked to San Antonio to ask the governor if he could establish a colony of Anglo-American settlers in the Texas area. The governor, Antonio María Martínez, initially met the request with disdain, but, through the lucky intervention of a mutual friend, the plan was eventually approved. Moses Austin began preparations to settle his colony on the Colorado River, but died soon after returning home from San Antonio.

In July 1821, Moses's son Stephen F. Austin chose to fulfill his father's dream of establishing a colony in Texas, but decided to settle along the Brazos River rather than the Colorado, noting the area's fertile soil and abundant populations of deer and black bear. In the following month, Stephen F. Austin became the impresario, or manager, of the endeavor, and began plans to move 300 Roman Catholic families to the river settlement.

During the next two years, Austin gathered families and arranged to meet a boat, the *Lively*, at the mouth of the Colorado to begin work on the colony. Unfortunately, the *Lively* made a navigational error and came to shore at the mouth of the Brazos. William W. Little and Joseph Polly led 15 men 90 miles upstream, and established a settlement that they called the "Fort on the Bend," or "Fort Bend." Because the *Lively* never reached the Colorado River, Austin presumed that the ship and its passengers were lost at sea. Life was hard for the settlers, but they successfully constructed Fort on the Bend without Austin. In August 1822, the settlers experienced their first Texas drought, and named themselves the "Forlorn Fifteen." Along the way, they heard—and believed—persistent rumors of Austin's death.

The two groups reconnected in the following year. As a result, the Mexican government (Mexico had declared independence from Spain in the intervening time between Moses Austin's audience with Governor Martínez and the establishment of the colony) approved a grant of 15,000 square miles for Austin's Colony, situated between the Brazos and Colorado Rivers. In 1824, Austin gave himself 22.5 leagues, or 99,630 acres, of that grant. Of that amount, five leagues, or 22,140 acres, were located on Oyster Creek. Austin later released his claimed land to others.

In 1830, the Mexican government stopped colonization efforts in the area, and a new era in Texas history began: the Texas Revolution. The city of Velasco, located at the mouth of the Brazos, became the second port in Texas to perform customs inspections. When settlers tried to bring a cannon through the port to help upstream colonists on June 26, 1831, the "Battle of Velasco" ensued. On March 6, 1836, the Texas Declaration of Independence was signed by members of the Convention of 1836 in Washington-on-the-Brazos, a township in the lower basin of the Brazos. Washington-on-the-Brazos is now a historical site, and is located in an unincorporated section of Washington County.

On April 17, 1837, Velasco became the site of the Battle of the Brazos River, a conflict between the Texan and Mexican navies. The battle, between the Texan schooner *Independence* and two Mexican brigs, ended with the eventual capture of the *Independence* and her crew. A number of injuries resulted from the battle along with several deaths, but there was little serious damage to the ships on either side.

Several months before the battle, however, the Brazos had served as the burial route for the "Father of Texas." In December 1836, Stephen F. Austin died from pneumonia in Columbia, which was the state capital at the time. Following his death, the steamship *Yellowstone* carried his body down the river to the family plantation at Peach Tree, in what is now Brazoria County.

Following the Texas Revolution, many lower Brazos River communities were Union-occupied in the Civil War. After this the area stabilized, and its inhabitants moved on to rebuild their civic structures and local economies. In the years that followed, hurricanes and flooding on the Brazos River mitigated success, and droughts brought despair. But, as the Industrial Age began to flourish, the communities forged together into what would become a new economy. The first sugar cane plantation was built on Fort Bend's Oyster Creek in 1840, and soon, the lower Brazos River basin would be known as the "Sugar Bowl of Texas."

The first canal in the area, built in 1857, connected Oyster Creek with West Galveston Bay and the Brazos. The 14-mile stretch became part of the Gulf Intracoastal Waterway around the mouth of the Brazos.

Today, the lower Brazos River basin and the coastal prairie's canal system provide the lifeblood of Texas to one of the nation's most important metropolitan regions.

# *One*

# Wrestling the Brazos

The mighty Brazos River meanders through more than 1,000 miles until it reaches the Gulf of Mexico. Stretching from its confluence in Stonewall County to the gulf, the Brazos passes through six distinct Texan ecosystems. The Brazos is also—along with the Rio Grande—one of only two major Texan rivers that drain directly into the Gulf of Mexico. These two rivers have built a substantial portion of the gulf deltas, though the Brazos dumps into the gulf without an intermediary tidal basin. The Brazos also collects more water flow every year than any other Texas river.

Surface and groundwater aquifers—such as the Ogallala in its upper basin—feed the Brazos's vast flow. Its basins also have a natural ability to capture vast amounts of rainwater, filling the river like a bathtub. These characteristics help to give the river its fame and temperament.

In its natural state, the Brazos had many rocks, shoals, bars, snags, bends, and rapids. Historically, droughts affected its levels as strongly as hurricanes or high upstream rainfall, leaving it with an undependable flow. Furthermore, the river's natural mouth featured a shifting bar, which could fluctuate between 4 and 10 feet in height. This meant that the natural Brazos River could flood violently and with little notice, destroying towns, boats, and human lives.

Just a few years after establishing his colony, Stephen F. Austin realized that the river mouth would create problems. In 1824, he learned that only 16 miles separated the Brazos's mouth and the deep waters near Galveston. A year later, he proclaimed that settlers could build an inland waterway between the Harbor of Galveston and the Brazos River. He said that canals would be the key to mastering the waters of this new land.

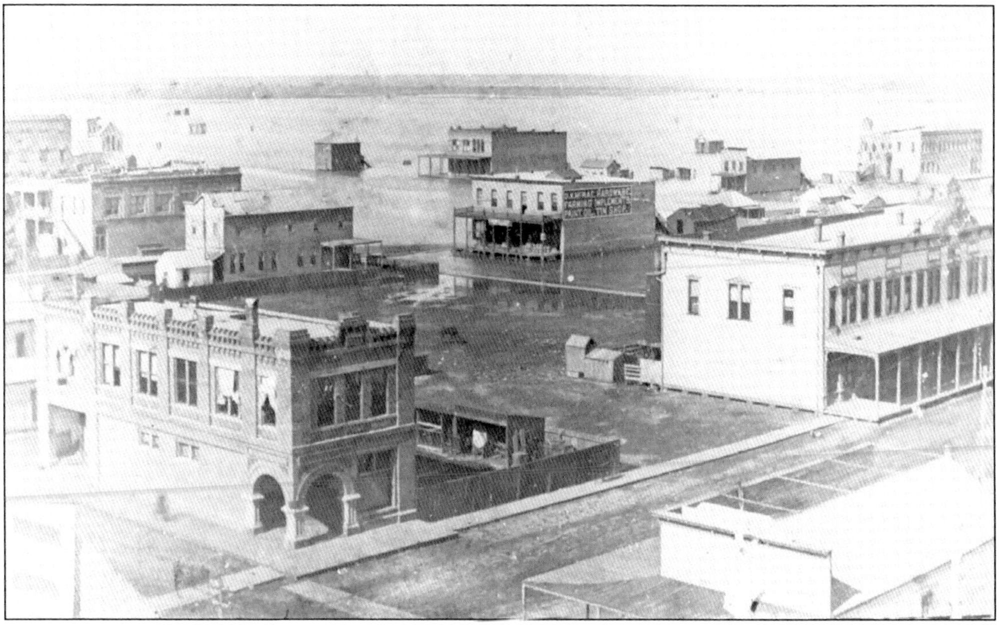

The Brazos River exhibited torrential floods that devastated communities. The Gulf of Mexico and the river were unpredictable in their natural state and could suddenly rise, as the gulf does here in Velasco in the 1840s. Boats were used when walking became impossible. (Courtesy of Brazoria County Historical Commission.)

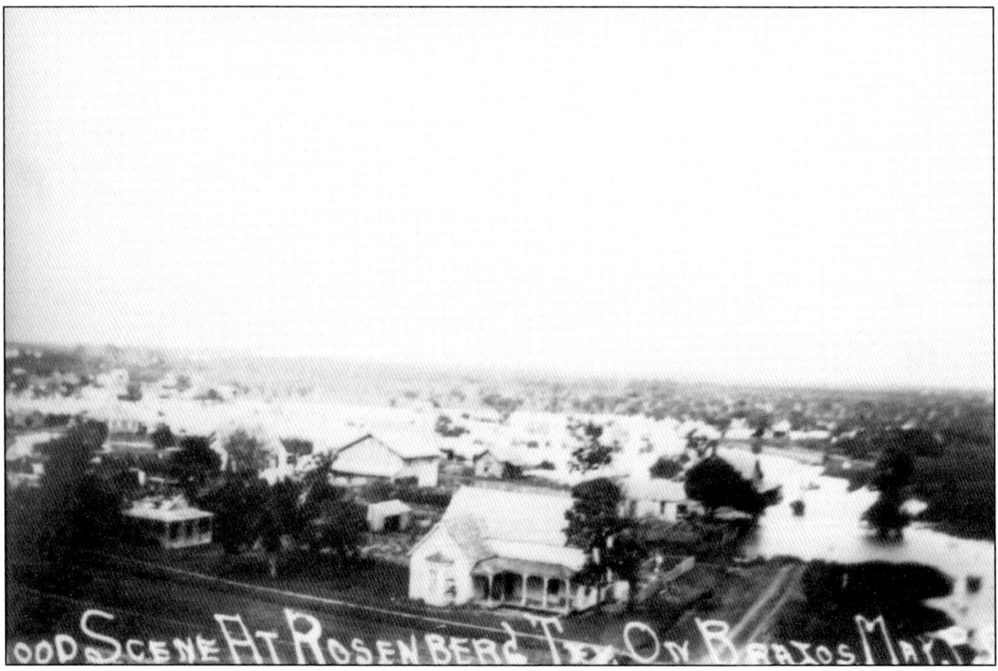


Hurricanes and upper basin rainfall often caused the Brazos River to rise, and unpredictable flooding was common. The town of Rosenberg experienced many floods and was nicknamed "The City of Mud." Significant flooding occurred in 1913, 1922, 1929, and 1957, but less devastating flooding occurred often enough to be considered a part of life. (Courtesy of Fort Bend Museum.)

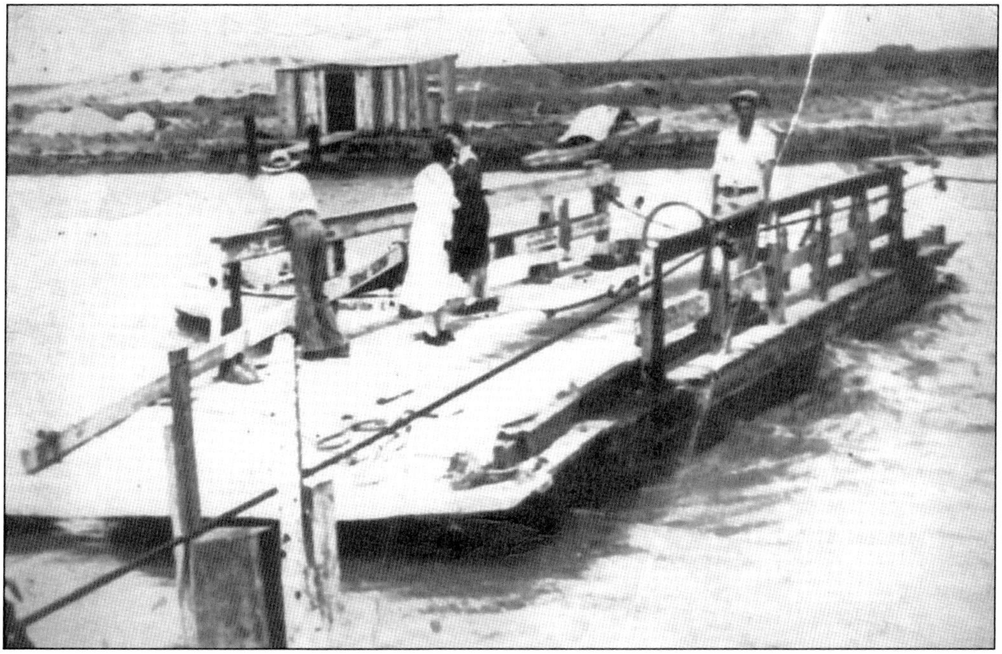

Ferries were the foundation for transportation throughout the history of the Brazos River. Settlers used them along the entire length of the Brazos. Even after work began on the Intracoastal Waterway, these ferries were still frequently used. Pictured here from left to right, Jack Morris of Freeport, Mrs. Bess, and Hollia Warneke cross at the Surfside Canal ferry in 1931. (Courtesy of Joseph Pessarra.)

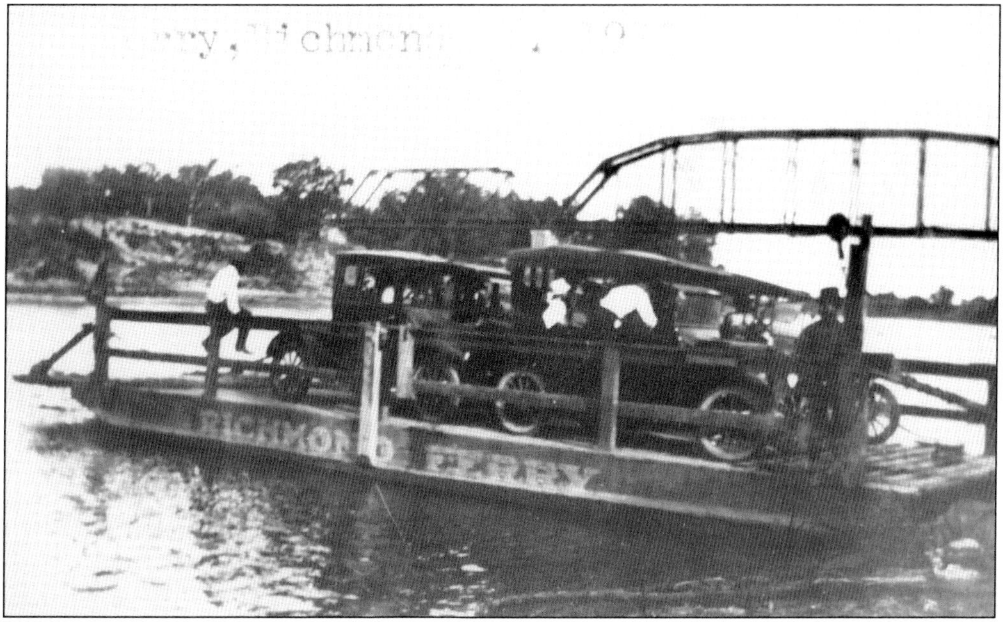


The Richmond Ferry was an important component in commerce and personal transportation. It connected parts of towns and river communities. Even after the railroad came to the area, the community still needed ferries for local shuttling. These waterways were the "local highway systems" of the time, and people used them daily. (Courtesy of Fort Bend Museum.)

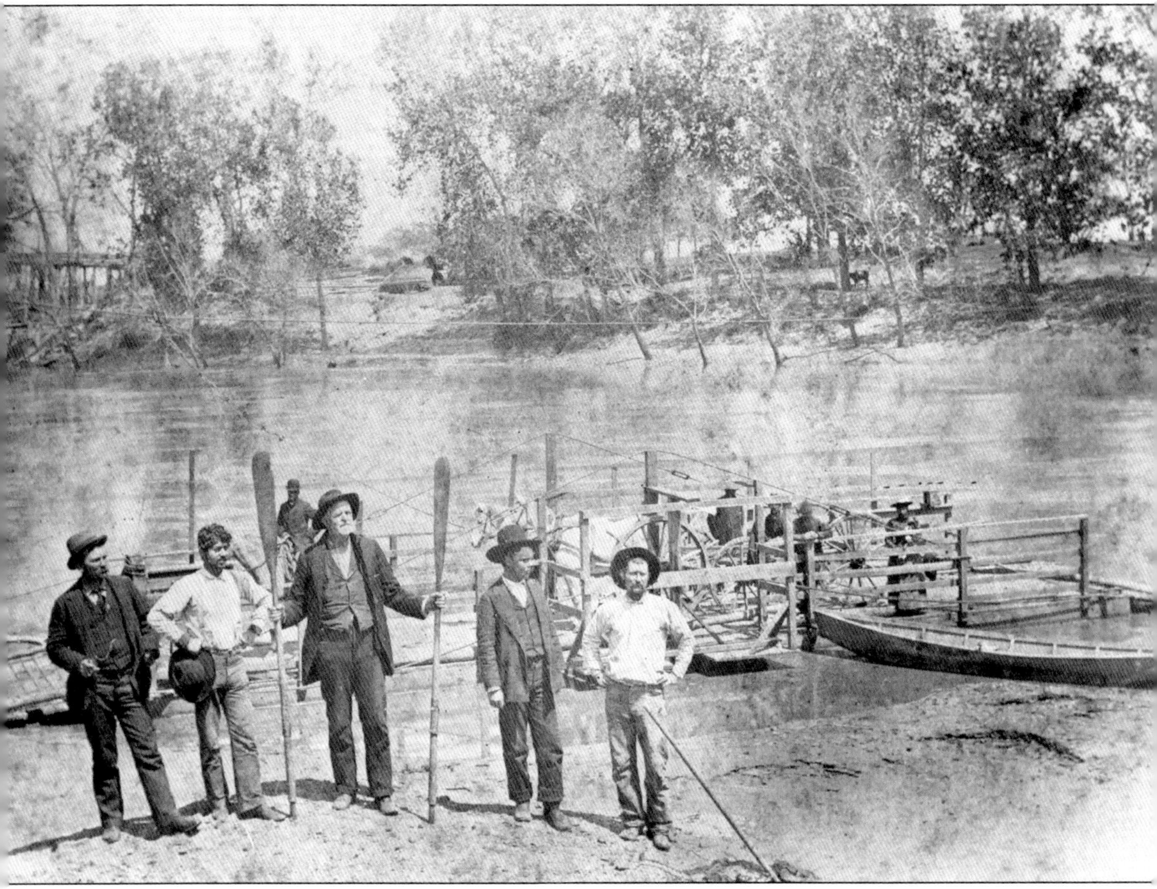

Since there were no roads in the region, Austin's Colony quickly established ferries to move large quantities of goods. In 1823, a ferry operating out of the town of San Felipe was one of the reasons that Austin made San Felipe the unofficial capital of his settlement. River ferries became the regional transportation system, and were highly important to commerce and the local economy, moving cattle, people, and later, automobiles. Thompson's Ferry, Mosely's Ferry, and others operated throughout the 19th century and into the 20th century. Ferries were so important to travel that, during the Texas Revolution, Sam Houston ordered troops to defend the ferry and burn San Felipe. Without a ferry, Santa Anna could not advance. Eventually, the use of ferries began to wane in the region with the introduction of roads, railways, and bridges that often followed the path of the original ferry crossing. (Courtesy of Fort Bend Museum.)

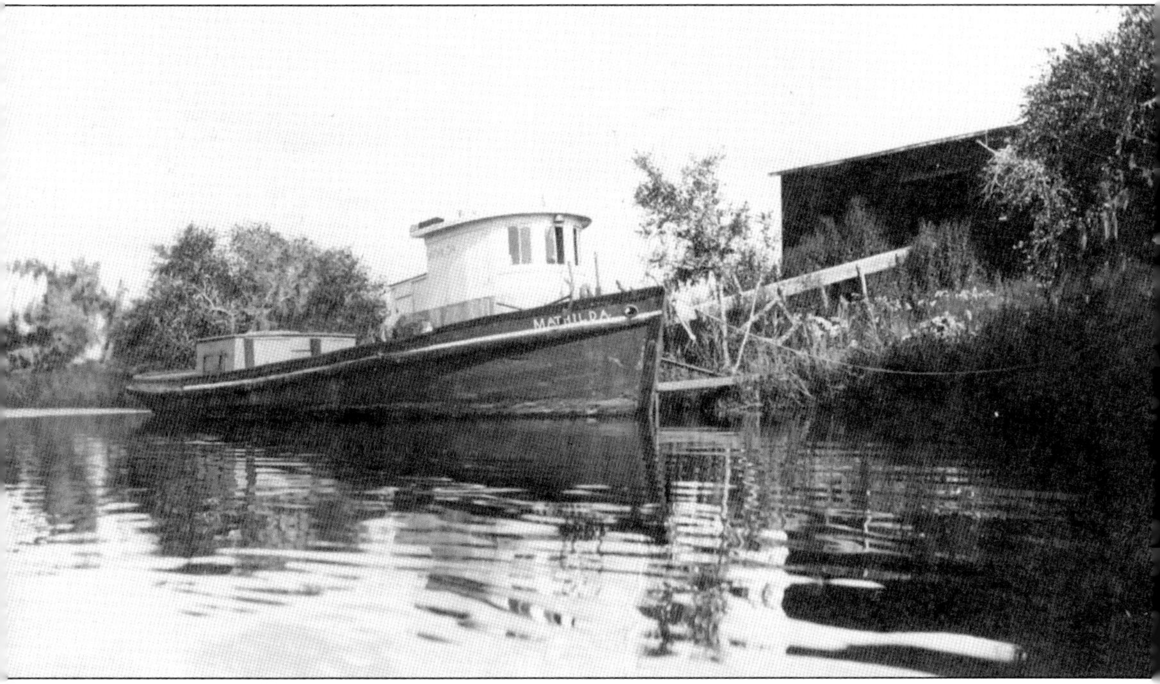


Between the establishment of the Austin's Colony and the 1850s, government and economic leaders spent money and time trying to tame the mouth of the river. Within a few years of establishing the colony, Austin surmised that a man-made waterway would become critical to avoiding the mouth of the Brazos. The Brazos's mouth easily destroyed ships and boats as they attempted to make the turn through its tempestuous waters; by 1848, few insurers would provide coverage for its navigation and five percent was added to the price of any goods that had to pass around the sandbar. The *Mathilda* (pictured) was one of the vessels that hauled rice between the lower Brazos and Galveston, and routinely navigated the river mouth.

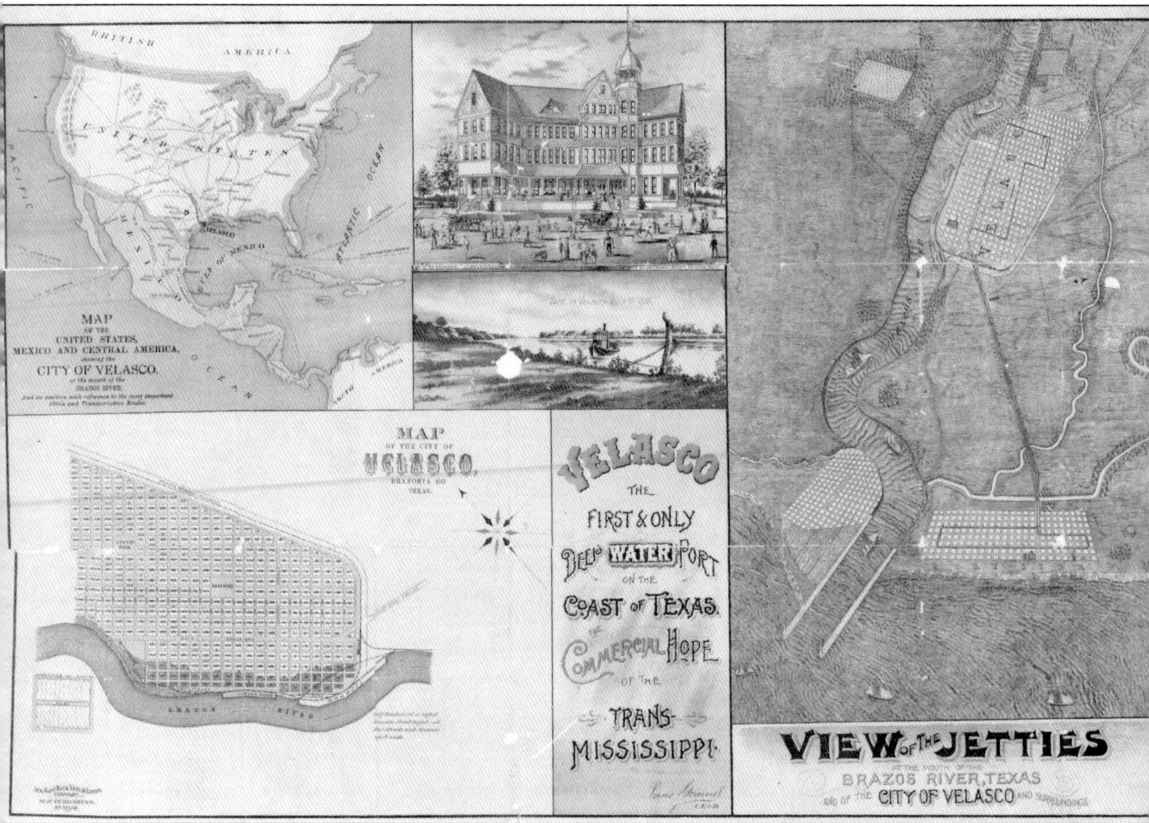


While the colony's leaders wrestled with how to tame the mouth of the Brazos, developers were heralding the benefits of river-town living. Promotional maps such as this one by the Brazos River & Channel Dock Co. described the crops, goods, and commerce that could make a person a good living in the area. On this map, the inland and deep-water cities are considered the prime places to relocate. "The royal road to commercial supremacy is by water," it states. "Railroads develop and people large areas. Rapid and easy transportation make the inhabitants of villages, towns and even farms neighbors." The piece says water communities do not build great cities, but communities. It goes on to state that railroads do not make cities, and that, "It is not in the nature of things that they should."

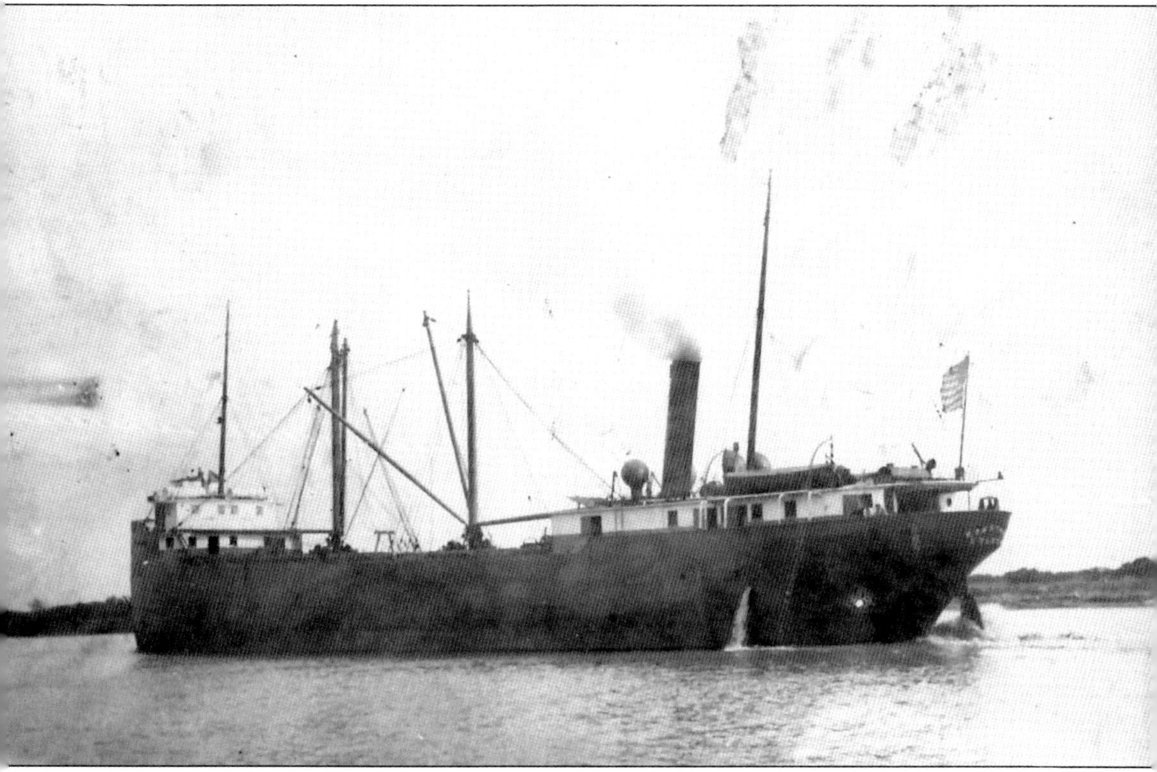

The connection between the gulf and the Brazos was an important component in convincing eastern investments to relocate to Velasco and the lower river region. In its natural state, the Brazos dumped directly into the gulf, which meant that direct inland access was available. "No rock-bound coast or stretch of barren sand divides farm from sea," stated the promotional map from the Brazos River & Channel Dock Co. in about 1892. This vessel travels along the port in an undated photograph. At the turn of the 20th century, Velasco capitalized on the complaints that the Port of Galveston was too expensive, and that crops needed to get to market more quickly after harvest. Velasco was touted as the answer to the Trans-Mississippi water commerce route. Port authorities even promoted a 50¢ pilotage and port charge. They claimed that this cost was less than at any other port on the Gulf of Mexico.

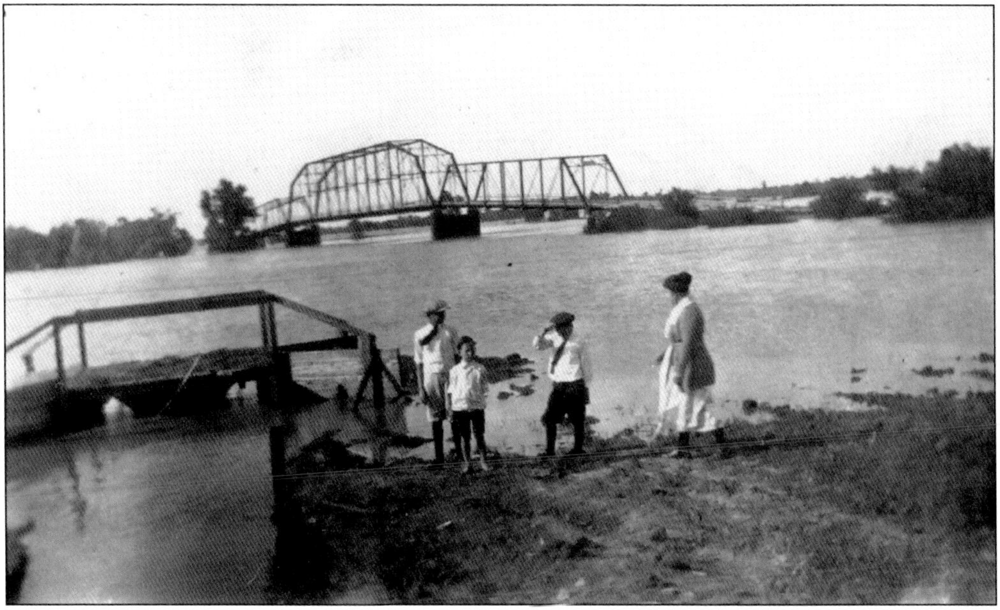

Following the Civil War, one of the first railroads constructed in the area was the Gulf, Colorado and Santa Fe. Galveston citizens sponsored it because it would avoid Harris County and the city of Houston. Houston often quarantined goods from Galveston during yellow fever scares, and Galveston residents suspected that the quarantines were an economic ploy. Galveston business leader Henry von Rosenberg served as the first president of the line, which began construction in 1875. It reached Richmond over the Brazos River in 1879, Brenham in 1880, and Belton in 1881. In 1886 it became part of the Atchison, Topeka and Santa Fe system. Later, residents named Rosenberg, Texas, after the railroad's president. (Both, courtesy of Fort Bend Museum.)

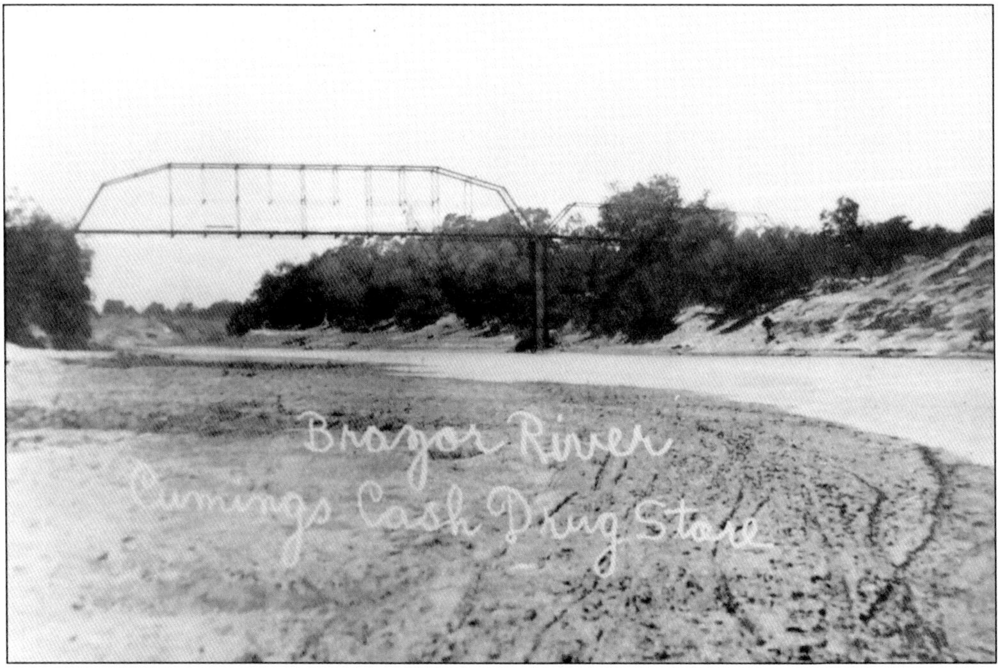

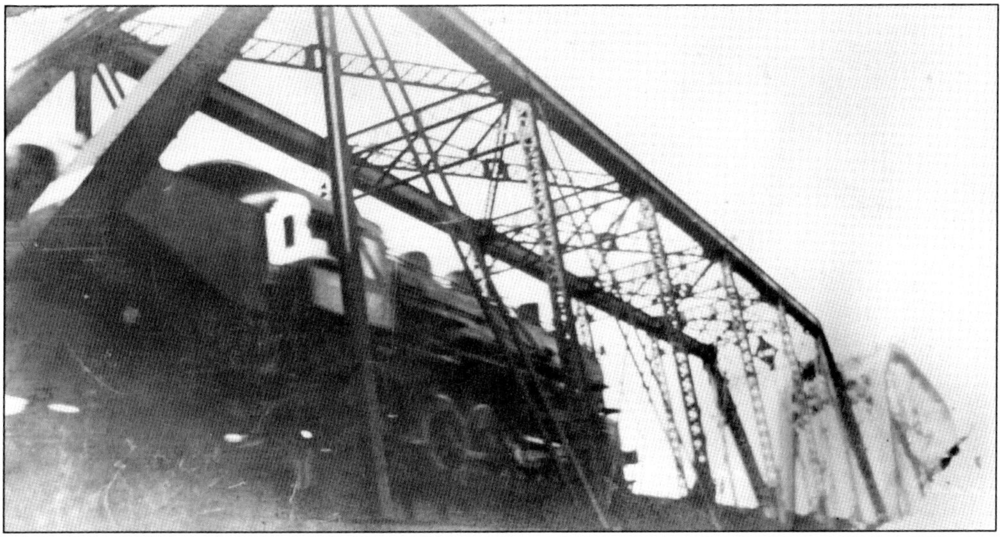

Roads were harder to come by than rail. In 1850, Houston businessmen tried to build the Brazos Plank Road. They planned to grade a road from Houston to the Brazos River and then cover it with planks so that ox wagons could move goods along it. Counties were responsible for the roadways, however, and funding was often scarce. Additionally, overland routes in the area were often muddy and difficult. The Brazos Plank Road was never built, and transportation continued to focus on rail-to-port routes. Roads remained scarce in the area until 1917, when Texas created the State Highway Commission. Soon gasoline automobiles rolled into town, spurring a renewed interest in roads and bridges, and construction began on the Brazos River Bridge in 1922. (Both, courtesy of Fort Bend Museum.)

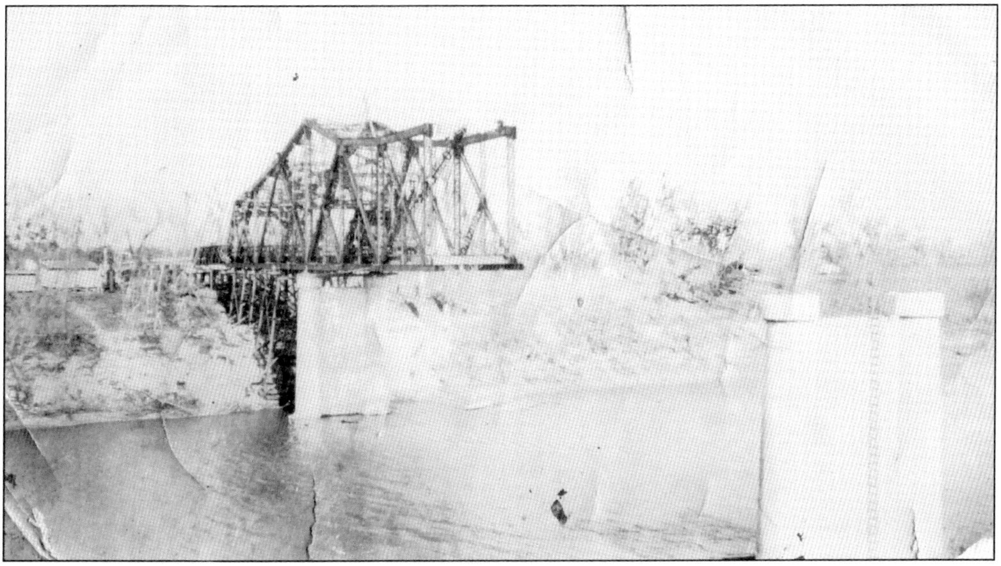

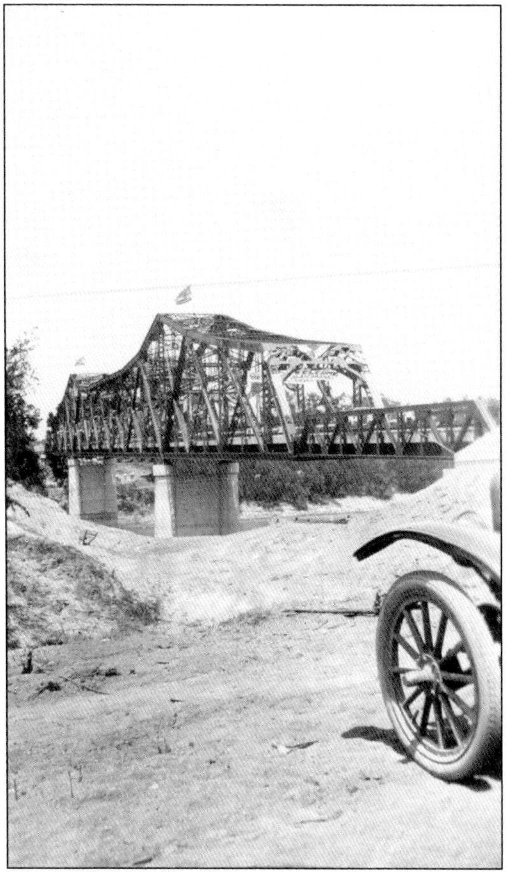

Residents dedicated the Brazos River Bridge on a bright and breezy day in 1922. They heralded the event with a massive Rosenberg community party. Flags—including a large Imperial Sugar sign—adorned the bridge, and residents had their photographs taken as they walked over the span. Despite this, the river would remain an essential part of river town life. (Courtesy of Fort Bend Museum.)

Rail became an important part of moving sugar, rice, and other goods to market. It transported these products between Velasco and Galveston. It also bolstered Fort Bend County and allowed the region to become a transportation hub and agricultural leader in the coming decades. (Courtesy of Fort Bend Museum.)

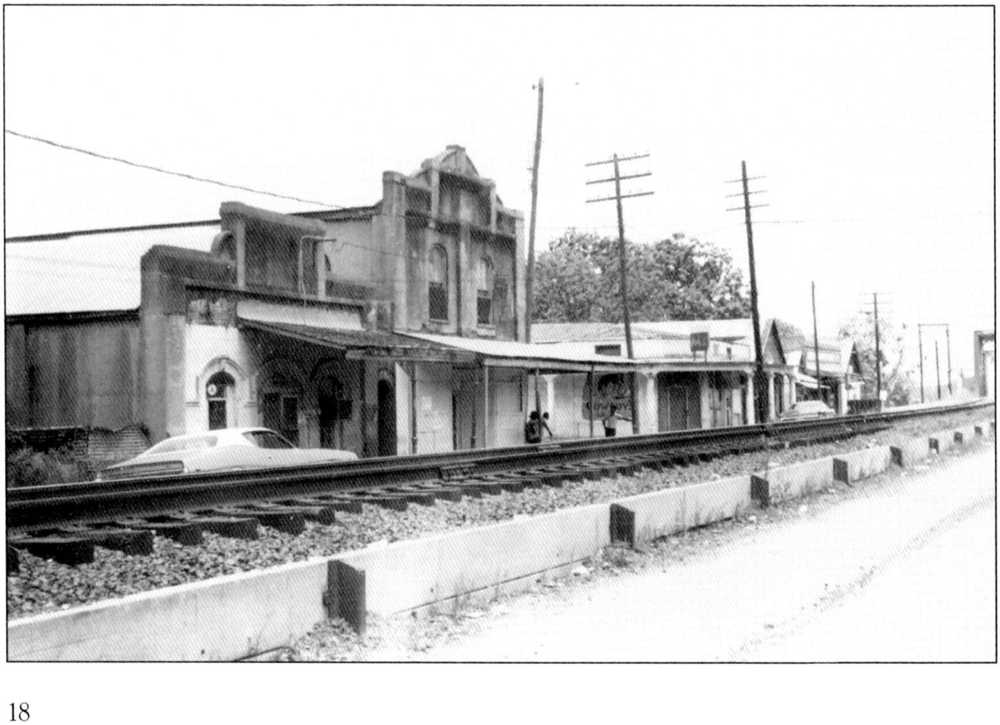

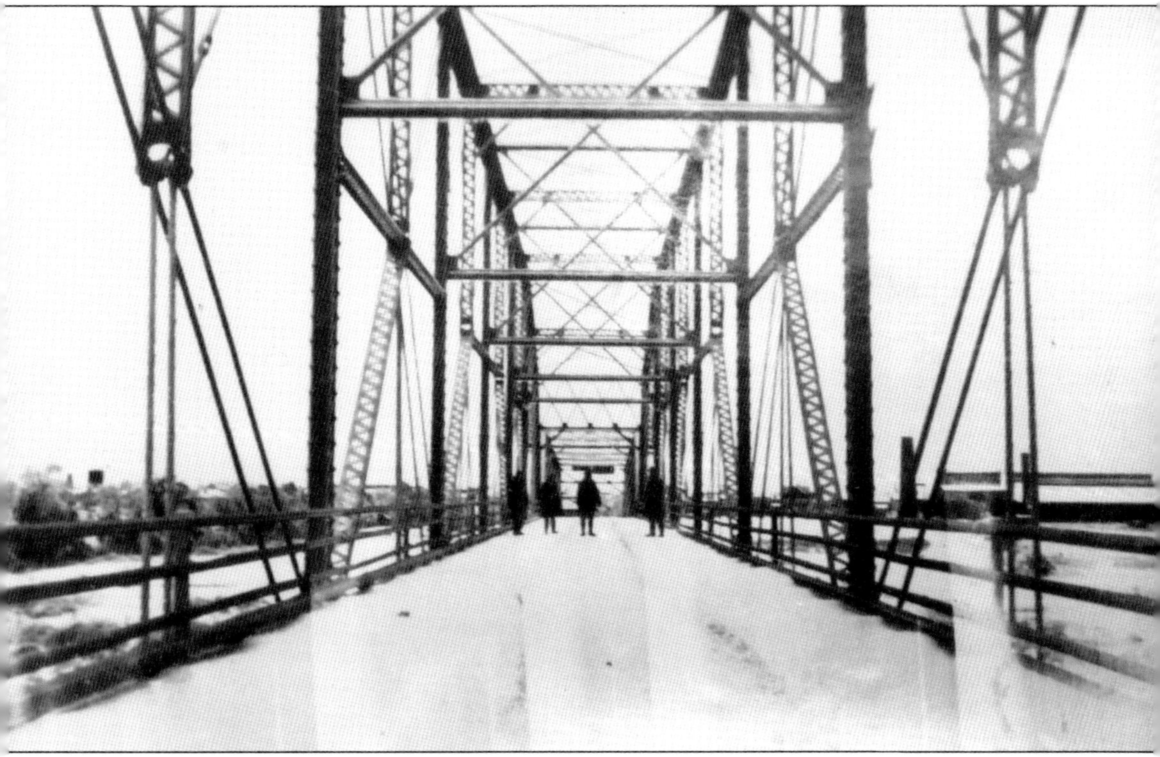

Sometimes the lower Brazos river towns experience snowstorms, such as this one in 1924. The climate along the lower river is mild and subtropical, with Southeastern winds that benefit the coastal prairies and seasons that vary less than on other parts of the Brazos. The area can be humid in spring and summer, but, in late autumn and in winter, "northerners" bring chilling winds as often as once a week. In its lower region, the Brazos River experiences winter freezes that can be devastating, but they do not last as long as those in communities along the upper basin. Silt from these upper basin communities travels along the river, and eventually dumps into the gulf. For years, this exasperated attempts to dredge the channel, and created the treacherous, shifting sandbar at the river's mouth. (Courtesy of Fort Bend Museum.)

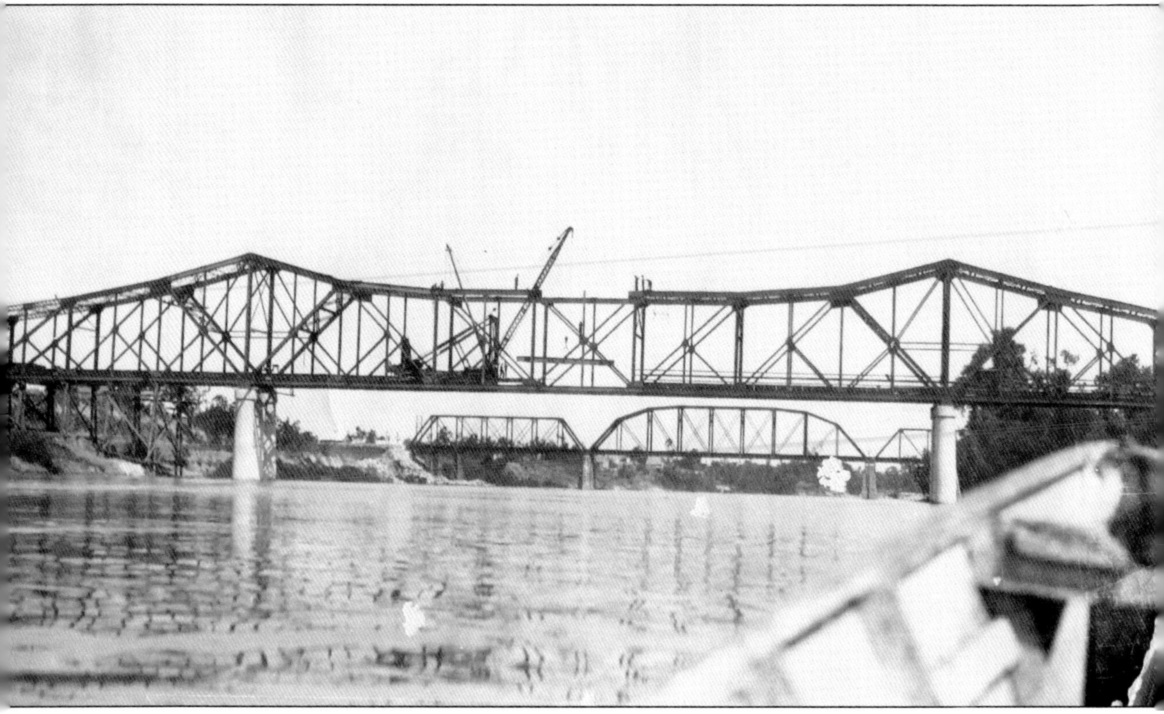

Roads did not exist in the area when Austin's Colony was first settled, and early explorers never ventured inland. In 1855, much attention was given to river and port travel, but overland routes were described as a mere collection of straggling wagon ruts. Transporting freight by road was not desirable, as wet roads slowed travel. This made rail more preferable until the gasoline automobile changed the game in the beginning of the 20th century, and the state took control of roads away from the counties. Following the dedication of the Brazos River Bridge in 1922, the lower Brazos River had all the conveniences necessary for modern growth. Imperial Sugar repositioned the center of the Sugar Bowl; Velasco's deepwater port had jetties; and rail, auto, and marine transportation solidified the connection between Fort Bend, Brazoria, and Galveston Counties. All of these forms of transportation can be seen in this photograph. (Courtesy of Fort Bend Museum.)

# *Two*

# The Farm Crops and Ranch Cattle

When settlers arrived at Austin's Colony, they chose river and creek land that had a dense growth of green cane, which signaled good drainage. Austin didn't mind this decision because, by the terms of his grant, he could not give the settlers land fronting the Gulf of Mexico anyway.

While settlers chose their land because cane grew there, they wanted it cleared for other crops. Corn was the most important crop in the area, with cotton a close second. Another important food crop was the sweet potato, because the slaves could eat it and it was a good substitute for bread.

Cotton was one of the first crops shipped from Austin's Colony. Before the establishment of the Republic of Texas, the cultivation of cotton was predominately confined to the lower Brazos River. The river offered easy transportation that other regions did not, and planting further inland produced smaller crop yields of inferior quality, which earned less at market. Jared E. Groce, dubbed the "Father of Agriculture," was the owner of Bernardo Plantation. He cultivated the area's first cotton crop and owned the first cotton gin in Texas. In 1823, he also sent the region's first cotton shipment to New Orleans.

When Austin arrived, millions of cattle roamed the Texas prairies from the Sabine River in the east to the Rio Grande in the west. The cattle may have been left over from the Spanish missions. In 1833, the Department of the Brazos stated that 25,000 head of cattle roamed freely in the region. By Mexican law, settlers could get more land if they intended to raise cattle. In 1825, the government allowed a farming family to have 77 acres, but a family raising livestock was eligible for 4,251 acres. This meant that most Austin's Colony farmers were also ranchers.

Raising the cattle was easier than selling them, however. Beginning in the 1830s, Austin's Colony used the Opelousas Trail, which meant that they drove their cattle from Velasco, and then to Anahuac, where they merged into the trail that took them to New Orleans. During the drive the cattle had to swim rivers. To start a river crossing, a cowboy would grab a steer by the horns, back it into the river, and swim with it until the remainder of the herd followed.

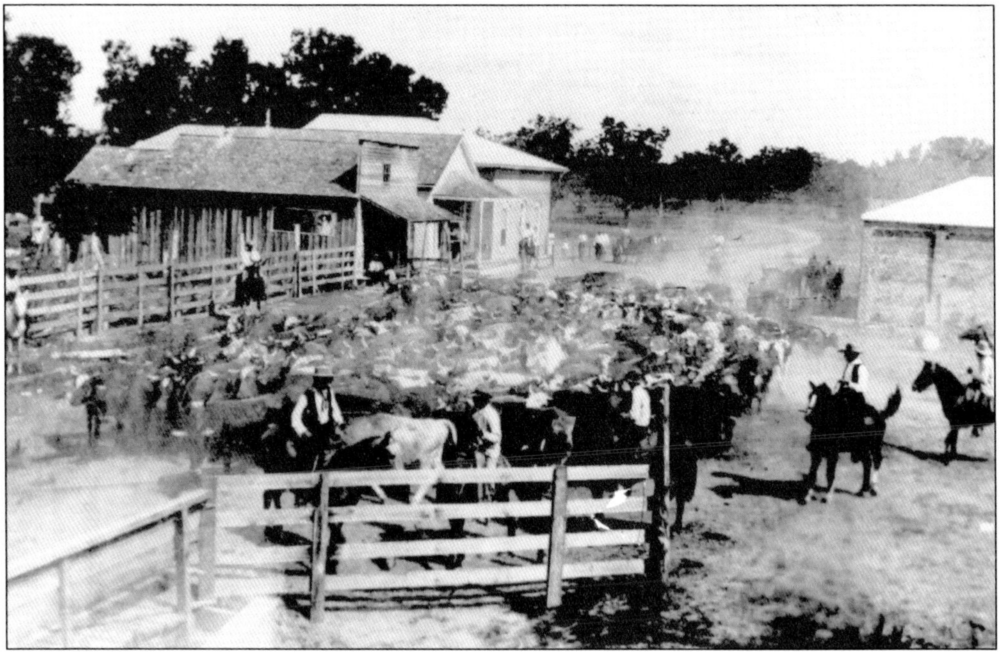

Cattle ranching on the Brazos is as old as the Austin's Colony. To maintain their land agreement with Mexico, settlers would purchase domestic cattle from Louisiana and other parts of the United States, as well as Mexico, because native cattle were too wild to breed. In this photograph from 1912, cattle approach the new Brazos Bridge. (Courtesy of Brazoria County Historical Commission.)

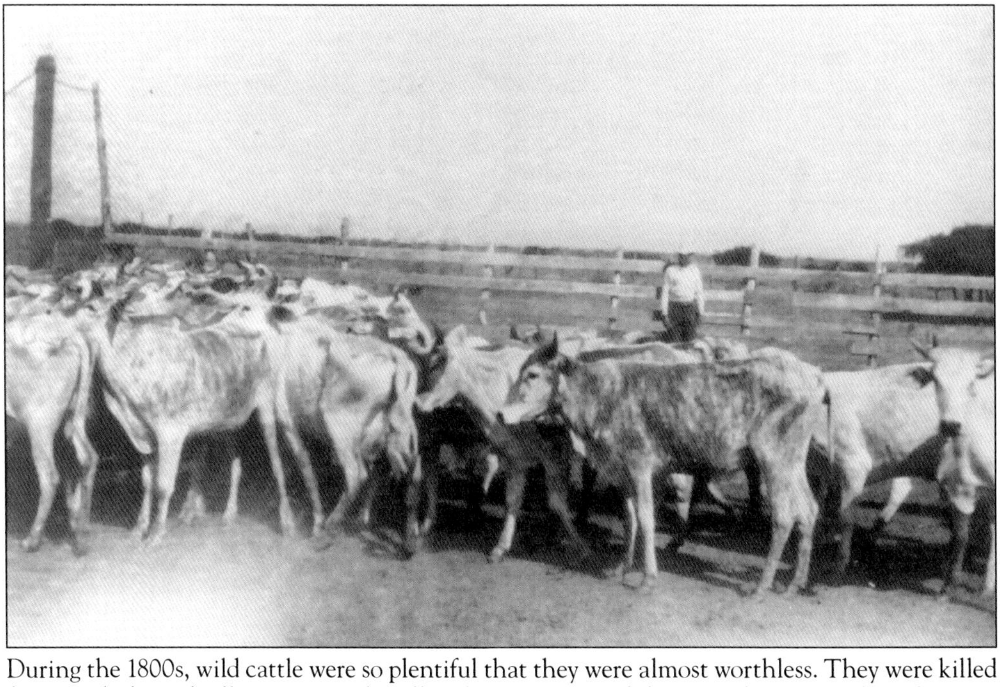

During the 1800s, wild cattle were so plentiful that they were almost worthless. They were killed for sport, hide, and tallow. As a result, tallow factories covered the coastal prairies. These factories could consume 100 to 300 head of cattle per day, and the meat was cast to the hogs or anyone else who wanted it.

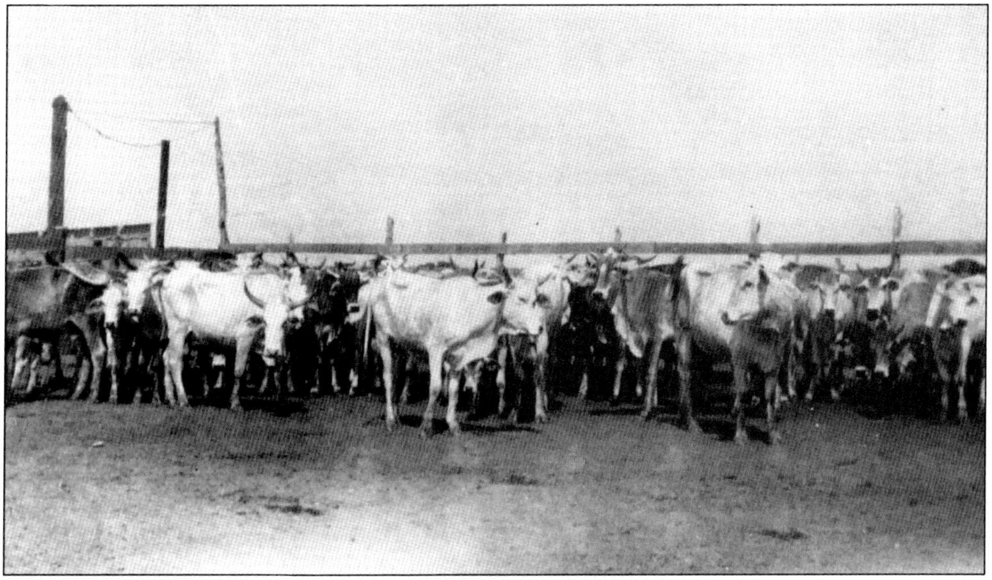

In the 1830s, Velasco was a stopping point for the local cattle drives. Austin's Colony cattle would move along the river mouth until they merged into the Opelousas trail at Anahuac, where they went on to New Orleans. This continued until the 1860s, when Galveston's port became large enough to ship the animals.

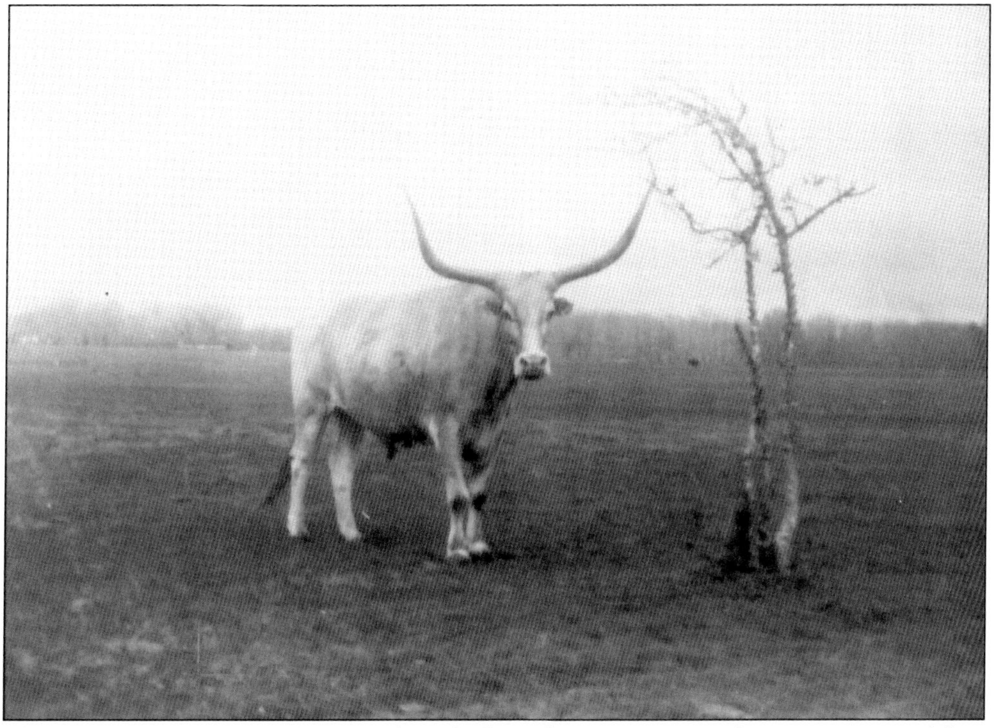

This is a photograph of the last Longhorn bull on the 20,000-acre Robert E. Lee Stringfellow ranch, located near the mouth of the Brazos. Stringfellow, who was born in Brazoria, owned a meat market in Velasco in 1890 that fed the workers building the city's jetties. His wife, Nannie, operated the ranch after Robert was injured in the 1932 hurricane.

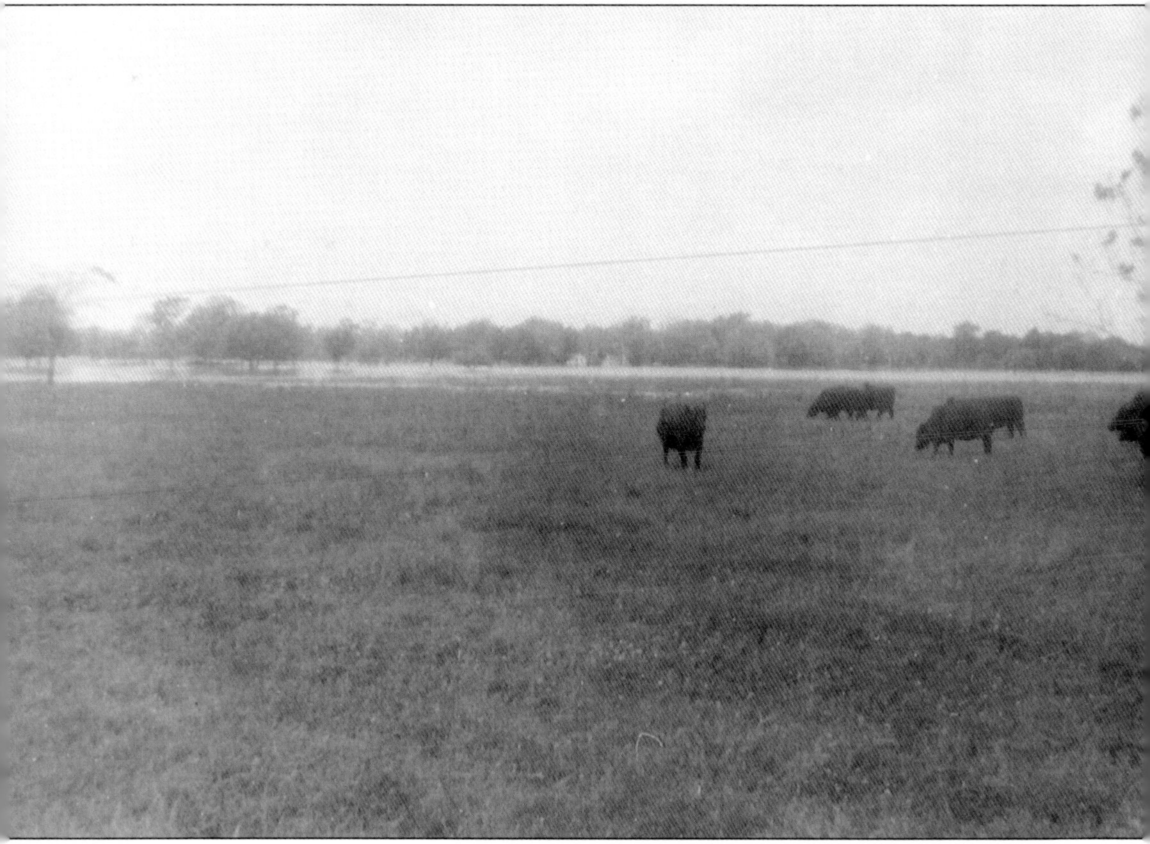

The lower basin's original cattle population was wild, and some people considered them fiercer than buffalo. For decades, settlers tried to tame and improve the animals, with little result. This changed in 1906 when the estate of A.H. "Shanghai" Pierce first imported the Indian Brahma to the region. Pierce, a shrewd Wharton County businessman, spent years searching for ways to improve the Texas cattle industry. He eventually settled on the Indian Brahma and made arrangements to import them, but died several years before the first animals arrived. Reports show that his executives only received the cattle after promising that they would not kill the animals. The imported Brahma changed the Texas cattle industry due to several important characteristics—such as their thick hides and ability to safely graze in the hot Texas sun—which were passed on when the animals were bred with the local population.

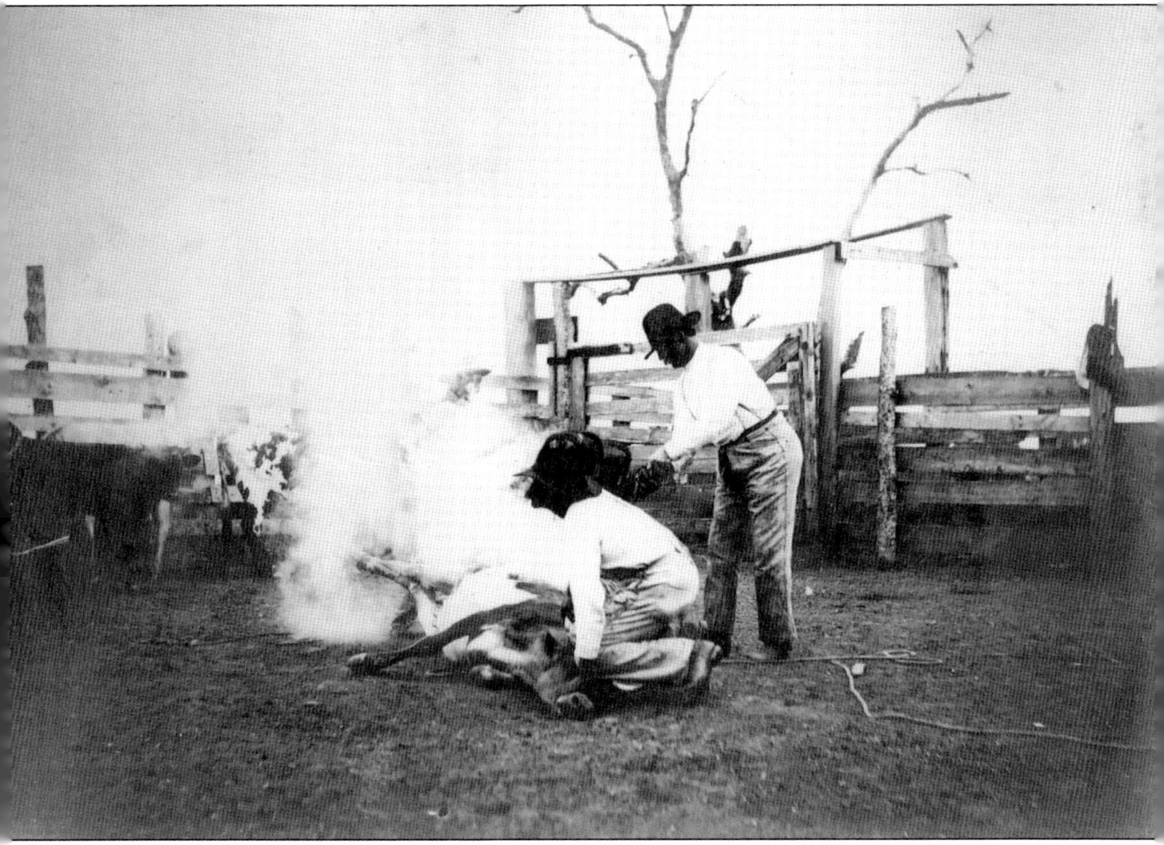

None of the cattle discovered by the early settlers had marks or brands. These wild cattle were corralled and branded early on in Austin's Colony, and for decades after. Taming these animals was problematic due to the sheer numbers that roamed the gulf coast prairies, but barbed wire, corrals, and branding made it easier to commercialize the cattle industry.

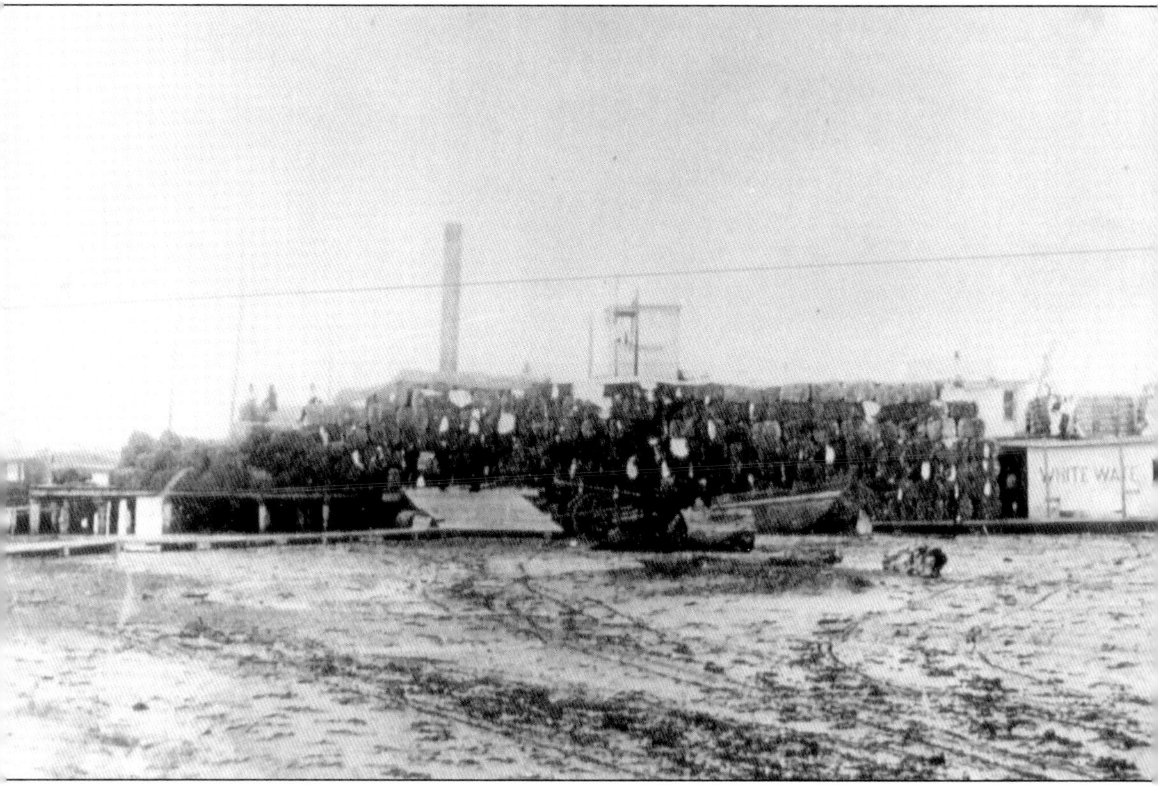

With the shipment of his first crop in 1823, plantation owner Jared E. Groce helped to establish the viability of the cotton industry along the Brazos. Within a decade, the region had 33 cotton gins between San Felipe and Brazoria, and local fields commonly yielded two bales per acre. Velasco remained a vital port in the modernization of the cotton industry until the early part of the 1900s. Eventually, Groce would also be instrumental in developing formalized water management on the lower Brazos River.

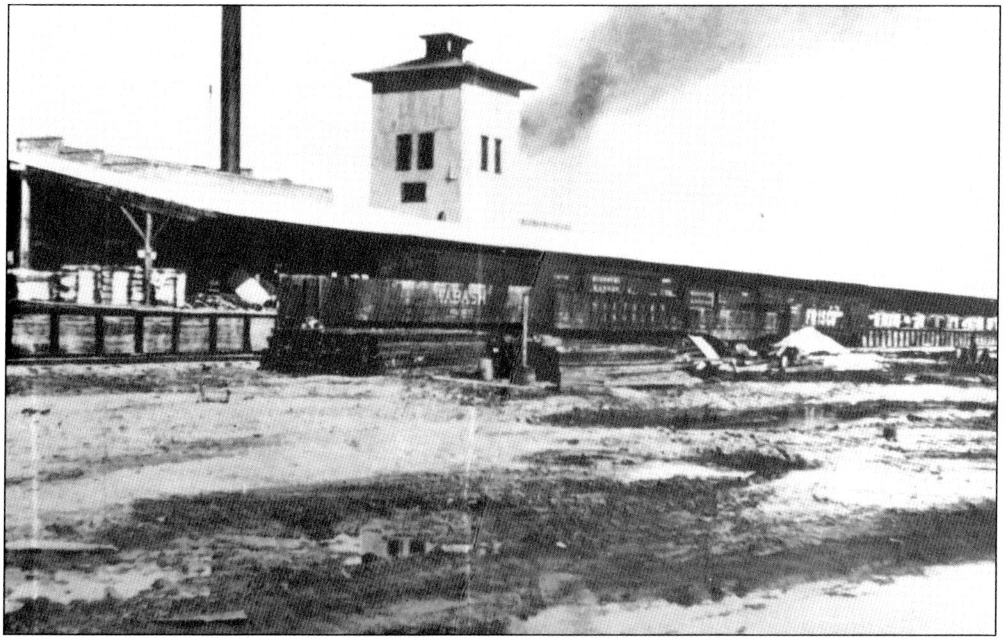

Cotton production throughout the lower Brazos River meant settlers needed access to several ports. Cotton left from ports at Velasco and Galveston as well as Texas City. Texas City dredged an eight-foot channel in 1893. It was 43 feet long and featured a 1.5-mile-long port. By 1910, two hundred and thirty-nine ships were using the Texas City port each year. Despite this, Galveston continued to dominate the Texas port industry. For example, in 1917, it shipped 490,921 bales of cotton. By comparison, Texas City shipped about half of that amount. About 25 percent of the state's cotton went through Galveston, and through the 1920s, Texas City absorbed its overage. The port boasted warehouses big enough for 100,000 bales of cotton, and two cotton compressors. (Both, courtesy of Texas City Museum.)

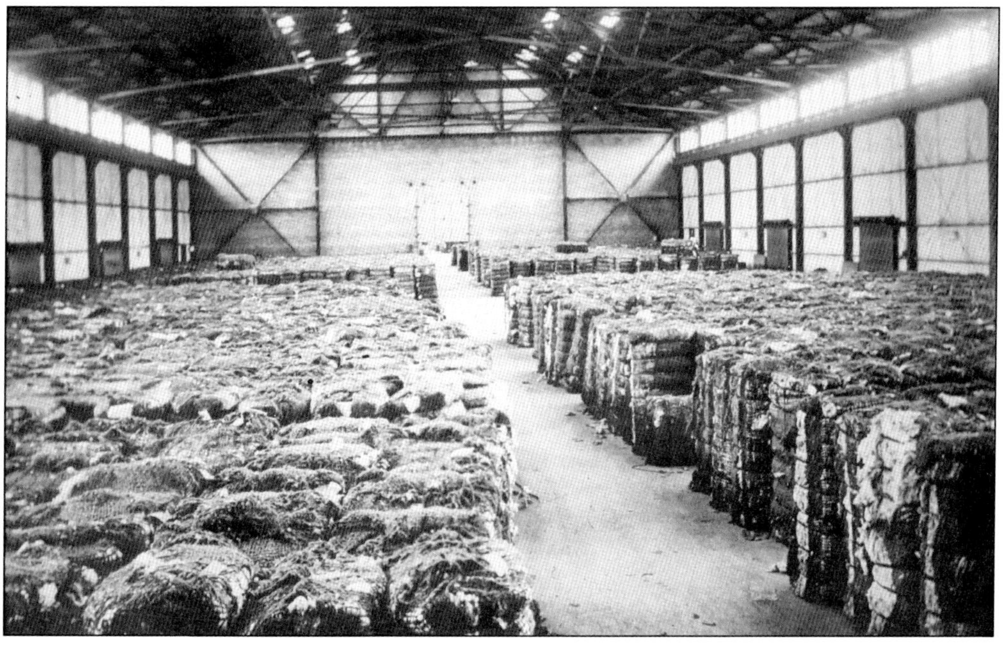

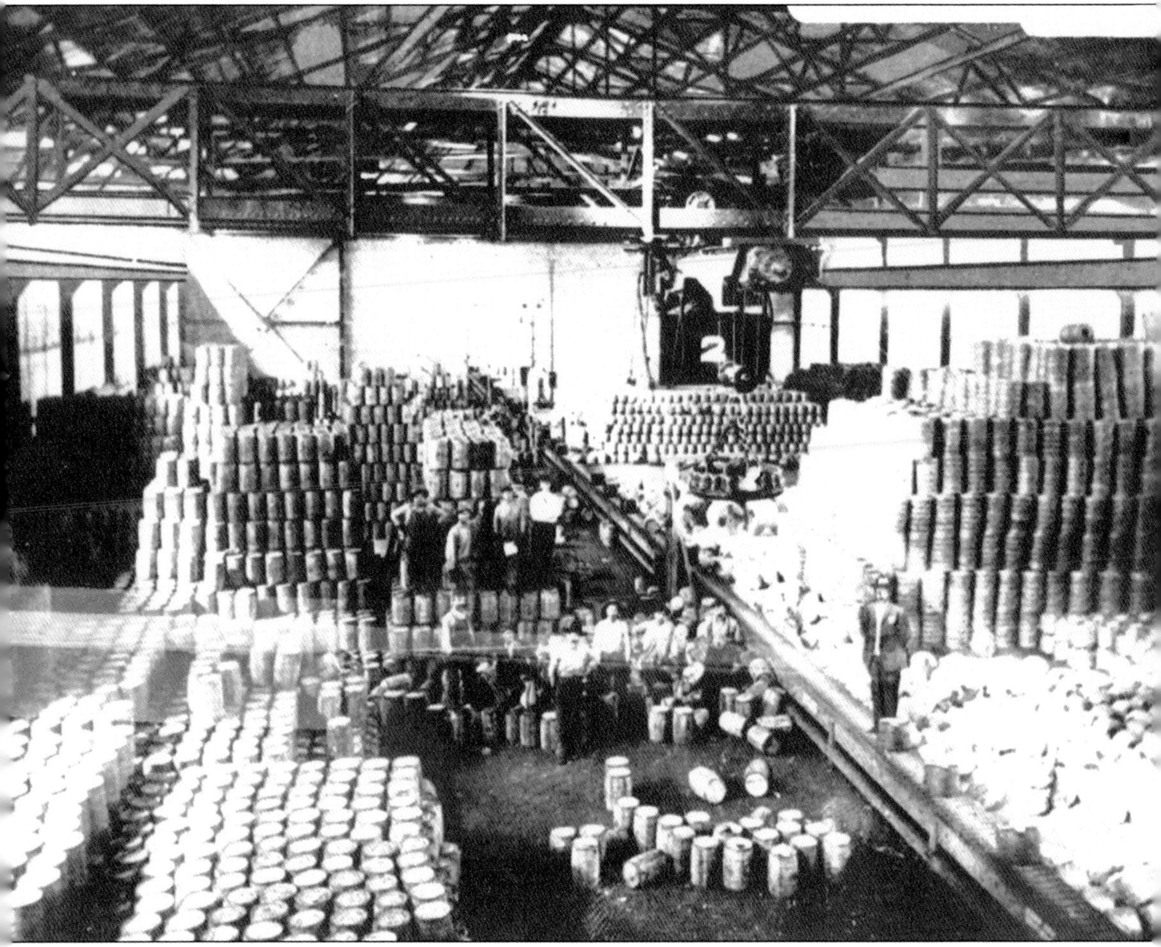

During the 1920s, Texas City began to shift its focus from agriculture to oil. It promoted the quality of its facilities, access to inland rails, and lower rates among its attractive features. The decline in cotton or crop shipments around 1917 did not concern port officials. They had already captured five oil company tank farms, the Knox Process Corp. (a gasoline-cracking refinery), and the Stone Oil Co. These companies operated alongside the port's crop business. Before the decline, Texas City had a grain elevator, fig preserving plant, and various warehouse businesses. This photograph is from 1912, when the port moved 665,901 cotton bales, which was the peak for crop shipments. (Courtesy of Texas City Museum.)

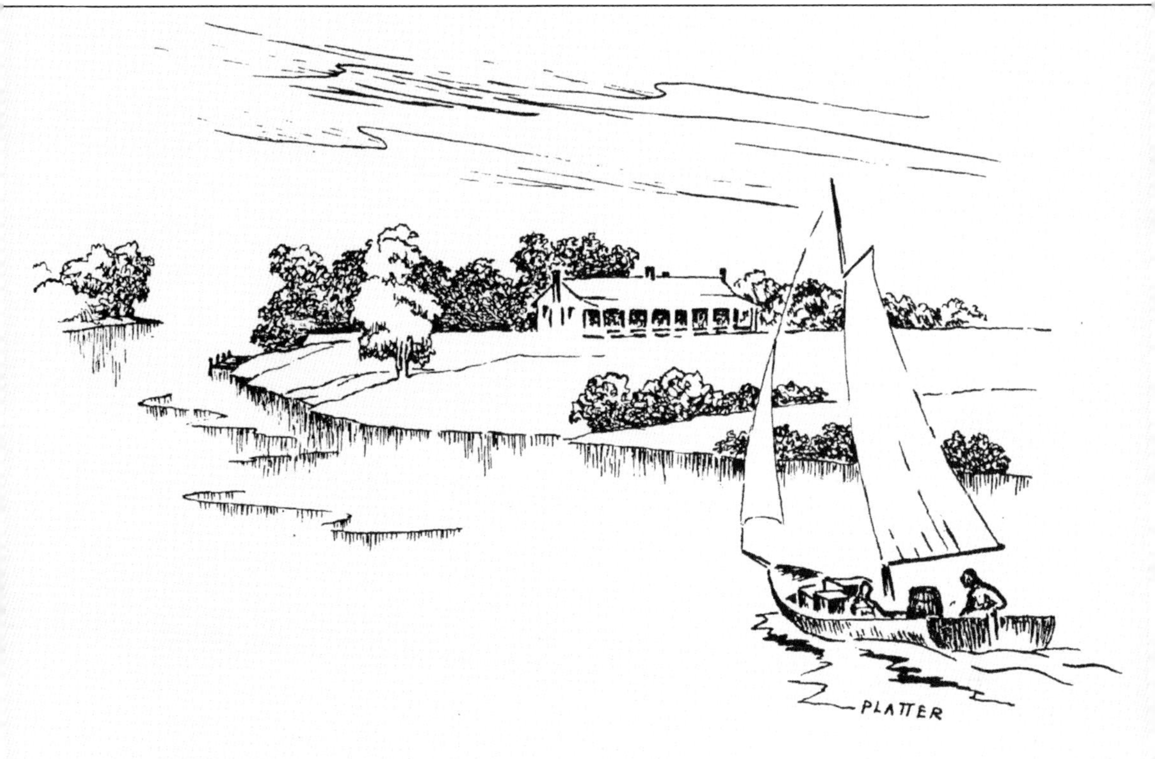


Reterio, located on the east bank of Oyster Creek, became a cotton plantation in 1847. Moses Austin Bryan, Stephen F. Austin's nephew, owned the plantation. He arrived in the region in 1831, serving as his uncle's land clerk, but, by 1860, Bryan owned nine slaves and had accumulated a net worth of almost $100,000. This established him as one of Brazoria's most wealthy residents. Reterio was not part of the Sugar Bowl, and instead raised corn, potatoes, and cattle along with its cotton crop. After the Civil War—in which Bryan served as a major in the Confederate army—many Texas plantations deteriorated and disappeared. As a result, plantation photographs are difficult to find. Sketches or drawings, such as this illustration, are more common.

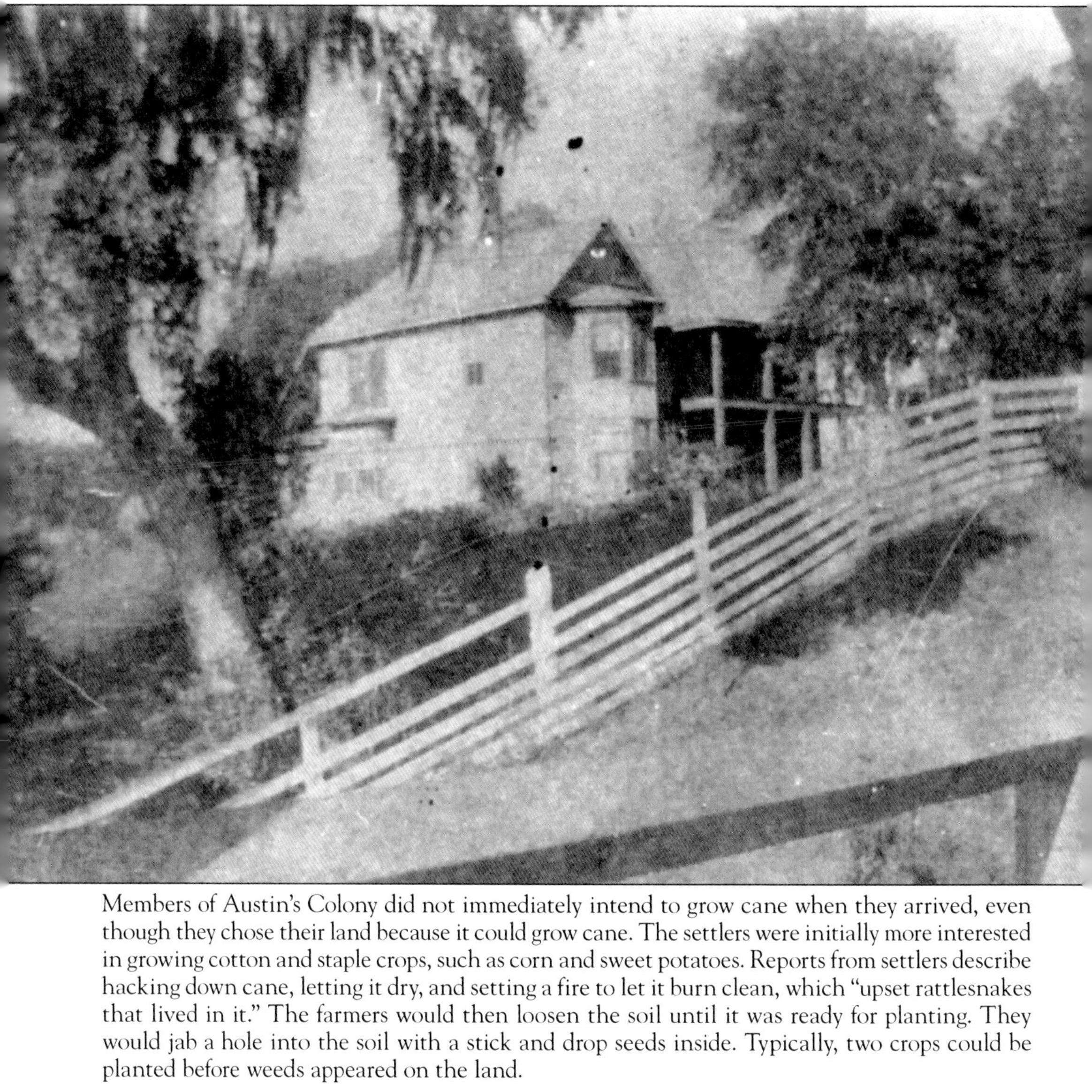

Members of Austin's Colony did not immediately intend to grow cane when they arrived, even though they chose their land because it could grow cane. The settlers were initially more interested in growing cotton and staple crops, such as corn and sweet potatoes. Reports from settlers describe hacking down cane, letting it dry, and setting a fire to let it burn clean, which "upset rattlesnakes that lived in it." The farmers would then loosen the soil until it was ready for planting. They would jab a hole into the soil with a stick and drop seeds inside. Typically, two crops could be planted before weeds appeared on the land.

# *Three*

# The Sugar Bowl Plantations

Sometime before 1755, a Spanish mission, Mission San Jose y San Miguel de Aguayo, built the first Texan sugar mill in San Antonio. The success of this venture meant that Moses Austin knew future settlers of the lower Brazos River basin could grow sugar cane on their farms.

Stephen F. Austin also understood this, and, by 1828, his colony had a sugar mill. In 1830, Austin noted that local farmers had adapted at least 70,000 acres for growing sugar. By 1833, he listed sugar as a major crop, and within seven years, Austin's Colony had developed a thriving economy. By 1840, there were 10 to 15 large sugar mills in the area, and the commercial production of sugar began. By 1850, the settlers had grown the area's 45 sugar farms into a fully realized plantation system. Twenty-five of these were located in Brazoria County, and most of them were built along the Brazos River. This plantation system was the foundation of the "Sugar Bowl," a term used to describe the region until the mid-20th century. A large plantation could produce 1,200 hogsheads—equaling about a million pounds—of sugar per year. Some reports state that the industry was prosperous and grew quickly, causing the price of molasses to fall to the point that it was worthless.

Eventually, Fort Bend wrangled the position of leader of the Sugar Bowl from Brazoria County, and it never lost the title. In 1925, Imperial Sugar, the centerpiece of the Fort Bend sugar industry, produced one million pounds of pure, refined sugar per day. Imperial Sugar was an important fixture in the area, and helped to modernize Fort Bend and the sugar industry. For example, in 1948, Imperial Sugar had the only air-conditioned sugar packing room in the world. This was the centerpiece of a $4 million renovation.

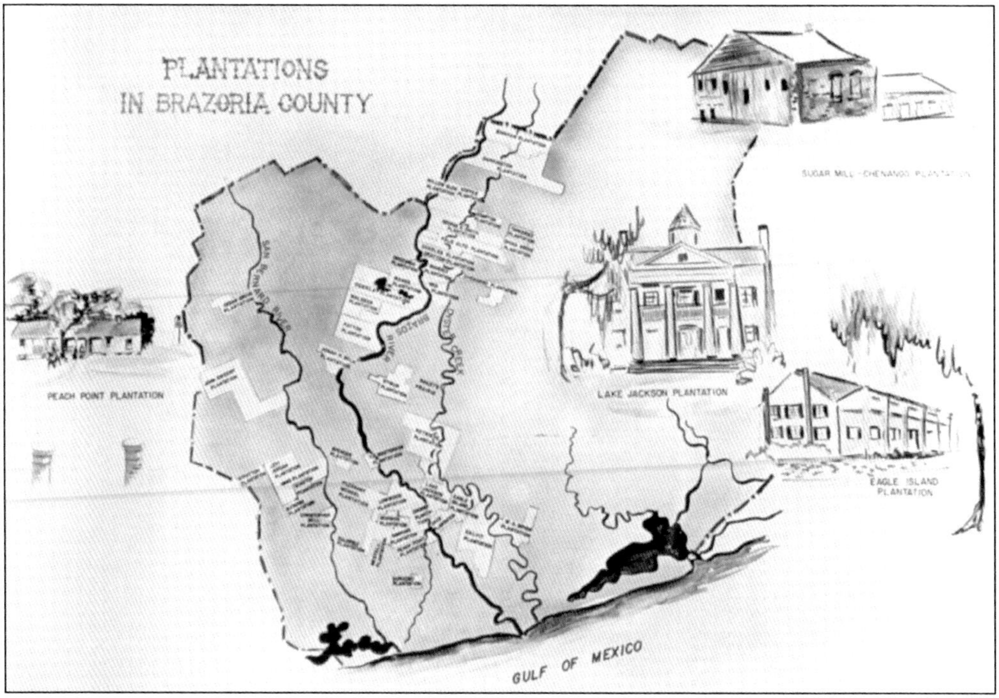


The majority of the Sugar Bowl plantations were located along the Brazos River on or near the riverbank. Settlers initially built their farms on the river to give themselves easy access to the water, and the ferries that provided local and regional transportation. Eventually, railways would speed traffic to Galveston County, and canals would connect the deep waters of the gulf to the river that fed these thriving towns. (Courtesy of Don Hutson.)

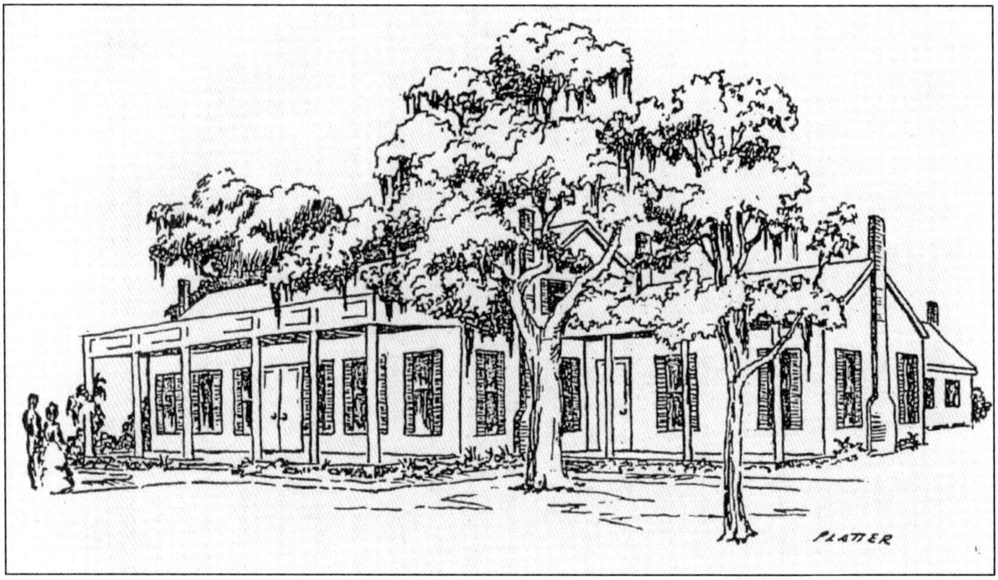


Eagle Island was a 16,000-acre plantation located on Oyster Creek. It belonged to Sarah Groce, whose father, Jared Groce, had owned the first cotton gin in Austin's Colony. Eagle Island had a brick sugar mill with two kettles, and featured a backup machine system so that slaves could keep the mill operating efficiently.

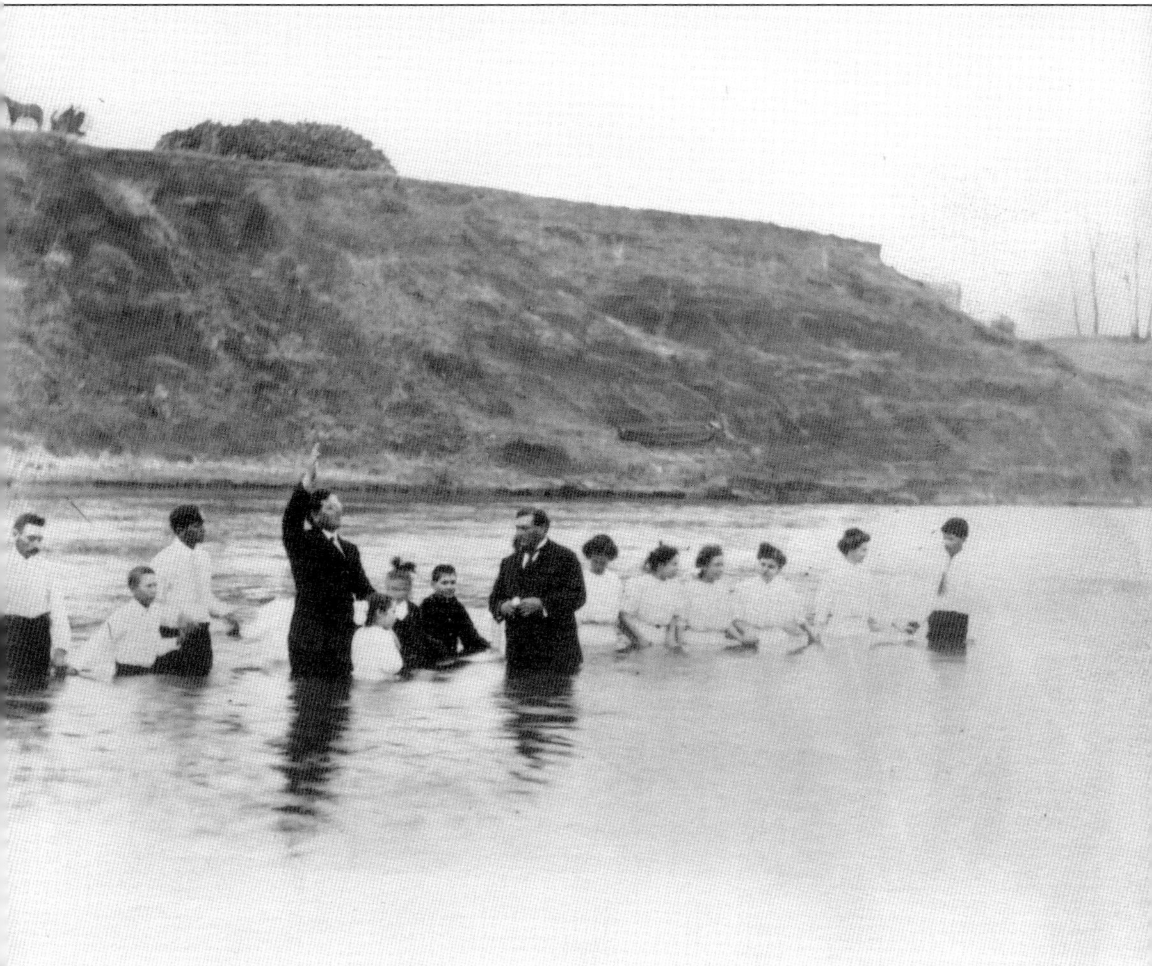

Life centered on the Brazos River. It was a focal point for economic development and community spirit, and people often gathered at the water for baptisms. Stephen F. Austin had recruited Roman Catholics for the colony, as a requirement for colonization mandated by the Mexican government. He had also sought out educated and moneyed colonists who could handle the challenges of being a pioneer.

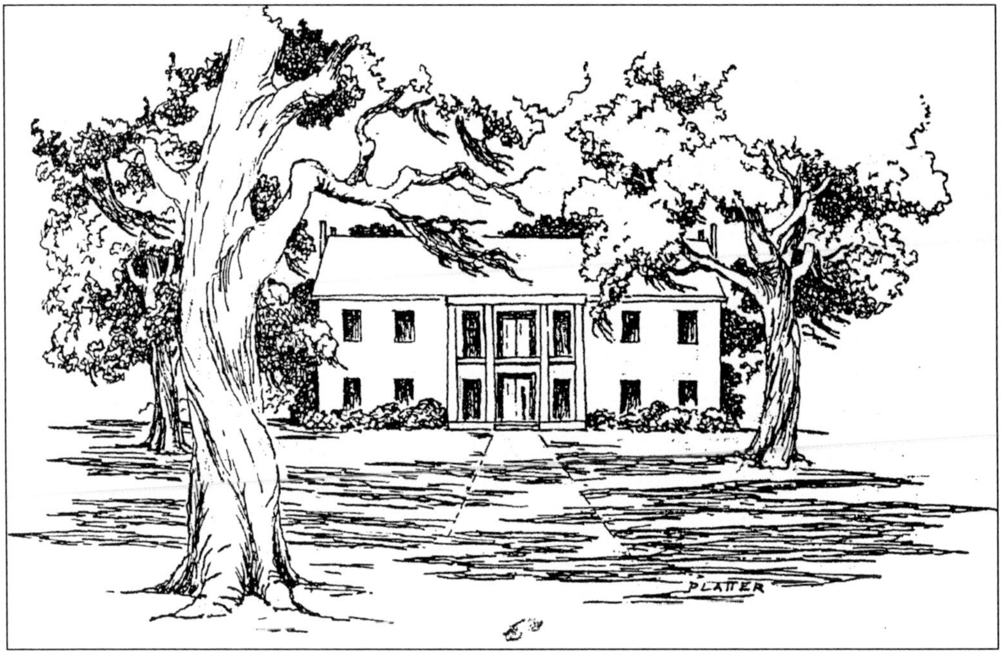


Pleasant Grove was a sugar plantation, located on the river in Brazoria. It featured brick construction on the main house, the sugar mill, and the slave cabins. After the owner, Leander McNeel, died, the plantation was plunged into 43 years of court disputes. The Texas prison system eventually purchased the property.

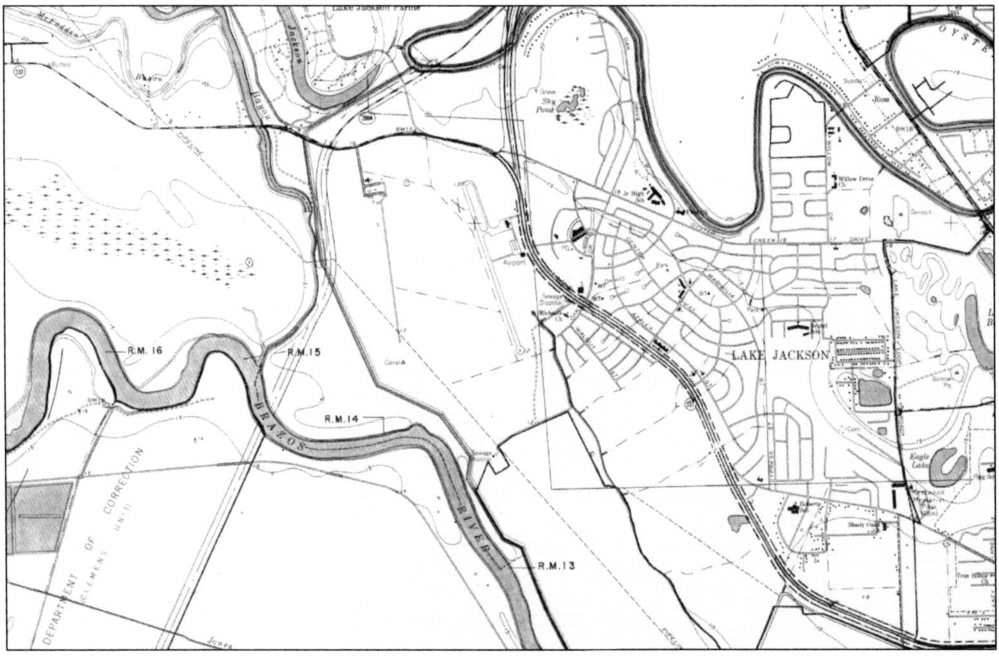


After the Civil War, convicts replaced slave labor, and Pleasant Grove became a part of the Clemens Prison Farm, visible at lower left on this map. The Texas prison system's lease lasted for 46 years, and the system helped these commercial plantations to rebuild and recover over time. In 1877, a local businessman, E.H. Cunningham, became the prison's convict lease system administrator.

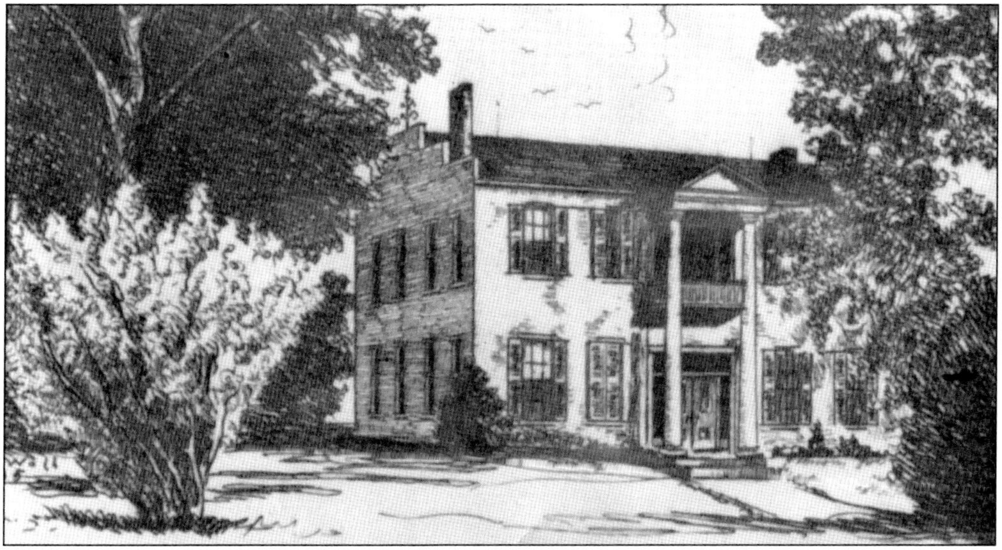

Local history and folklore record the Nibbs House as being a part of Walnut Plantation. Stories state that Sam Houston stopped to visit Mrs. Nibbs on his way to the Battle of San Jacinto. While he was there, the stories say, he bought his battle horse from her and then headed off to make history. Slaves built the house from bricks they made from Oyster Creek clay.

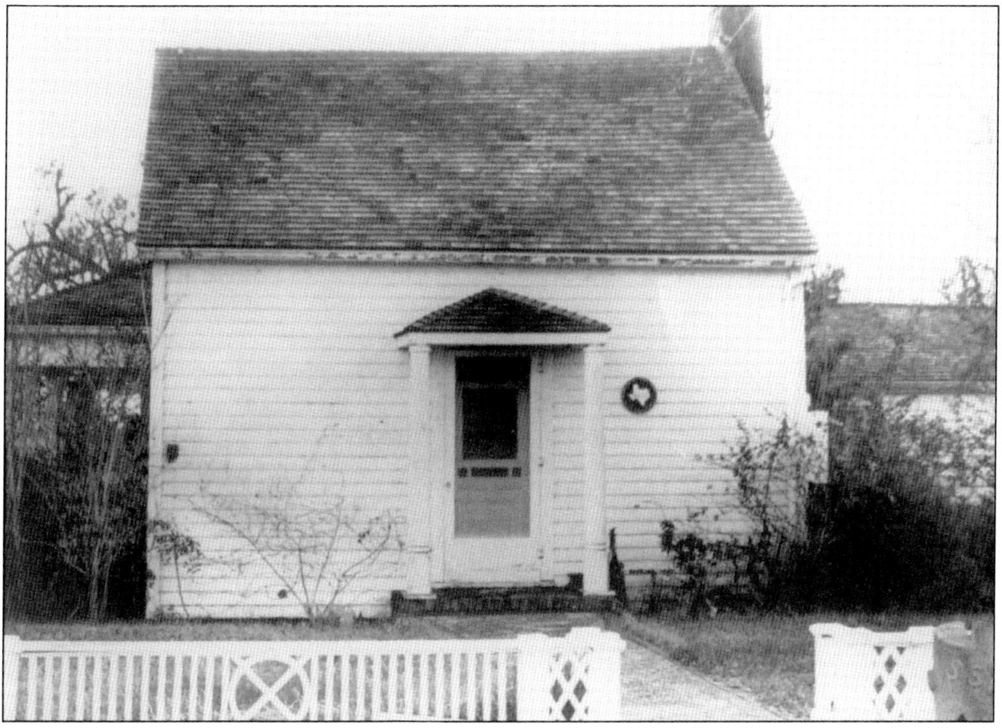

The plantation that Stephen F. Austin dreamed of became the home of his sister, Emily. Peach Point was built between Jones Creek and the Brazos River. Austin came to consider Peach Point as his own home and even wanted to be buried there, which he eventually was. In the mid-1800s, the plantation first produced cotton, and then sugar.

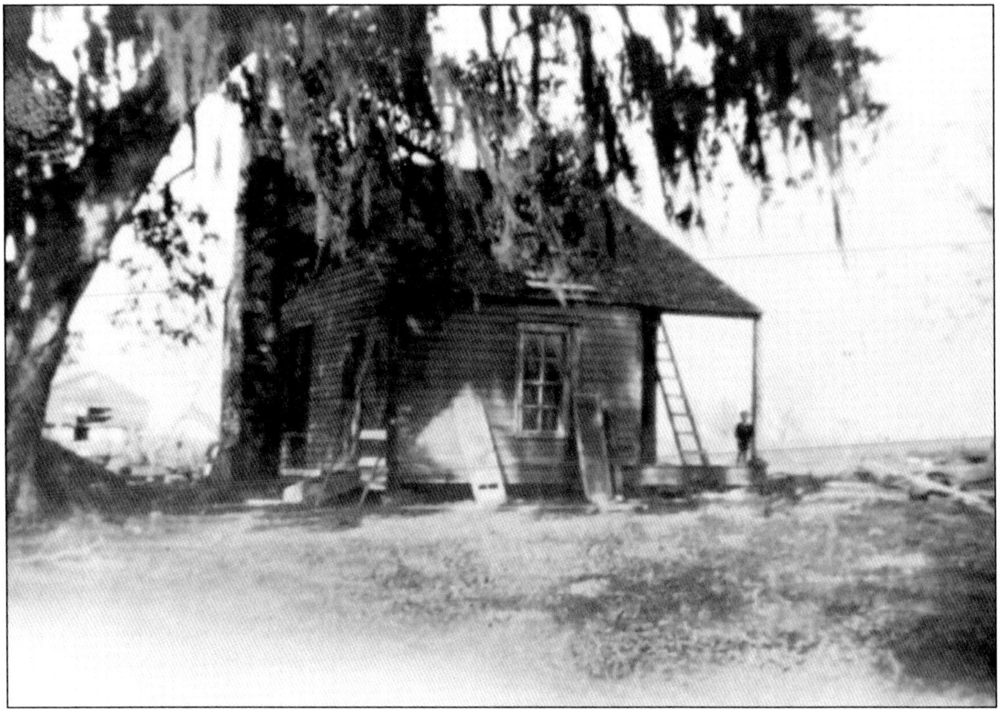

Like many plantations, Peach Point eventually fell into disrepair. Austin's office was among the structures allowed to decay. Pictured above, a small boy stands on the porch of the historic site. Below, an artist's sketch of the plantation shows the entrance to the farm, and the modest architecture of the main house.

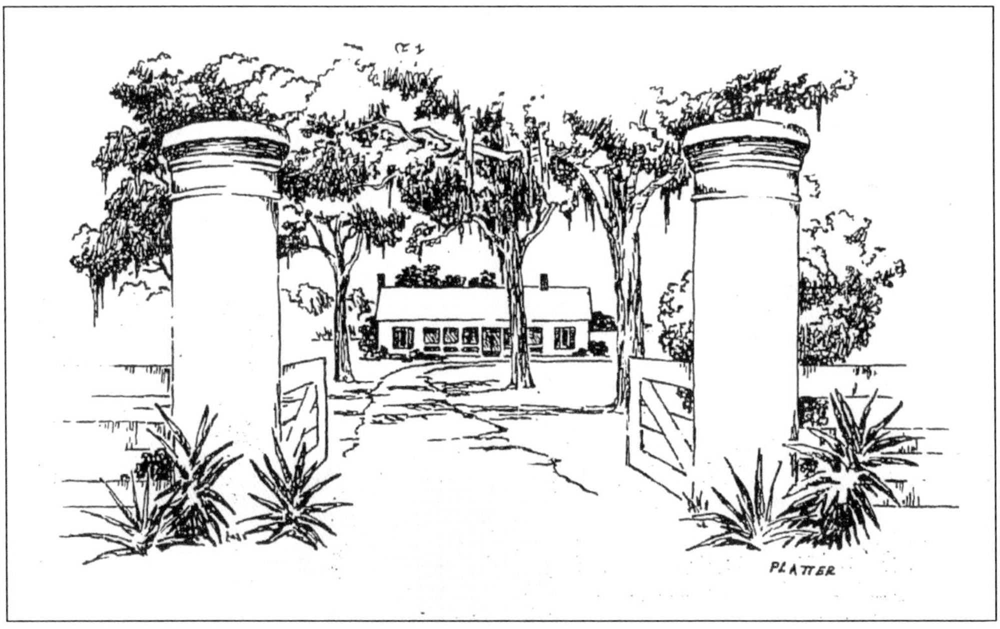

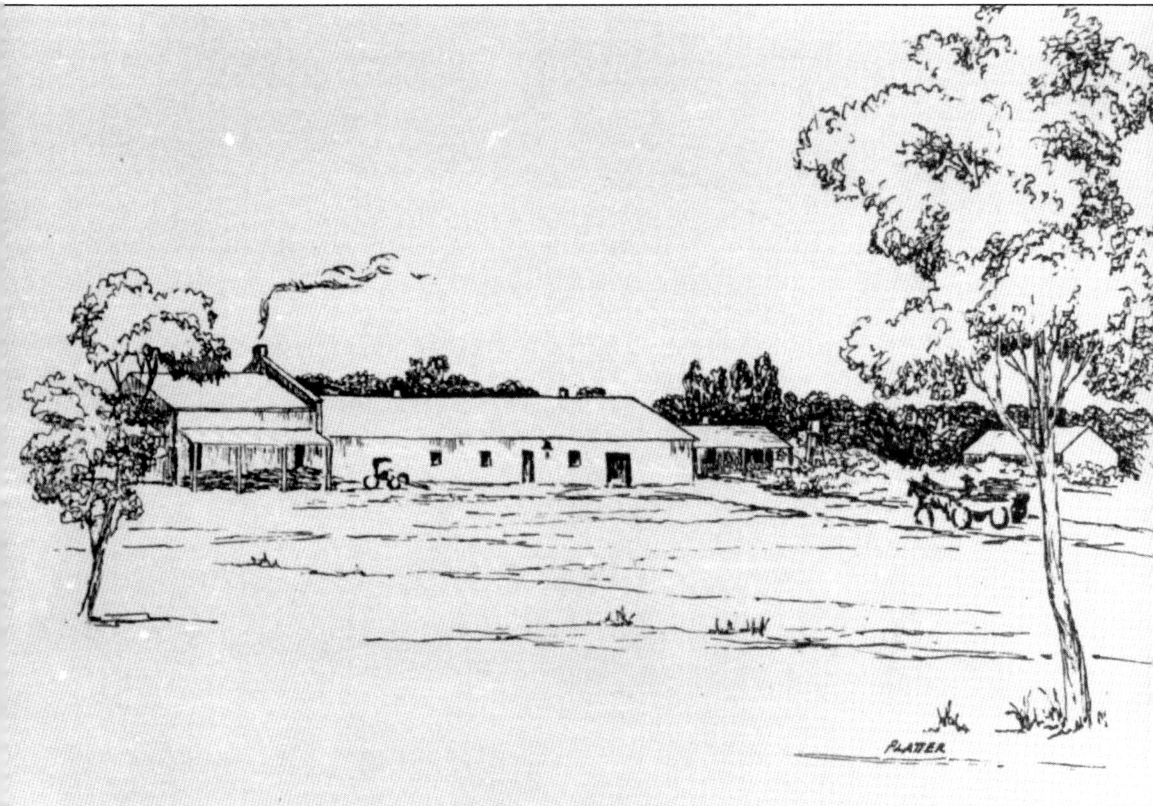

Chenango Plantation was a 1,300-acre Brazoria sugar plantation located near present-day Angleton. Its most infamous owner was Monroe Edwards, a Cuban slave smuggler. Edwards purchased the plantation—then called Point Pleasant—from Benjamin Fort Smith. Edwards and Christopher Dart, an old partner from Galveston, became smugglers in 1833. They used his plantation as a way station for slaves smuggled through Cuba. On their first trip to Cuba, they purchased 196 Africans for $25 each, and resold them for $600 each. The partners agreed to split a $100,000 profit, but Edwards tricked Dart. Instead of splitting the profits, Edwards altered the paperwork so that Dart received 50 percent of the plantation and a portion of the slave money. Unfortunately for Dart, Edwards had already sold the plantation for $35,000, and Dart's claim to the real estate was worthless. Edwards was jailed, but, after the trial, he fled and lived as a forger until the authorities captured him again. Edwards was sentenced to a term in New York state's Sing Sing prison.

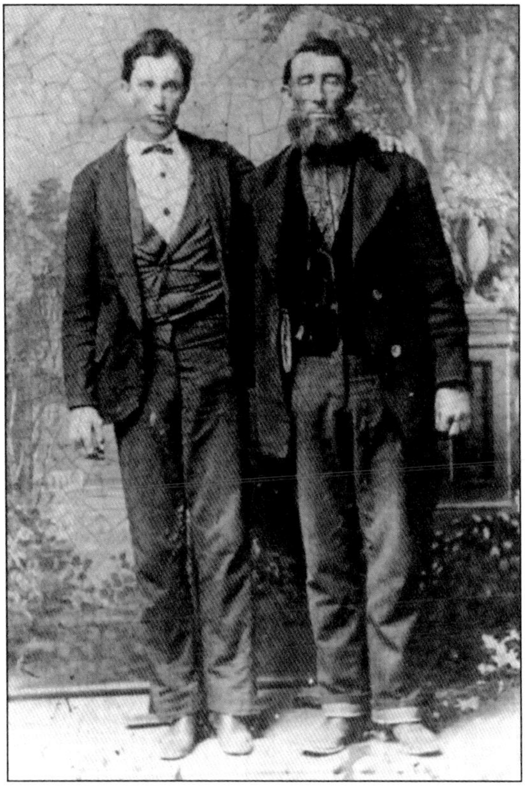

Chenango Plantation had its roots in Austin's Colon. Joshua Abbott, pictured on the right, had 4,428 acres on Flores Bayou that became part of the William Harris survey. Using some of the land set aside by this survey, Benjamin Fort Smith built the original, 3,000-acre Point Pleasant plantation. D.J. Moller of Liverpool is on the left in this photograph.

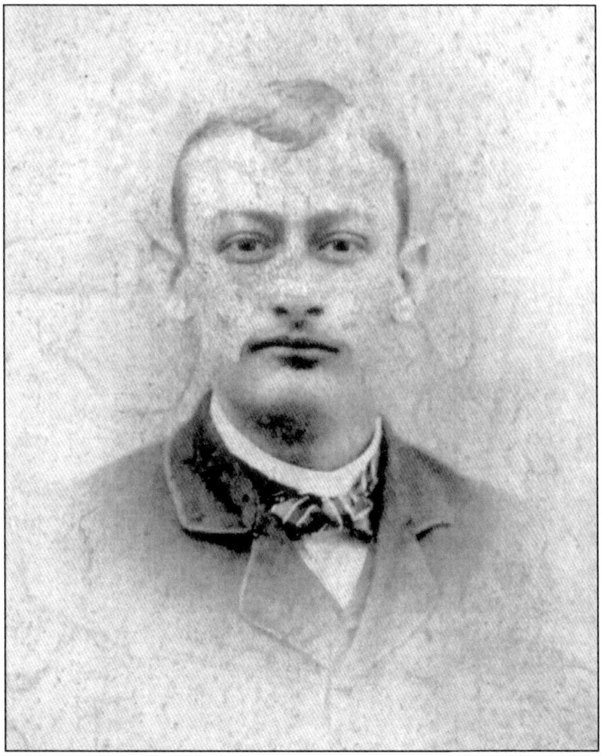

Bobby Thomas, stepbrother of Lon Follett, was born in 1860 in Liverpool. He was the son of Elijah Thomas, and was raised at the Chenango Plantation. Many people owned Chenango following Monroe Edwards's illegal sale of the property and the resulting bankruptcy.

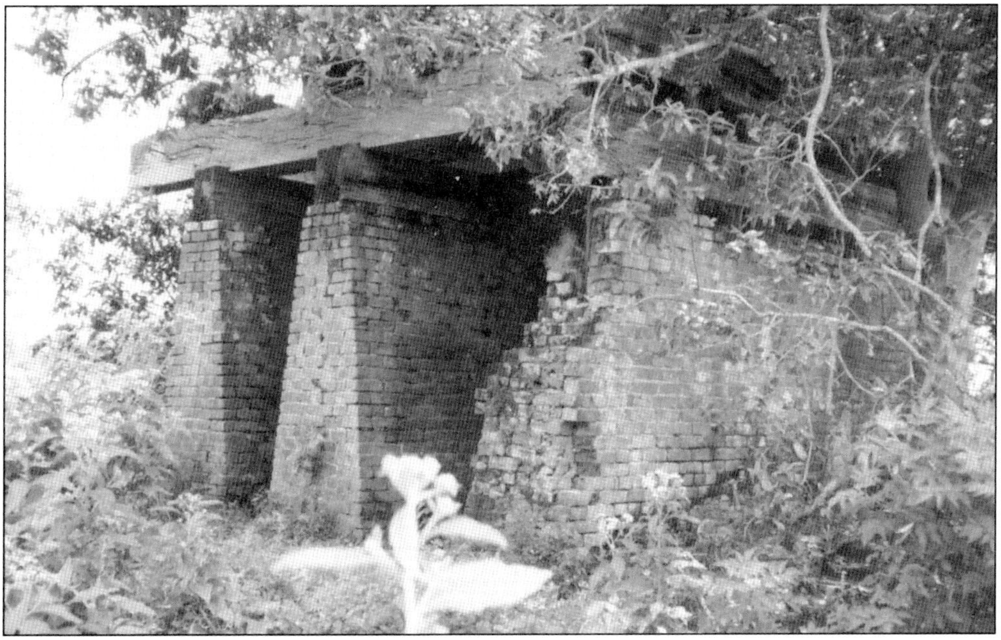

Edwards had plans to convert the original cotton farm into a sugar plantation. They constructed a sugar mill that became a landmark in the region following the Civil War. At one time, a small town—Chenango, Texas—formed around the plantation. The town had a post office that operated between 1869 and 1930, as well as a school that taught black children during segregation. The town also featured a train depot, a cotton gin, and a few businesses. Chenango never grew beyond 100 people, and the residents abandoned it sometime between 1930 and 1950. The plantation's sugar mill continued to deteriorate, and soon became a part of local folklore. The ruin was still standing when developers recently built the Chenango housing division; for a brief time, attempts were made to rally the community into saving the old structure. Experts have questioned whether the ruin is a sugar mill or simply another plantation building, but locals have dismissed this assessment.

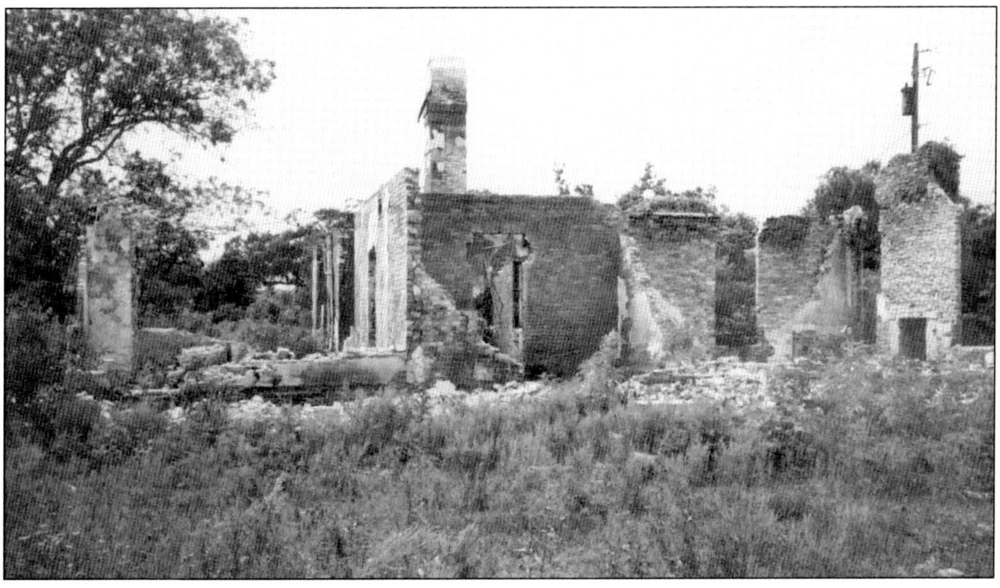

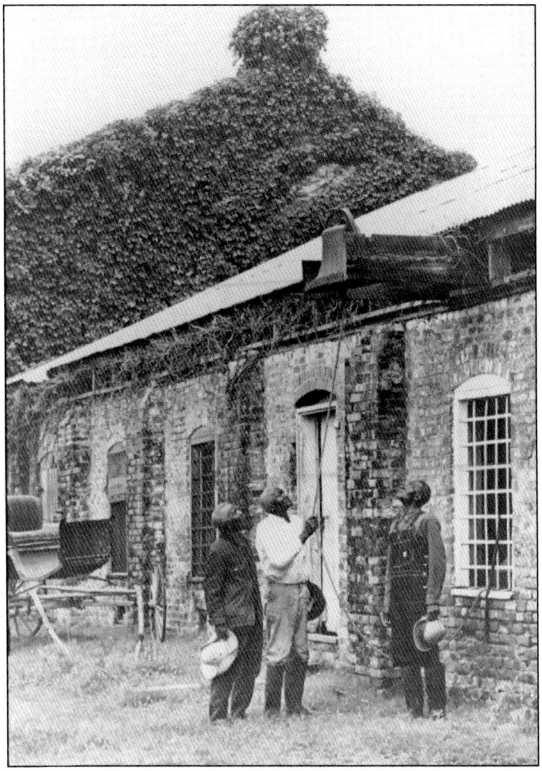

Slaves ring the bell at the Chenango sugar mill in this undated photograph. Texas abolished slavery in 1836, but smugglers devised ways to circumvent the law. Commonly, they would convince Cubans to become indentured servants for three years in exchange for Texas residency. The Cubans would sign the agreements, and, once at sea, the smugglers forced the Cubans to sign papers that voided the first agreements. The new agreements stated that each Cuban would work for a master for 99 years.

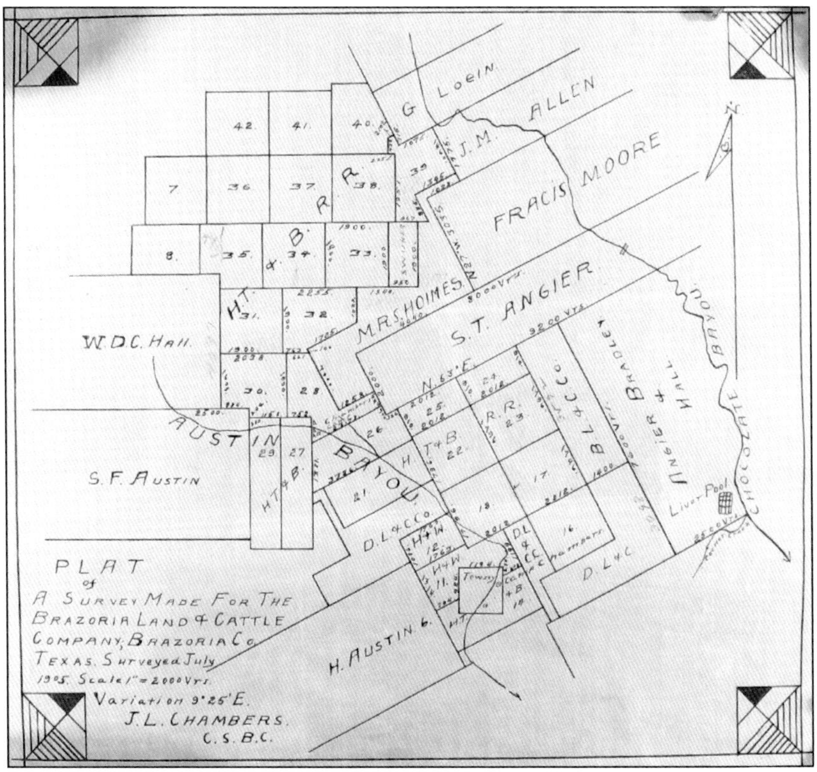


This Liverpool survey documents the W.D.C. Hall land. Hall was the settler who purchased the Chenango plantation from Monroe Edwards for $35,000. For his crimes, Edwards faced a trial in a Brazoria court, and was convicted by a jury.

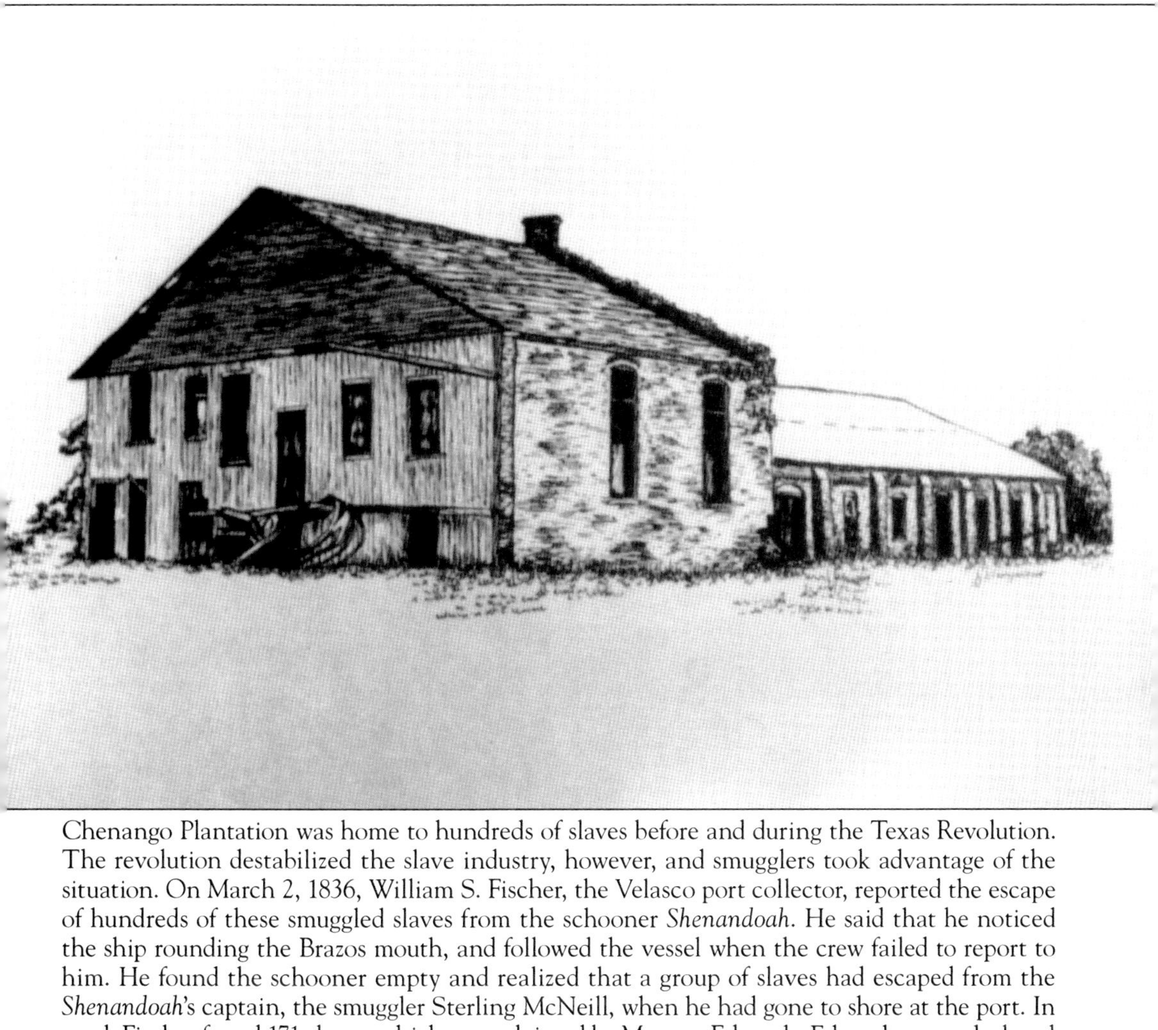

Chenango Plantation was home to hundreds of slaves before and during the Texas Revolution. The revolution destabilized the slave industry, however, and smugglers took advantage of the situation. On March 2, 1836, William S. Fischer, the Velasco port collector, reported the escape of hundreds of these smuggled slaves from the schooner *Shenandoah*. He said that he noticed the ship rounding the Brazos mouth, and followed the vessel when the crew failed to report to him. He found the schooner empty and realized that a group of slaves had escaped from the *Shenandoah*'s captain, the smuggler Sterling McNeill, when he had gone to shore at the port. In total, Fischer found 171 slaves, which were claimed by Monroe Edwards. Edwards secured a bond for the slaves and Fischer wrote that the outcome of the matter would be "the decision of the government." In the same report, a frustrated Fischer stated that "negro traffic" was increasing and that he needed more instruction regarding how to handle the situation. An earlier report describes how Edwards lost 124 slaves during the Mexican advance of 1835. (Courtesy of Brazoria County Historical Commission.)

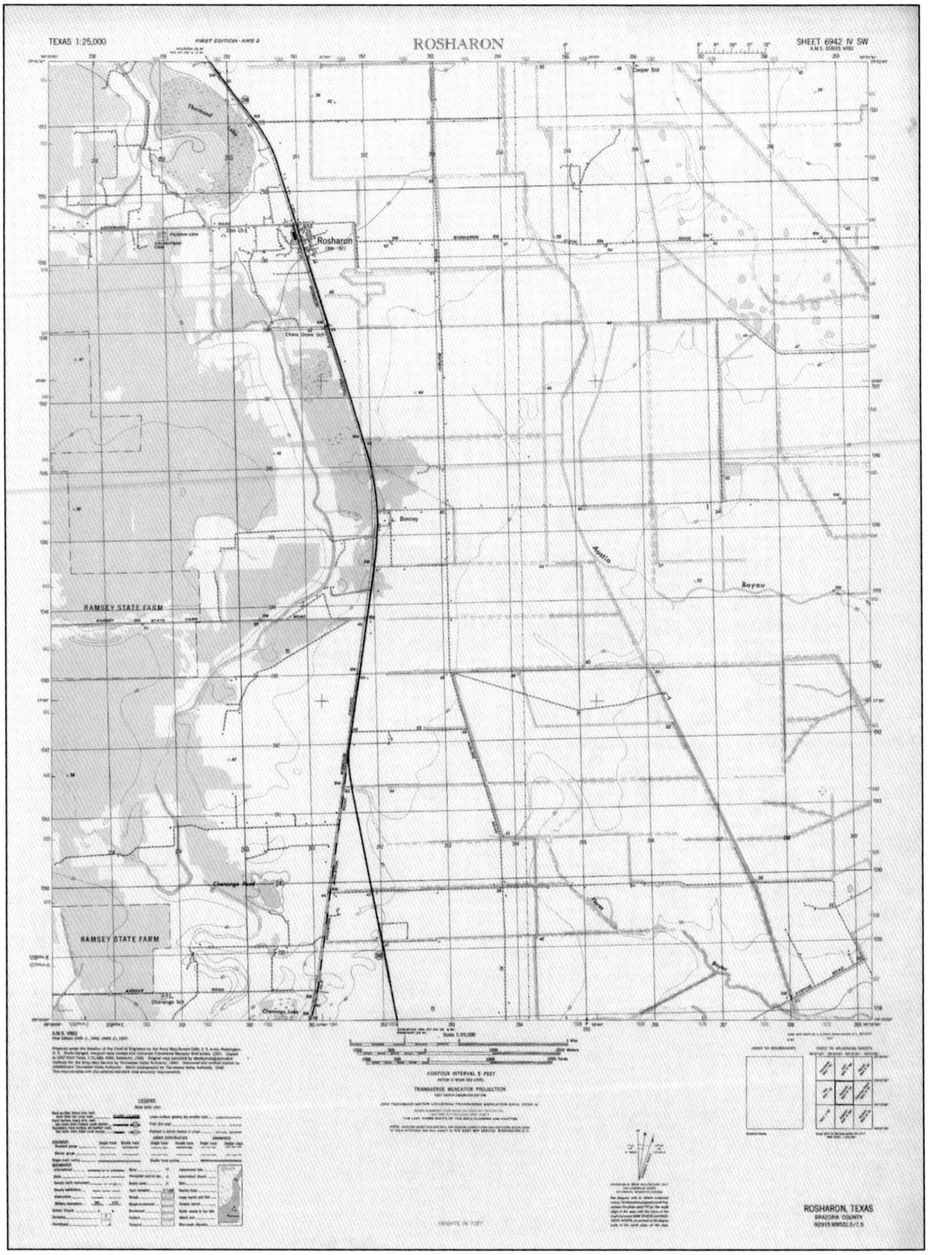


This map, drafted by the Army Map Service in 1947, illustrates the size of the Texas prison system's Ramsey State Farm. The collapse of the convict lease system began with a San Antonio newspaper investigation in 1910, but, even before that date, the Texas prison system was buying plantations outright. The state wanted to begin its own commercial agriculture system, producing its own sugar, cotton, corn, feed crops, and vegetables to provide for the prison system and other state agencies. Many notable plantations and farms became prison farms, including the Harlem and Blue Ridge Farms, Imperial Farms in Fort Bend, and the Darrington Farm and Retrieve Plantation in Brazoria. When this system failed, the loss of cheap labor effectively ended the plantation system as an economic force, but the introduction of rice growing to the region was about to cause a noticeable shift in the local agricultural economy.

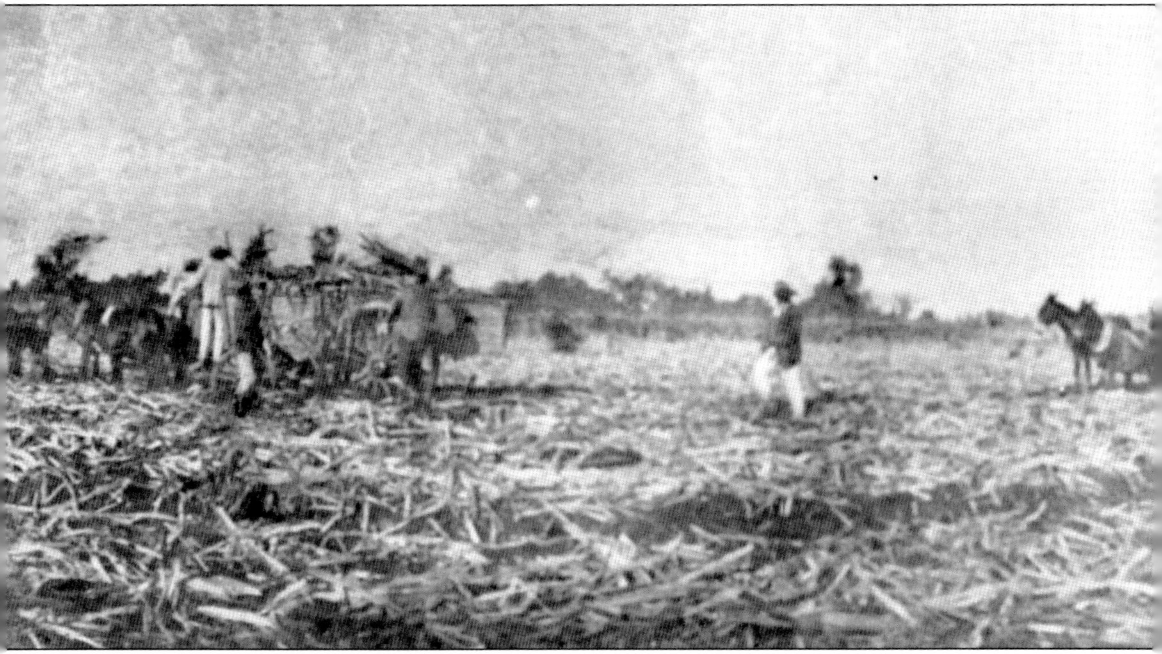

This undated photograph shows the harvesting and loading of sugar cane at the Masterson Plantation in Otey, Texas. In the beginning, plantations processed sugar cane to make both sugar and syrup, but by 1950, there was only demand for syrup. Consumers also prized fine white sugar, but the plantation mill kettles only manufactured the less valuable coarse sugar. Historians disagree on the date that commercialized sugar production began in the lower Brazos River, but it could have been as early as 1840. Brazoria, Fort Bend, Matagorda, and Wharton were all important to the Sugar Bowl. Both before and after the Civil War, Brazoria County led the state in sugar production. It could easily produce 10 times as much sugar as the other counties combined. In about 1910, Fort Bend—which entered the sugar industry in 1840 with the construction of the Williams Plantation—began to surpass Brazoria. (Courtesy of Brazoria County Historical Commission.)

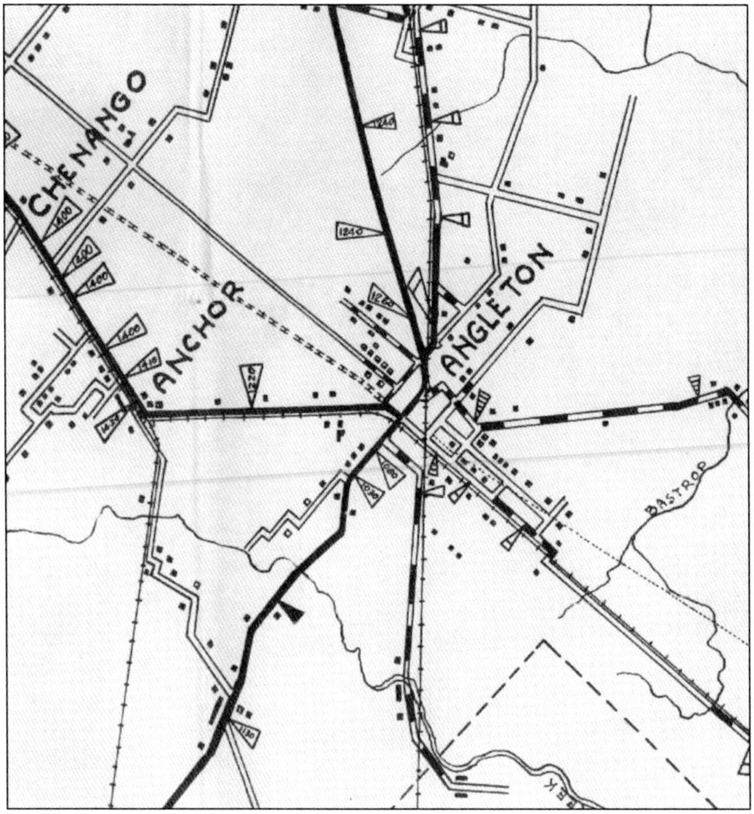


This Texas Department of Engineering map shows the towns of Angleton, Chenango, and Anchor in 1940. Chenango had a farm, and a road to Angleton (appearing as a line of H-shaped symbols) was under construction. A paved road already linked the town to Angleton. Within 10 years, Chenango would be abandoned, and Angleton would go on to be an important farm town.

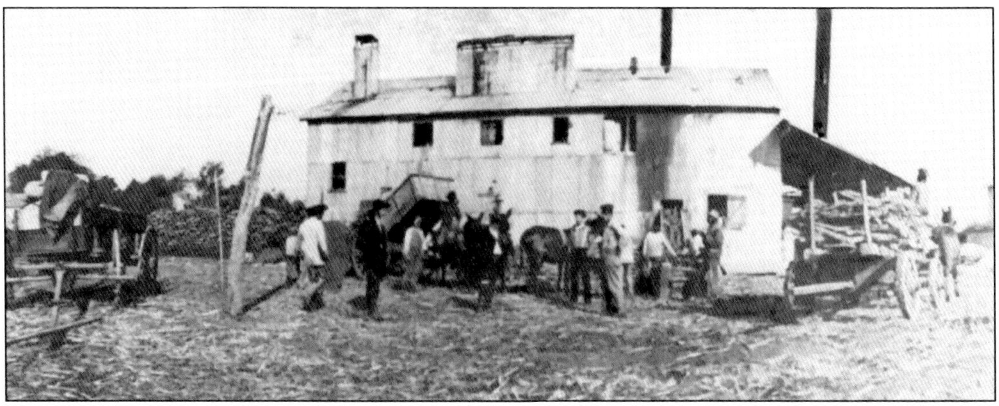

The Masterson Plantation, named for owner Thomas Masterson, was north of the Chenango school in Otey. It was a cotton and sugar plantation, and was one of two plantations that Masterson owned. In 1908, the Masterson Plantation became the Ramsey prison unit, with the town of Otey serving it. (Courtesy of Brazoria County Historical Commission.)

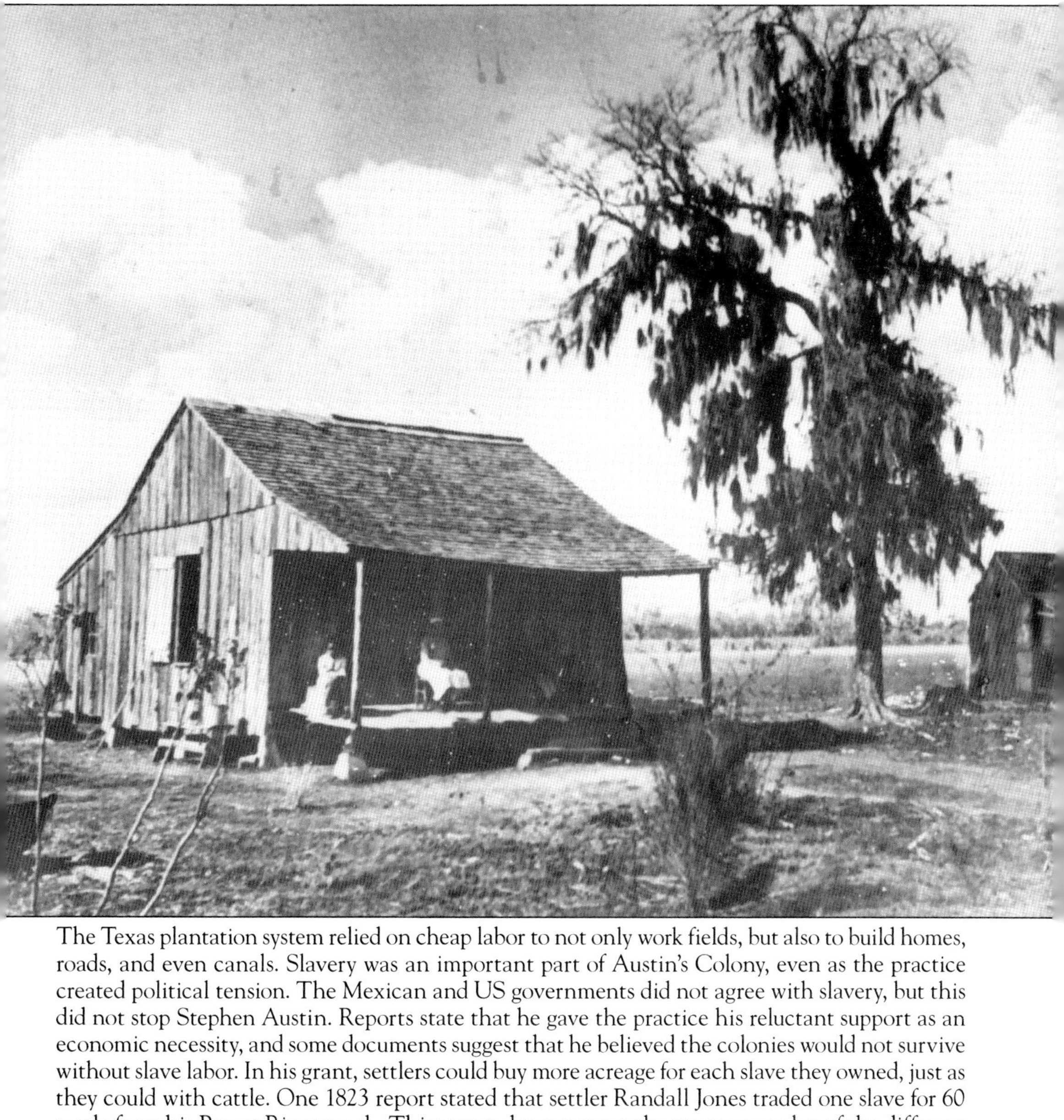

The Texas plantation system relied on cheap labor to not only work fields, but also to build homes, roads, and even canals. Slavery was an important part of Austin's Colony, even as the practice created political tension. The Mexican and US governments did not agree with slavery, but this did not stop Stephen Austin. Reports state that he gave the practice his reluctant support as an economic necessity, and some documents suggest that he believed the colonies would not survive without slave labor. In his grant, settlers could buy more acreage for each slave they owned, just as they could with cattle. One 1823 report stated that settler Randall Jones traded one slave for 60 cattle from his Brazos River ranch. This report demonstrates the monetary value of the different "properties" on a growing plantation. This undated photograph shows a tenant cabin in Fort Bend. (Courtesy of Fort Bend Museum.)

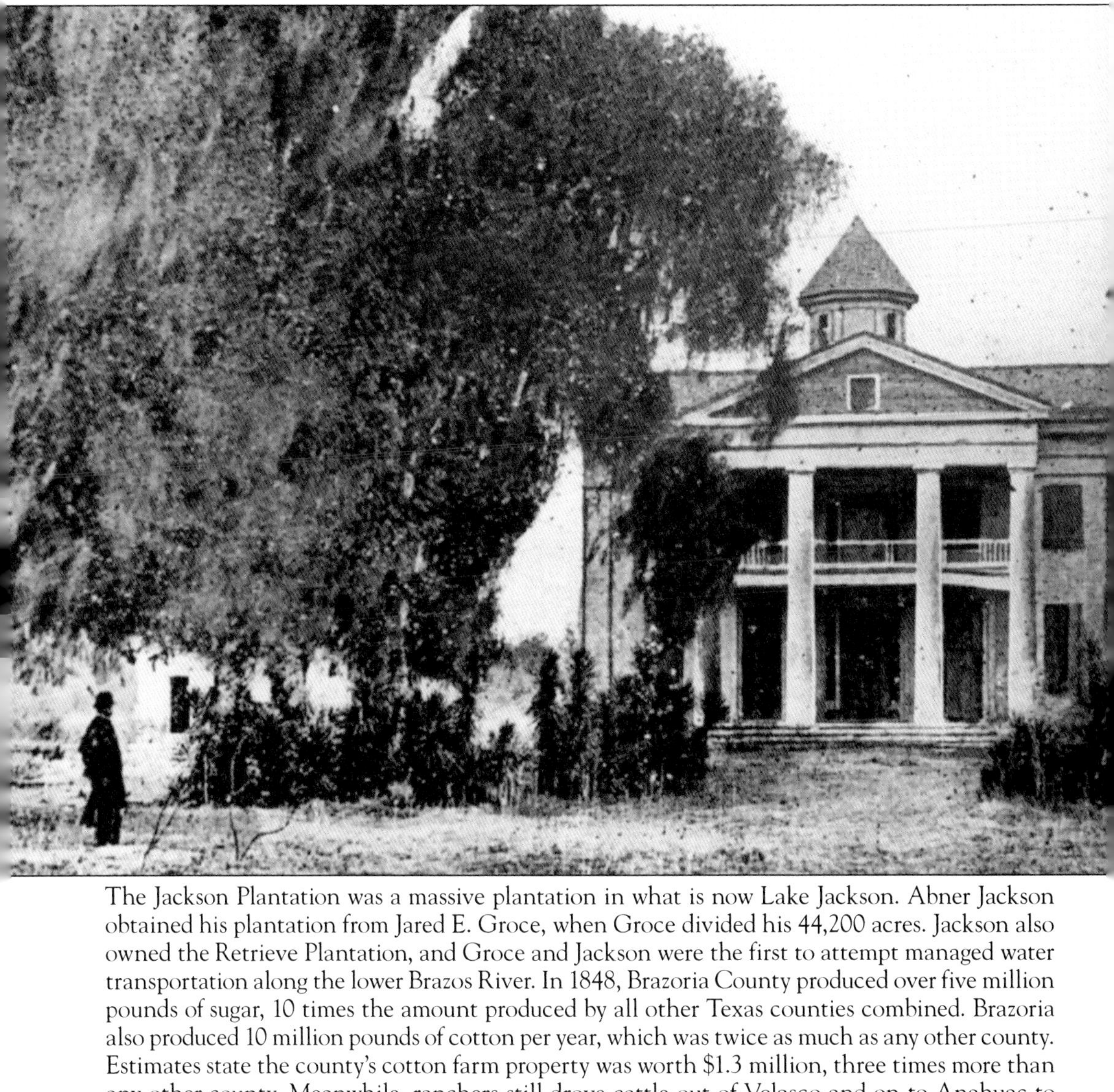

The Jackson Plantation was a massive plantation in what is now Lake Jackson. Abner Jackson obtained his plantation from Jared E. Groce, when Groce divided his 44,200 acres. Jackson also owned the Retrieve Plantation, and Groce and Jackson were the first to attempt managed water transportation along the lower Brazos River. In 1848, Brazoria County produced over five million pounds of sugar, 10 times the amount produced by all other Texas counties combined. Brazoria also produced 10 million pounds of cotton per year, which was twice as much as any other county. Estimates state the county's cotton farm property was worth $1.3 million, three times more than any other county. Meanwhile, ranchers still drove cattle out of Velasco and on to Anahuac to merge with the Opelousas Trail. This bustling pre–Civil War river economy needed to ship its products safely and quickly. To do this, plantation owners looked beyond the river and bayous to a new tool that would help keep their towns thriving: canals.

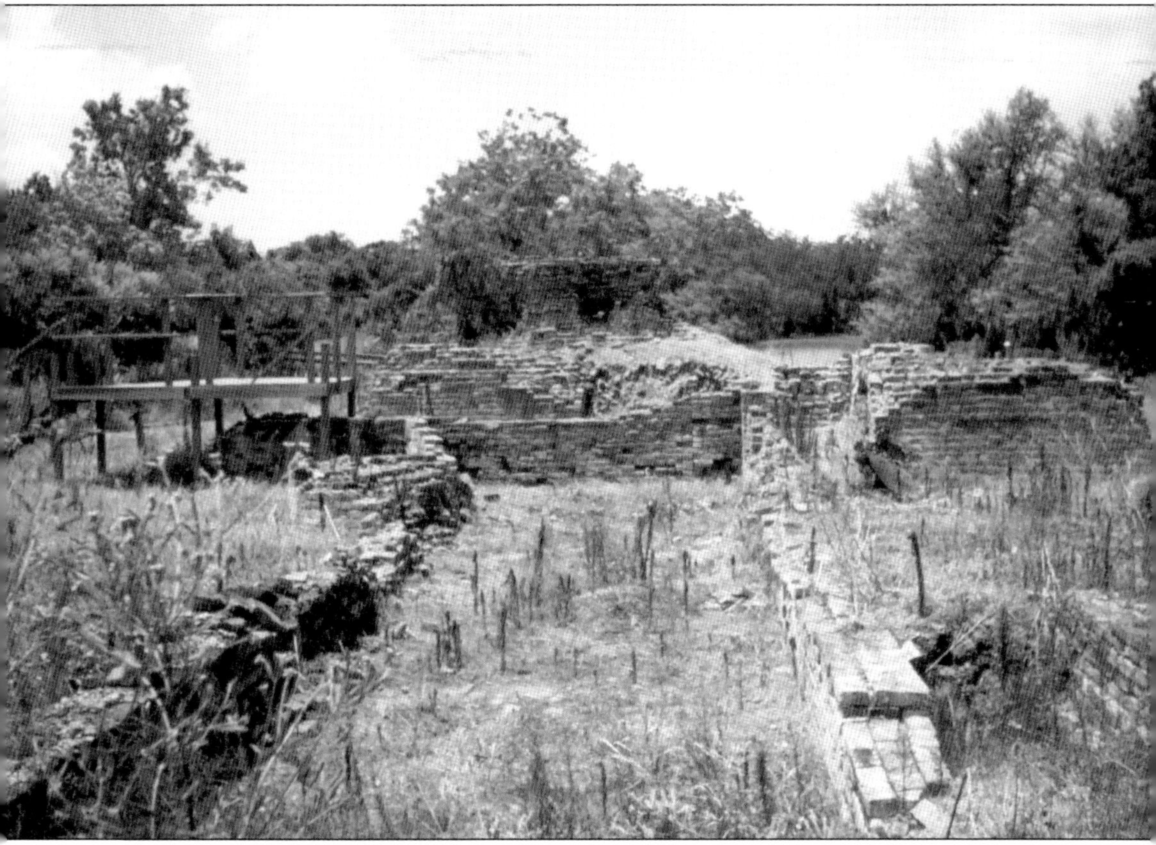

From the 1830s to the 1840s, plantation owners held meetings to entice investors with their proposed canal system. Austin and his people believed that a canal was the best solution to getting around the shifting sandbar at the mouth of the Brazos. On January 8, 1842, the Texas congress authorized $100,000 to the Brazos Canal Company to connect the Brazos River to the San Luis Pass. The idea was to dig a three-foot canal linking Oyster Creek to Bastrop Bayou so that vessels could avoid the mouth of the Brazos. The first step was to make a cut in Oyster Creek, but the project was plagued with problems—including the site manager's death by drowning. Abner Jackson took over the effort in 1845, agreeing to build a 24-foot-deep canal with a one-foot slope, which would have at least three feet of water in it. It would connect the Brazos River to Bastrop Bayou, and the bayou to San Luis harbor. Jackson began construction in 1846, and the project stretched over Jared Groce's five leagues of land and the Eagle Island Plantation. The ruins of Jackson Plantation are pictured here. (Courtesy of Brazoria County Historical Commission.)

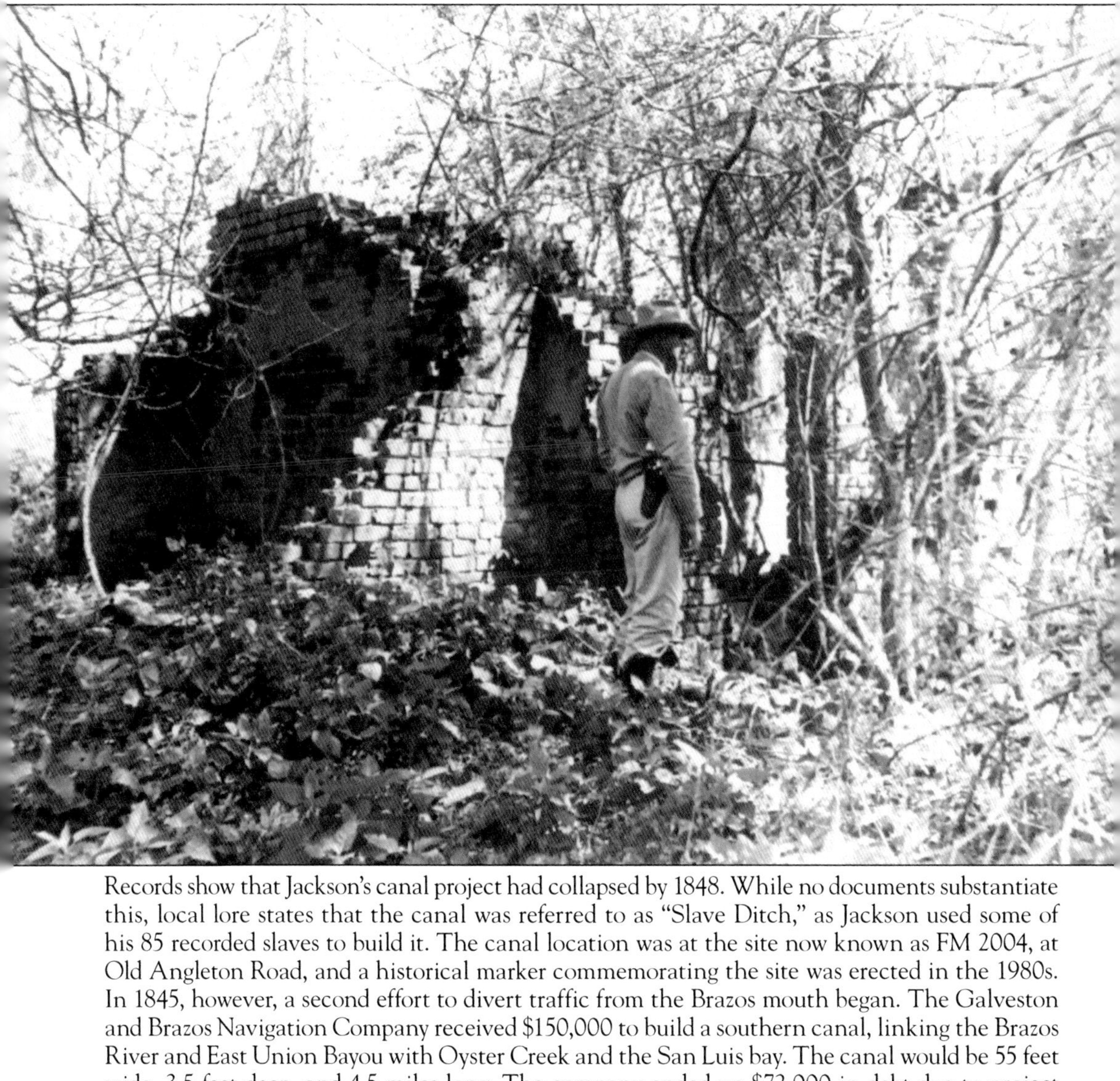

Records show that Jackson's canal project had collapsed by 1848. While no documents substantiate this, local lore states that the canal was referred to as "Slave Ditch," as Jackson used some of his 85 recorded slaves to build it. The canal location was at the site now known as FM 2004, at Old Angleton Road, and a historical marker commemorating the site was erected in the 1980s. In 1845, however, a second effort to divert traffic from the Brazos mouth began. The Galveston and Brazos Navigation Company received $150,000 to build a southern canal, linking the Brazos River and East Union Bayou with Oyster Creek and the San Luis bay. The canal would be 55 feet wide, 3.5 feet deep, and 4.5 miles long. The company ended up $72,000 in debt due to project delays, and the Galveston-Brazos Canal was abandoned until the post–Civil War Reconstruction period. Pictured here, "Cap" Brown stands at the ruins of the Lake Jackson Plantation, where the idea for the canal began.

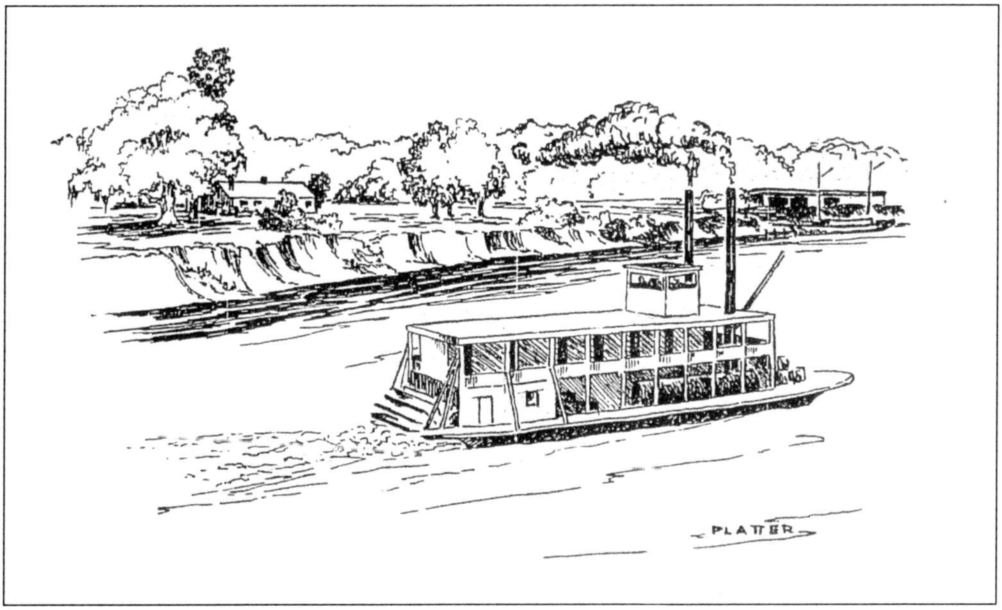


Thomas Phillip Crosby chose to settle on 1,000 acres on the lower Brazos River, and established Crosby's Landing. The landing catered to the local plantation owners by establishing docks for shipping and the receipt of goods from Galveston and New Orleans. When Stephen Austin died, the steamboat *Yellowstone* docked at Crosby's Landing bearing his body. In this A.A. Platter sketch, the landing can be seen on the bank to the right, with the Crosby homestead nestled in the distance.

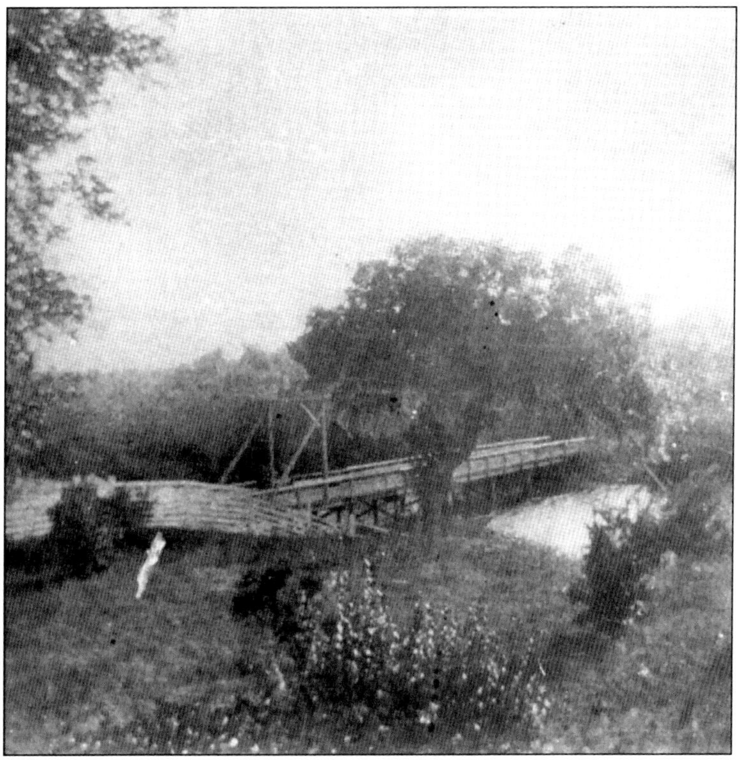

Settlers chose Chocolate Bayou as a shipping port, as it allowed them to circumvent the Brazos mouth. They would move their goods overland by wagon or ox to Liverpool, and then load the cargo onto sailboats to Galveston. The overland leg was difficult because the roads were not well built. Chocolate Bayou was also one of the most popular cattle ranching areas on the lower Brazos River.

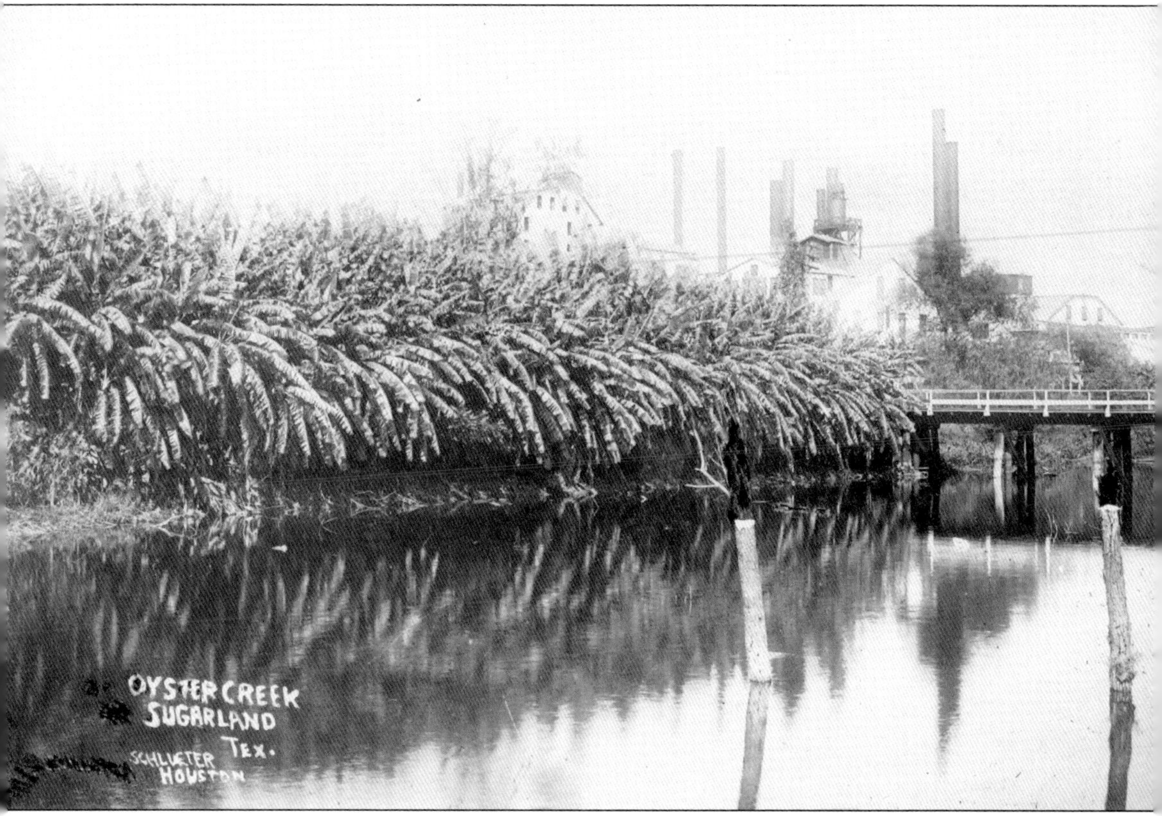


Oyster Creek was vital to the economic development of the region, beginning in the days of Austin's Colony through the growth of Imperial Sugar and Sugar Land. In 1901, J.M. Frost built a canal on Oyster Creek, which would become the American Cane and Rice Canal and be used to irrigate rice. At the time, community leaders called it a marvel of water management, and expected the canal to expand the economic system of Houston and the lower Brazos River region. Today, the Gulf Coast Water Authority's Canal A, near Sugar Land, moves water from Oyster Creek through Stafford, Missouri City, Manvel, Alvin, and League City. The canal then winds its way through Santa Fe and connects with the Briscoe to become Canal G. From there, the water continues through Dickinson and into Texas City and La Marque. All together, these man-made canals move Oyster Creek water up to 60 miles, supplying industrial and commercial areas south of Houston. (Courtesy of Fort Bend Museum.)

# *Four*

# Imperial Sugar

After the Civil War, E.H. Cunningham purchased Oakland Plantation. Oakland dates back to Austin's Colony and Samuel Williams. Nathanial Williams owned the plantation in 1840, before selling it to Benjamin F. Terry and William J. Kyle—both of whom left for the California gold rush in about 1852.

By 1879, E.H. Cunningham began building a community around his 12,500-acre property. The plantation had a large cane grinding mill for local cane, which converted the juice into syrup and plantation sugar. In 1891, Cunningham built a second sugar mill on Oyster Creek, dedicated to commercial production. In 1905, he changed the mill's name to Cunningham Sugar Company.

Labor for the mill was provided by Texas's convict lease system, which Cunningham administered with Col. Littleberry A. Ellis. The two men subleased convicts they didn't need to private farmers, which made the program more efficient. Cunningham and Ellis became quite prosperous, but not without developing a reputation. The convicts working the land came to call their fields the "Hellhole on the Brazos."

Meanwhile, the Cunningham Sugar Company was about to get new neighbors. I.H. Kempner and W.T. Eldridge purchased the adjoining Ellis Plantation in 1906. In 1908, they took control of the Cunningham property, and in 1917, they changed the name of the sugar refinery to the Imperial Sugar Company. Kempner said that the name referenced both the Imperial Hotel in New York and the raw sugar mill on the Ellis Plantation.

Kempner and Eldridge began modernizing the town around their land; in doing so, they began to shift the center of the Sugar Bowl away from Brazoria County. This move is illustrated by census data from 1910: Fort Bend had 6,775 acres dedicated to cultivating sugar, while Brazoria had only 2,000. Of the 13 sugar mills in Texas, four were in Fort Bend.

Imperial Sugar remained Texas's only sugar refinery, and went on to expand its market to 13 states.

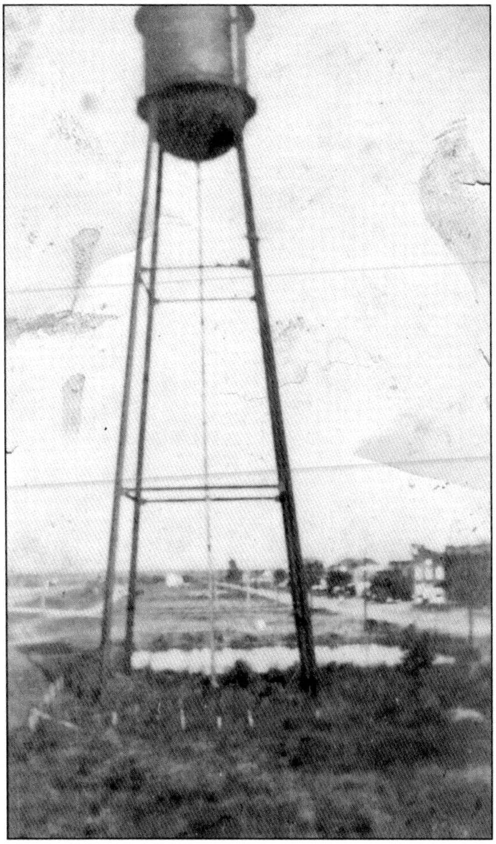

The water tower over Sugar Land was an important part of the modernized company town that Imperial Sugar was creating. After I.H. Kempner took control of the Cunningham refinery, the town transformed within a matter of decades. Behind the tower—in another show of modernization—a paved road has replaced a natural road that was "affected by weather." (Courtesy of Fort Bend Museum.)

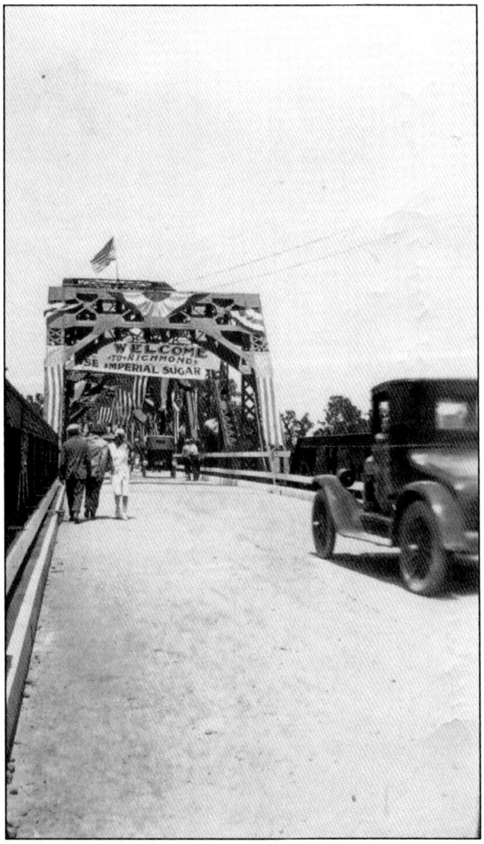


The Imperial Sugar Company was an active participant in the community. When the Brazos Bridge opened to traffic, Imperial Sugar celebrated its accomplishment with the pictured banner. The bridge was another sign that the refinery was increasing business in town, and improving the quality of life in "the town that sugar built." (Courtesy of Fort Bend Museum.)

The president of Imperial Sugar, I.H. Kempner Jr., sat for a formal photograph in November 1953. I.H. Kempner Sr.'s partner, W.T. Eldridge, was a tempestuous businessman who helped to build the Cane Belt Railroad and escaped conviction in two highly publicized murder trials. The two worked together until 1907, and upon Eldridge's death, Kempner said Eldridge was a "self-made man with considerable vision though at times, his ambitions triumphed over his judgment." (Courtesy of Fort Bend Museum.)

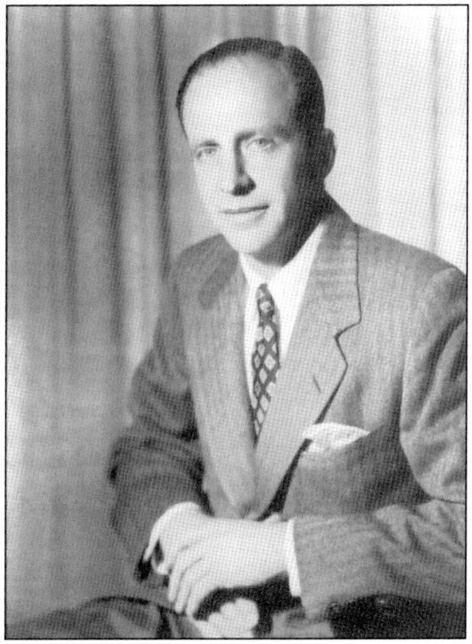

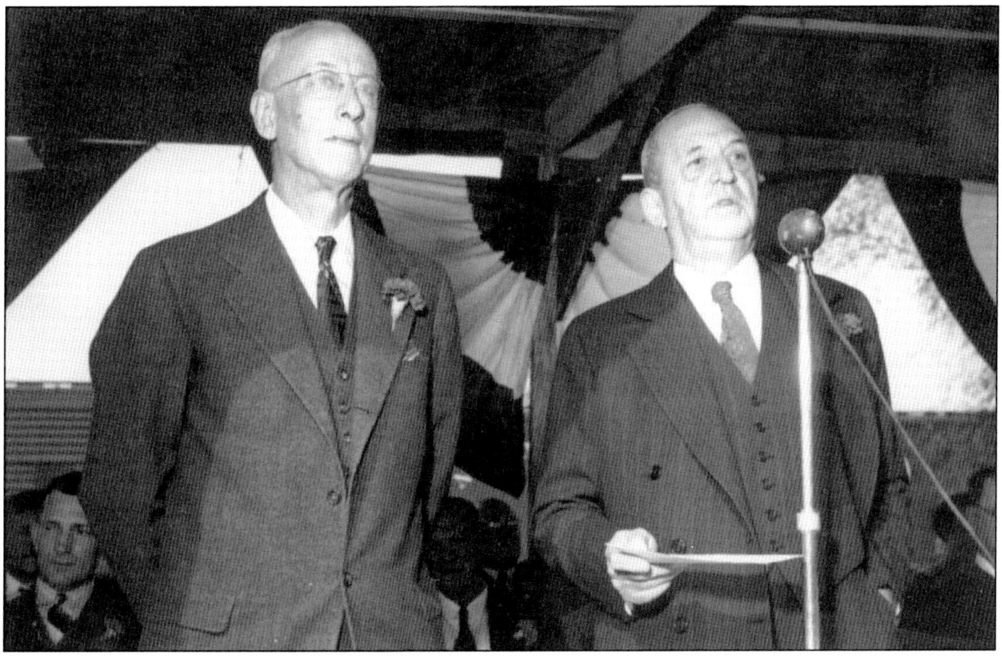

In this photograph from 1947, H.G. Thompson (left) and I.H. Kempner (right) speak at an employee dinner. Sugar Land was a private company town until 1959, when it incorporated and the Kempner family bought out the Eldridge interest in the company. Later, in 1989, Imperial merged with Holly Sugar and became Imperial Holly Sugar. The company began making beet and cane sugar. The refinery closed in 2003, but the legend of Imperial Sugar is deeply rooted in community history, and this has spurred local developments that pay homage to its name. The Imperial Sugar headquarters are still located in Sugar Land, although Louis Dreyfus Commodities—which has refineries in Savannah, Georgia, and Gramercy, Louisiana—purchased the company in 2012. Dreyfus continues to produce sugar under the Imperial Sugar brand, as well as Dixie Crystal. (Courtesy of Fort Bend Museum.)

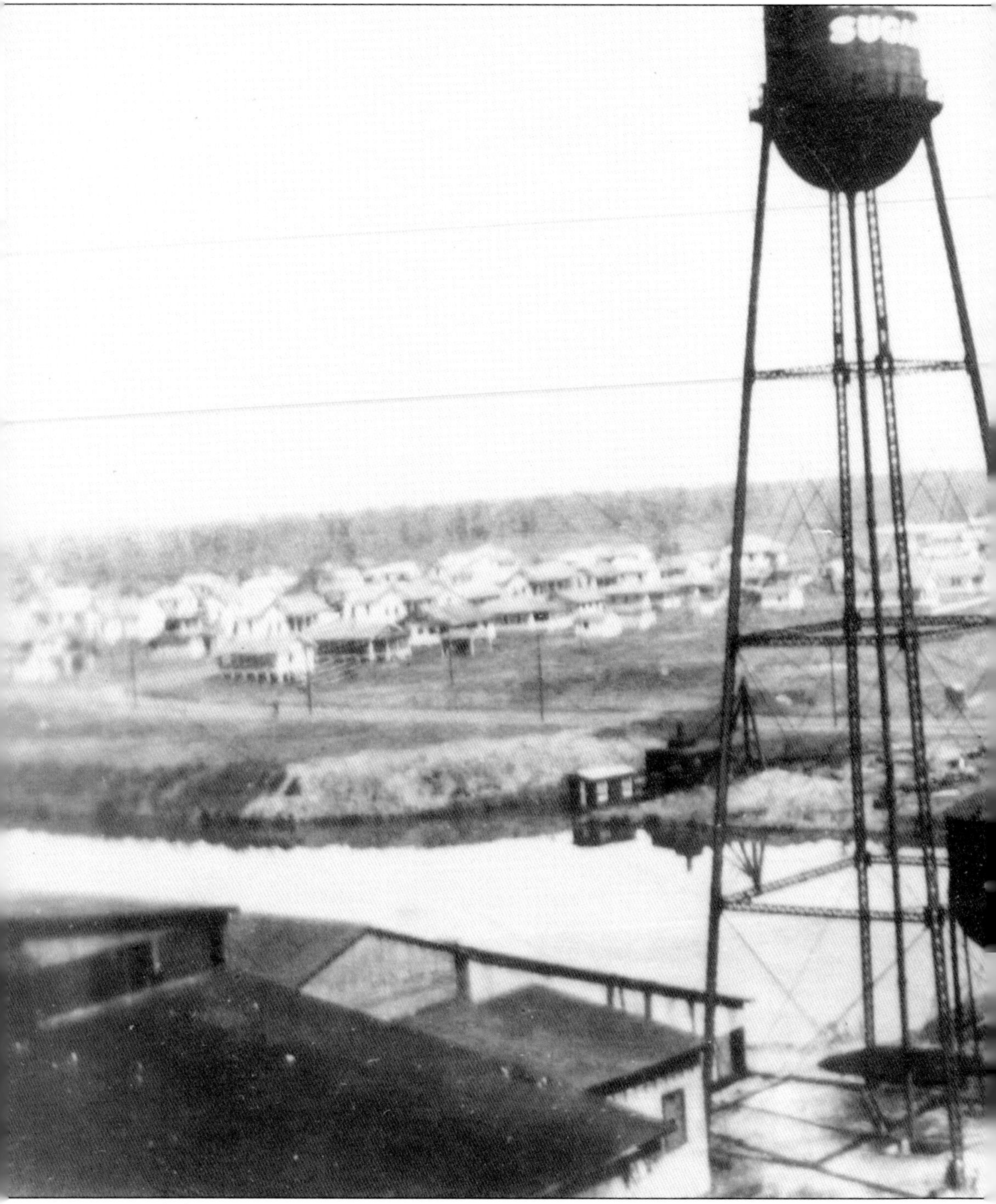

Situated along Oyster Creek, Sugar Land included homes built on stilts to protect against flooding. The town featured a hospital, a bank, a mercantile company, several stores, a paper mill, a cotton gin, and a feed mill, and functioned as a company town under the control of the Imperial Sugar Company. Kempner is also considered to be one of the men who created the commission form of city government, which Texas considers one option for official municipal governance. The

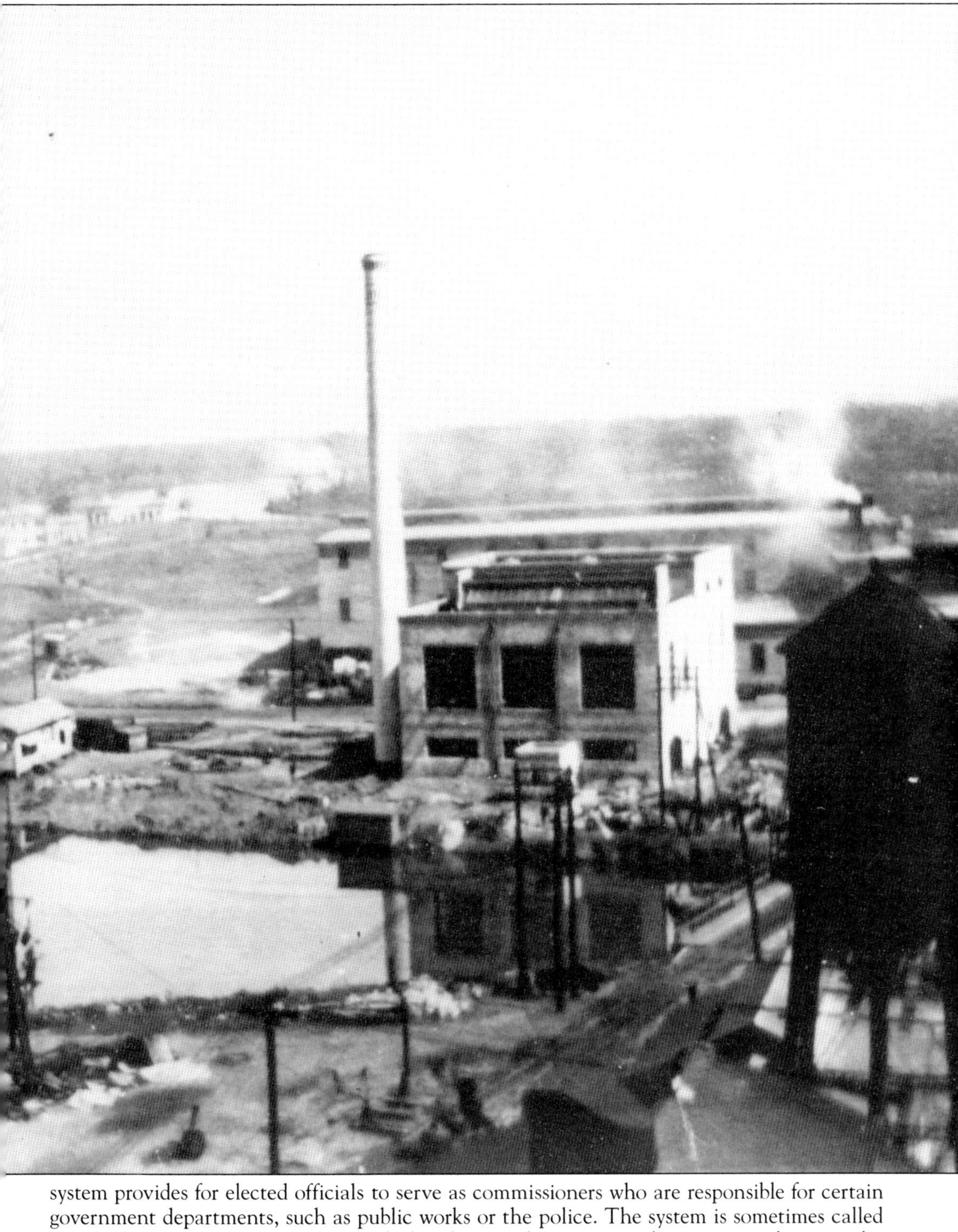

system provides for elected officials to serve as commissioners who are responsible for certain government departments, such as public works or the police. The system is sometimes called the "Galveston Plan," as it was created after the 1900 hurricane, and continues to be a popular choice for small- to mid-sized Texan cities. Today, Sugar Land operates under a council-manager government. (Courtesy of Fort Bend Museum.)

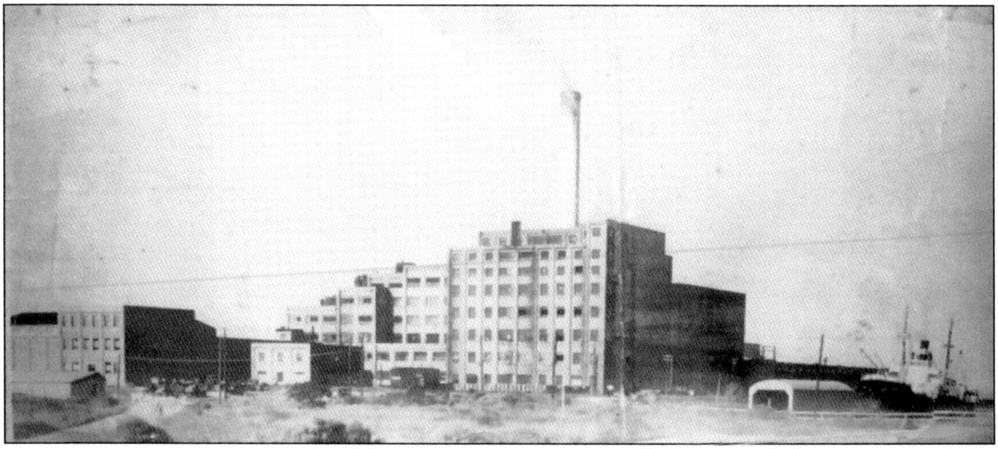

By 1930, Kempner had created a sugar monopoly along the lower Brazos River. In 1910, however, the Texas Sugar Refining Company became a legitimate competitor when it decided to build a portside refinery to compete with Imperial. Construction of the $5 million project began in 1923, with plans for nine buildings on a 10-acre tract of land. (Courtesy of Texas City Museum.)

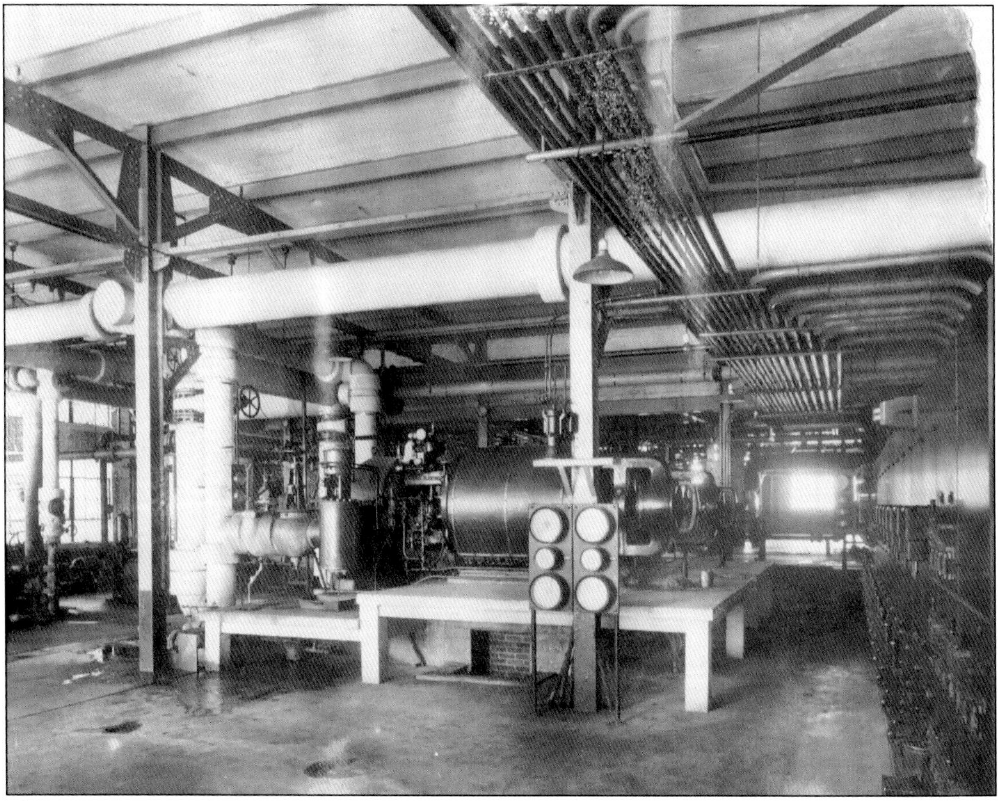

The Texas Sugar Refining Company produced sugar under a three-year contract with the American Sugar Refining Company, refining and packaging sugar under their label. The company employed 350 people, and produced one million pounds of granulated and powdered sugar per day. Until the refinery was built, the Texas City port only imported raw, Cuban sugar. (Courtesy of Texas City Museum.)

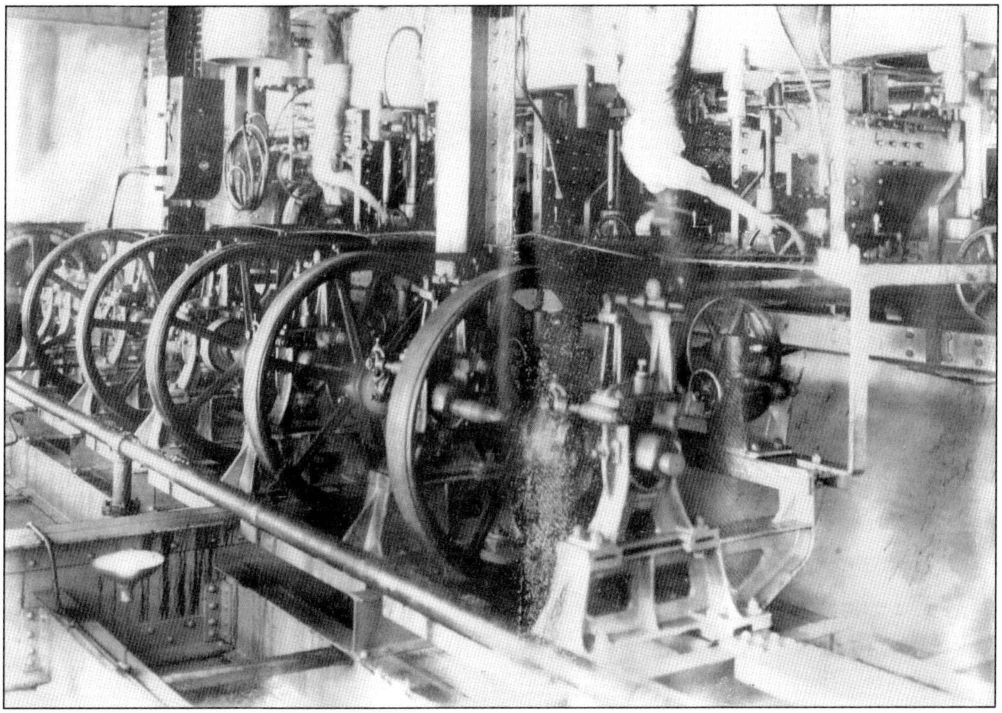

The Texas Sugar Refining Company was established by the Texas City Transportation Company, and utilized modern machinery similar to Imperial Sugar's. The company continued to produce at a high commercial rate, despite a lawsuit filed by the Chicago Title & Trust Co. The 1928 suit claimed that the company owed $3 million in outstanding mortgage payments. (Courtesy of Texas City Museum.)

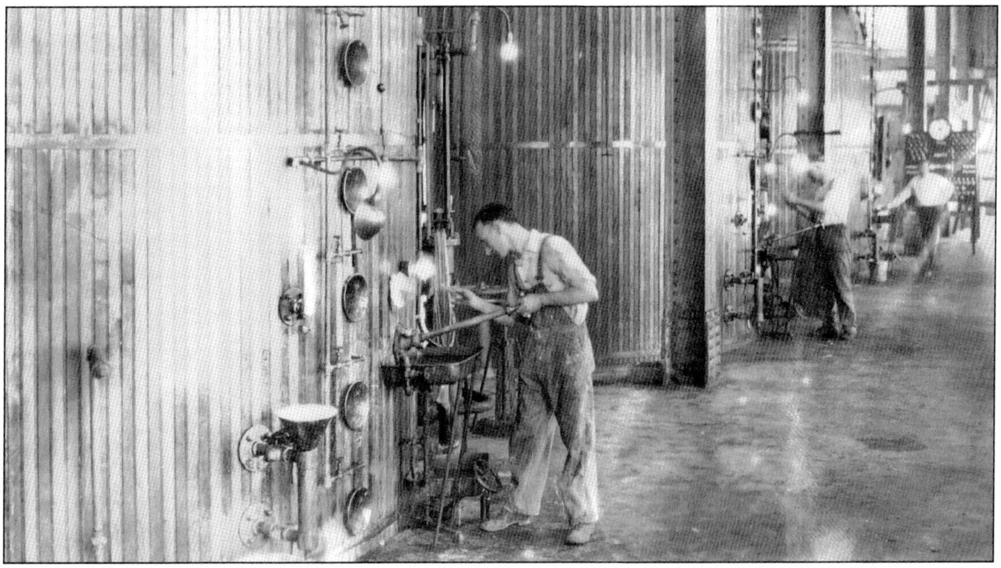

In 1929, Texas Sugar reorganized as the Texas Sugar Refining Corporation, and produced "Diamond Star" sugar until it ceased operations in 1932. The Chicago Title & Trust Co. lawsuit had finally thrown the company into bankruptcy, and the refinery was sold at a public auction for $2 million. (Courtesy of Texas City Museum.)

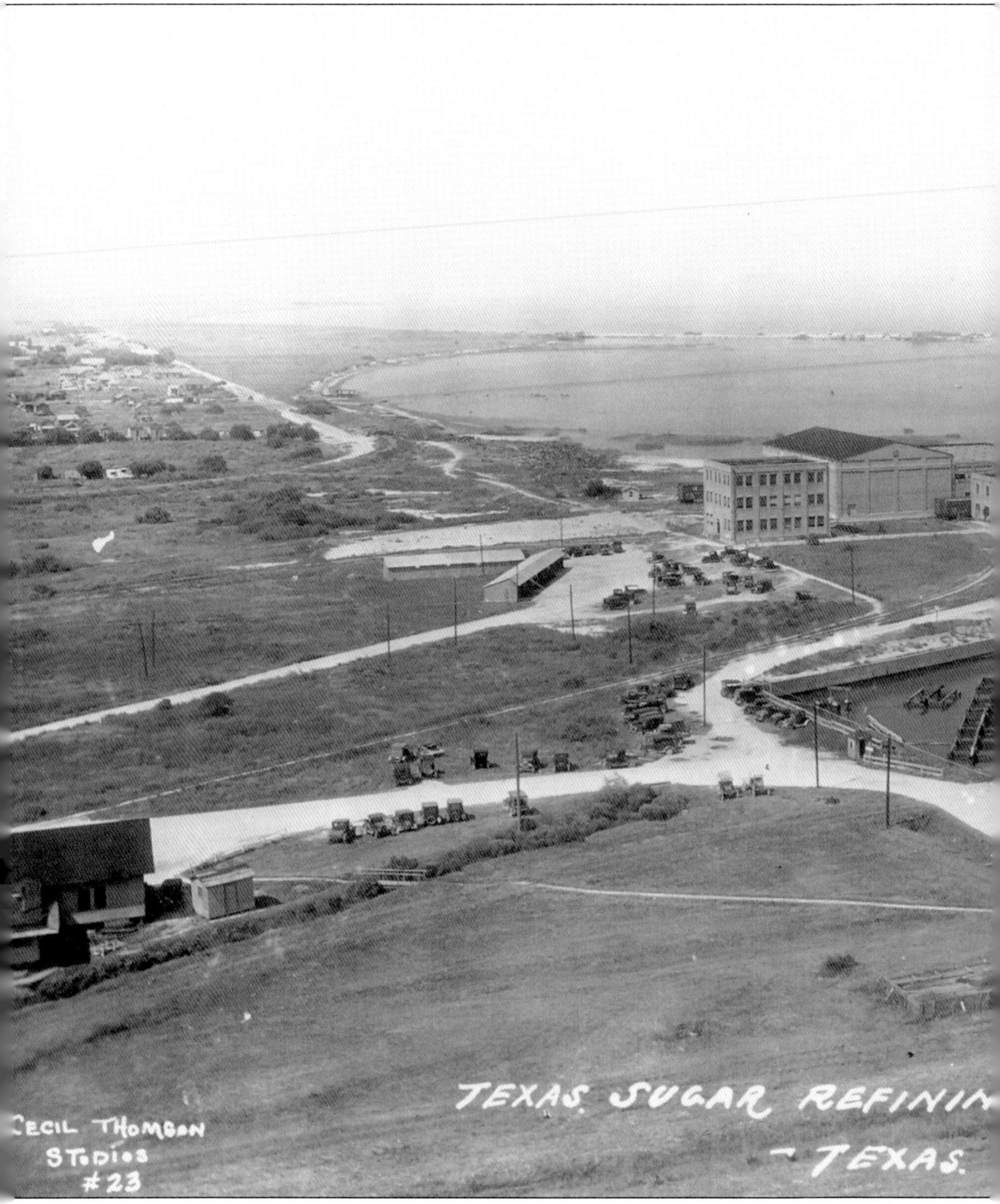


The Monsanto Chemical Company eventually purchased the refinery site to manufacture agricultural chemicals. In 1947, the cargo ship *Grandcamp* was docked at the Texas City port when a shipboard fire detonated a cargo of ammonium nitrate bound for the Monsanto plant. The resulting series of explosions is considered to be the largest industrial accident in the history of the United States, and the resulting rescue efforts claimed the lives of a large number of civilians

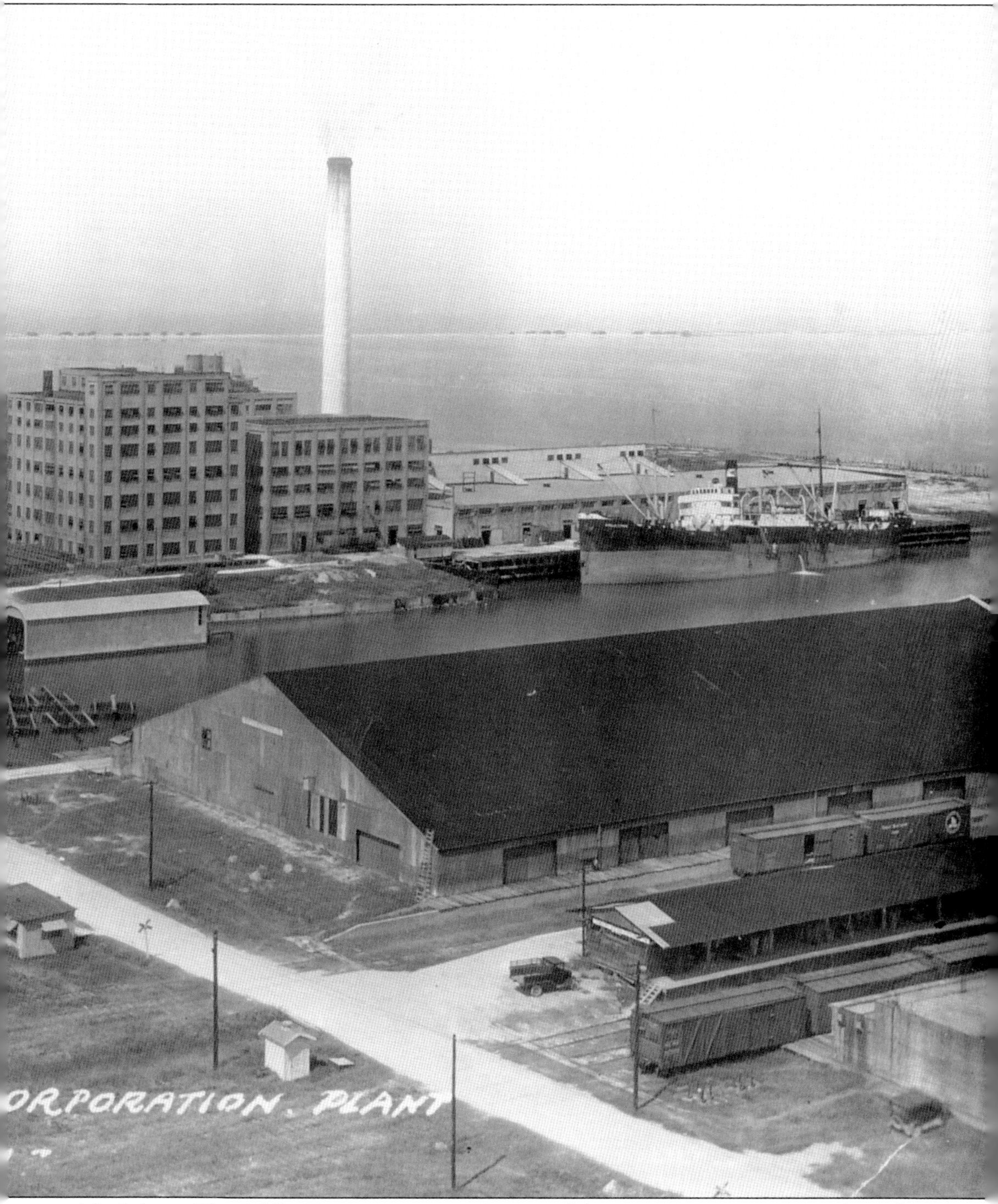


and firefighters. Thankfully, Texas City recovered as one of the most prosperous private industrial ports in the nation, and its connection with the lower Brazos River communities remains. The Gulf Coast Water Authority canal system stretches from the Brazos River to Texas City, and the Water Authority's main headquarters is just a few miles from the site of the original sugar refinery. (Courtesy of Texas City Museum.)

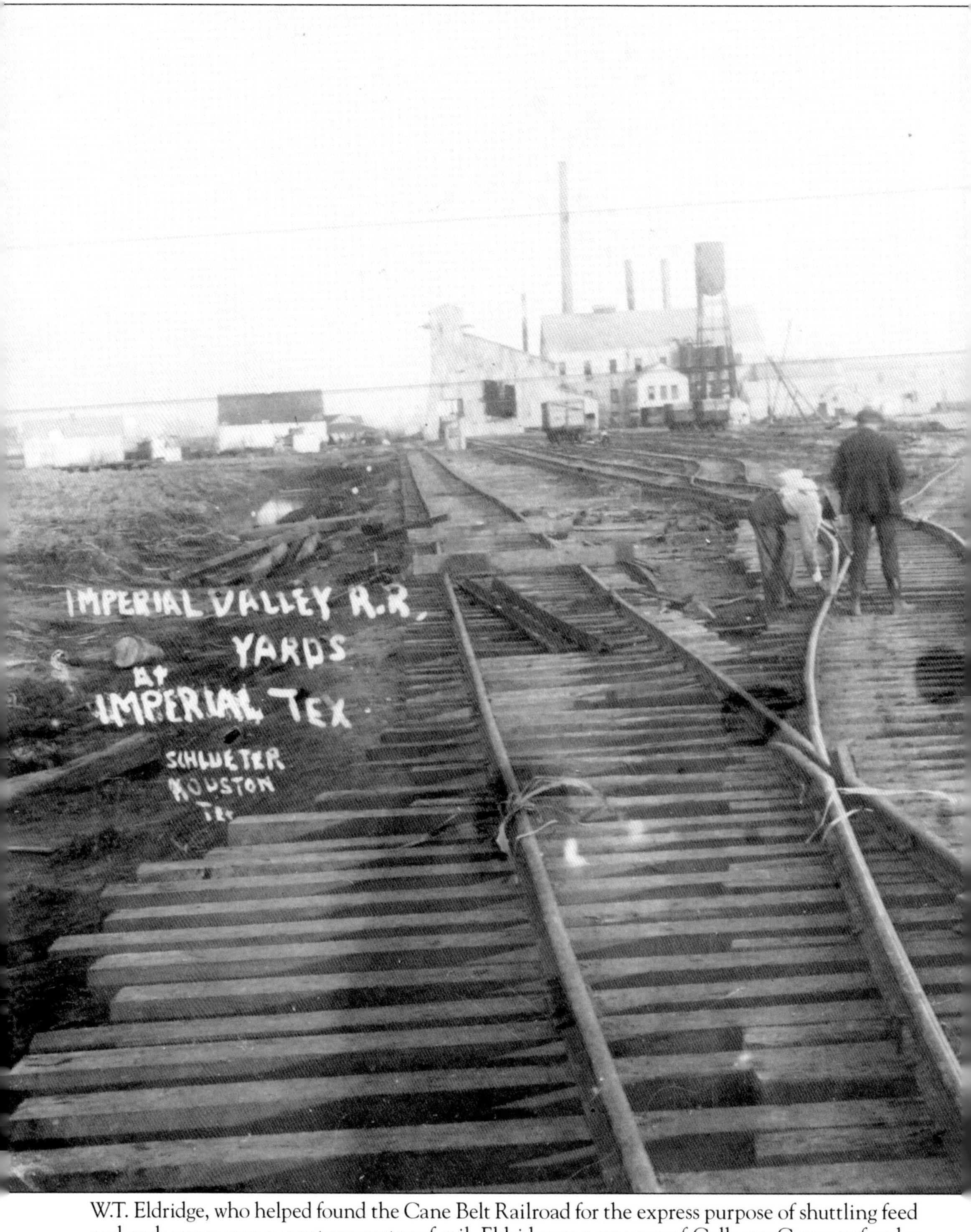


W.T. Eldridge, who helped found the Cane Belt Railroad for the express purpose of shuttling feed and cash crops, was a great supporter of rail. Eldridge was run out of Calhoun County after he was acquitted of the murder of his partner, Capt. William Dunovant, at which point he sold his portion of the railroad and invested in Ellis Plantation with I.H. Kempner Sr. Eldridge died in

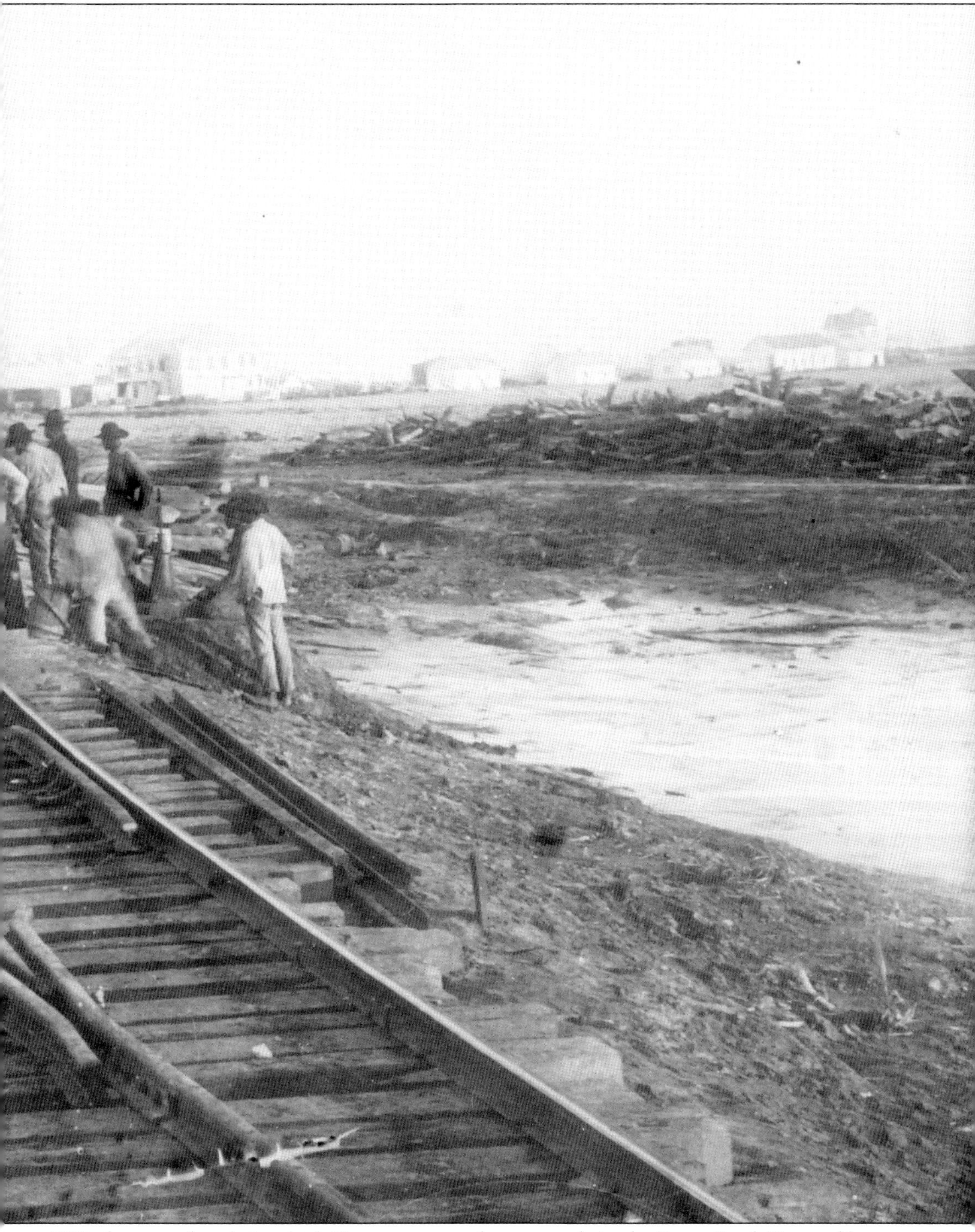

1932, the same decade in which Kempner created a monopoly in the Sugar Bowl. Pictured here, the Imperial Valley Railroad traveled through Sugar Land to transport sugar to Galveston port, diminishing Oyster Creek's role as a transportation route. (Courtesy of Fort Bend Museum.)

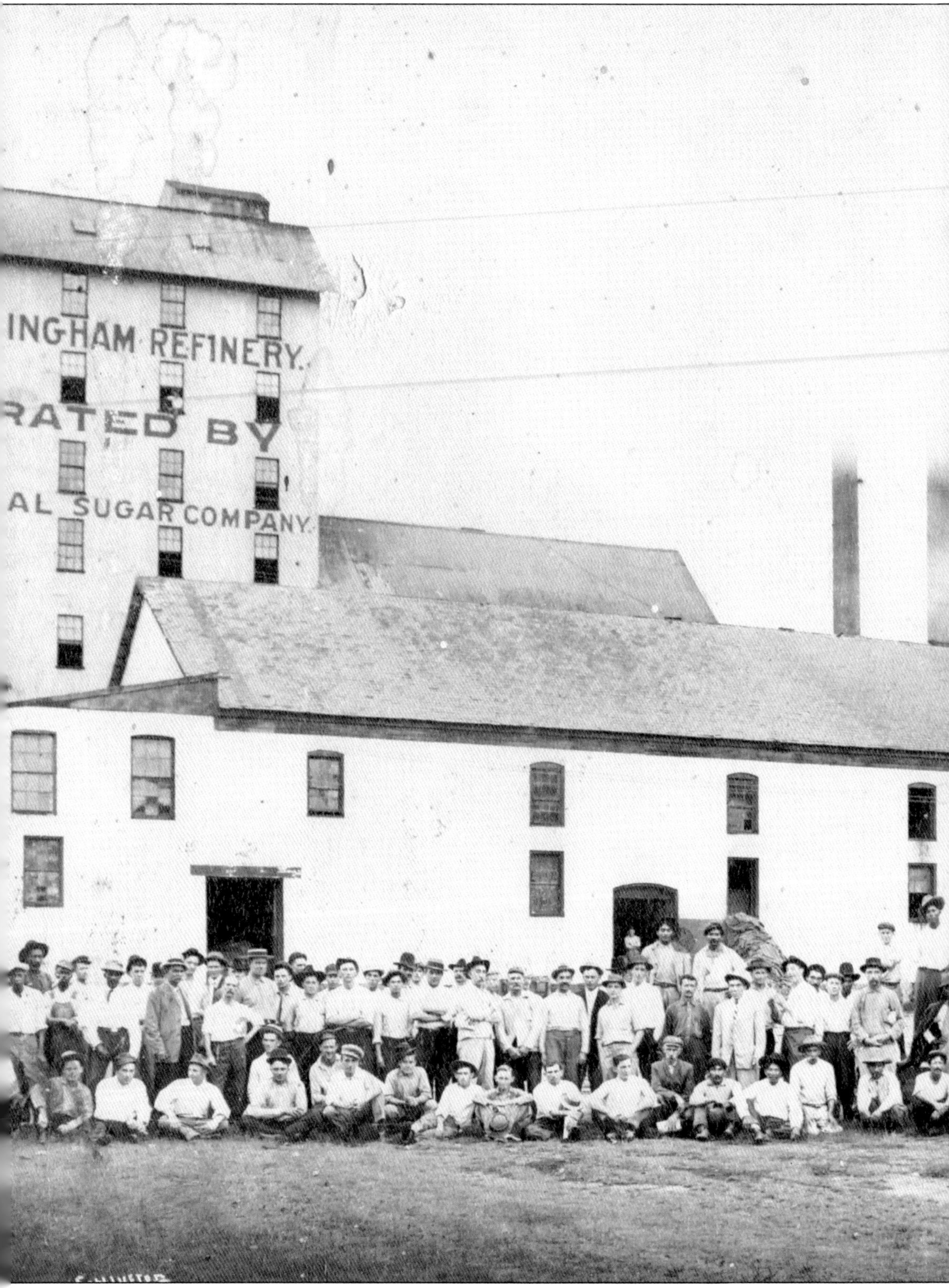
INGHAM REFINERY.
RATED BY
AL SUGAR COMPANY.

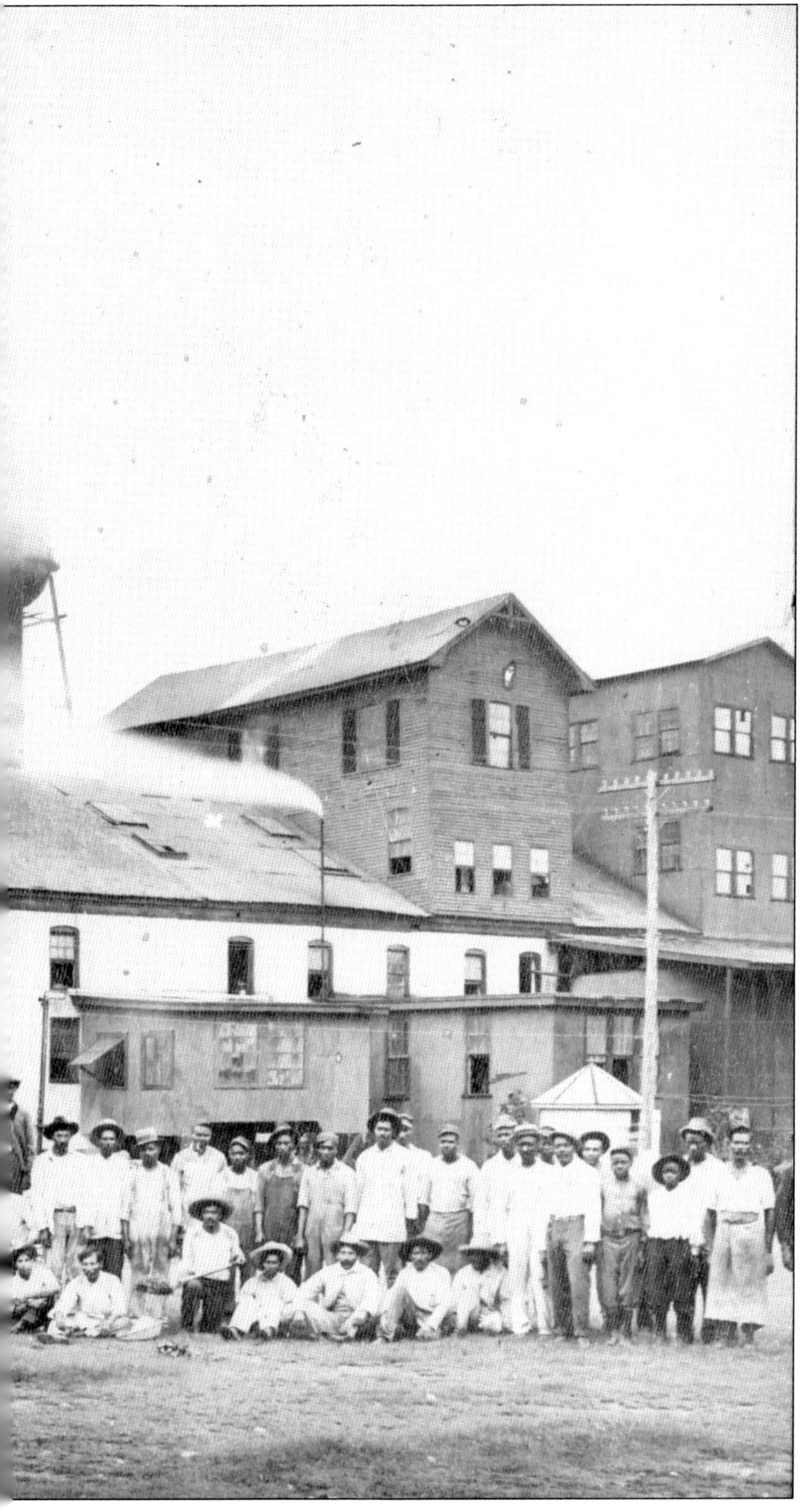

This photograph shows employees in front of the Imperial Sugar refinery. It was taken sometime after 1908, when Kempner and Eldridge took control of the Cunningham Refinery, but before they changed the name to Imperial Sugar in 1917. The building at the far left bears a painted sign reading, "Cunningham Refinery. Operated by Imperial Sugar Company." It was during this period that Fort Bend rose to prominence as the leader of the Sugar Bowl, and the refinery never lost its position as the centerpiece of the town. In 1925, the plant produced one million pounds of pure, refined sugar each day. After World War II, the company no longer produced its own cane, and raw sugar from Cuba and the West Indies was imported through Galveston. (Courtesy of Fort Bend Museum.)

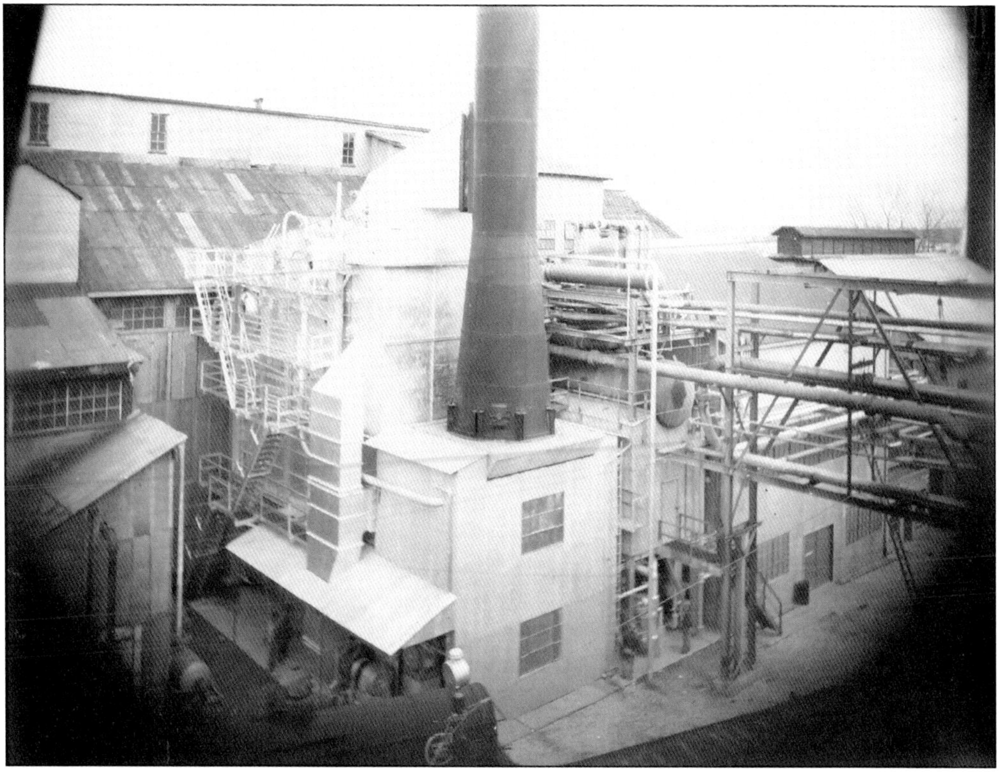

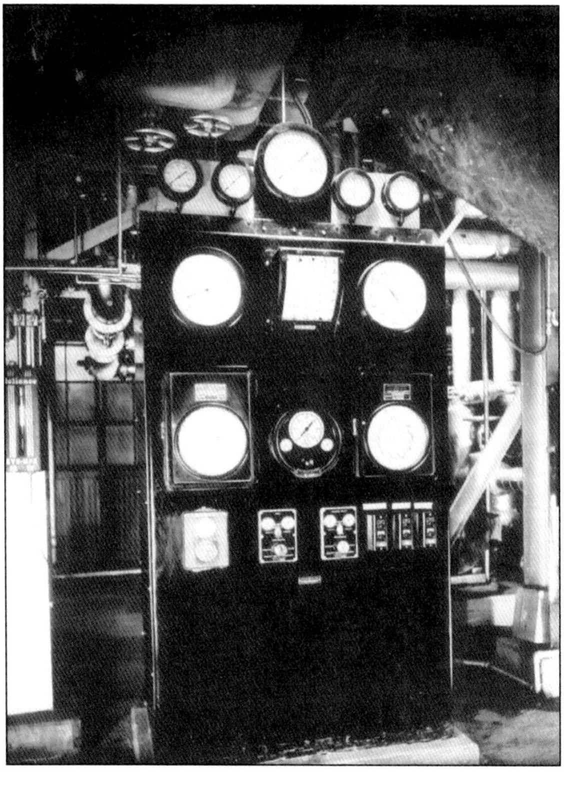

During the first half of the 20th century, the demand for refined white sugar outpaced that for the coarser sugar produced on the gulf coast prairies. Local cane growth decreased from 13,000 acres in 1910 to just 2,000 acres in 1950, but the increased market for refined product made this a period of great expansion for Imperial Sugar. A portion of the Imperial Sugar refinery can be seen here. (Courtesy of Fort Bend Museum.)

To capitalize on consumer demand for refined sugar, I.H. Kempner conducted a $4 million renovation of the refinery, which included the construction of the world's first air-conditioned sugar packing room. Decades later, when the company closed, museum curators inventoried the entire site for the community. Equipment such as this device was categorized, photographed, and logged. (Courtesy of Fort Bend Museum.)

## *Five*

# The Rice Belt

The Texas Rice Belt is a post–Civil War development and, like sugar, did not take long to become profitable for local farmers.

The belt produced 75 percent of the state's rice, and spanned from the Sabine River to the Rio Grande. By 1900, the belt was so prosperous that the federal government performed two studies of its irrigation system. They noted that the foundation for the crop's prosperity in the region was the "artificial" water supply system.

The weather in this area could fluctuate dramatically between wet and drought seasons. For example, in 1900, the Galveston Hurricane devastated towns in the region, but, in 1901, those same towns experienced a drought so severe that local lakes dried up. In the face of this, the canal system could be used to store water and protect towns.

Some speculate that Spanish missions may have used irrigation canals in San Antonio, but the first recorded reports of rice canals date to the 1880s, when farmers took shovels and dammed rainfall with levees. They would later cut these levees open when they needed water.

During the 1880s and 1890s, irrigation canals spread throughout Texas. By 1897, the entire state was using manmade canals to irrigate crops, but the coast country still had the highest concentration of canals. By 1902, coast country canals could stretch as far as 100 miles inland if a river was available to supply the canals. Eventually, the Brazos, Colorado, Guadalupe, and Rio Grande all supplied water to irrigation canals.

In this period, land developers constructed expensive canals that cost thousands of dollars, then sold the land and canals to settlers. The settlers, who had no information about the water supplying their land, soon started to lose money. Eventually, they lost enough money that the federal government began to take notice.

At one point, the secretary of state began to issue hundreds of canal system charters, but most never went past the paperwork stage. The Texas legislature also got involved when settlers wanted to gain control of their waterways, and in 1897, an amendment to the state constitution would have allowed landowners to issue bonds for irrigation canals. Unfortunately, voters overwhelmingly defeated the amendment. This is when the federal government noted that settlers might need to know more about the water systems they were managing.

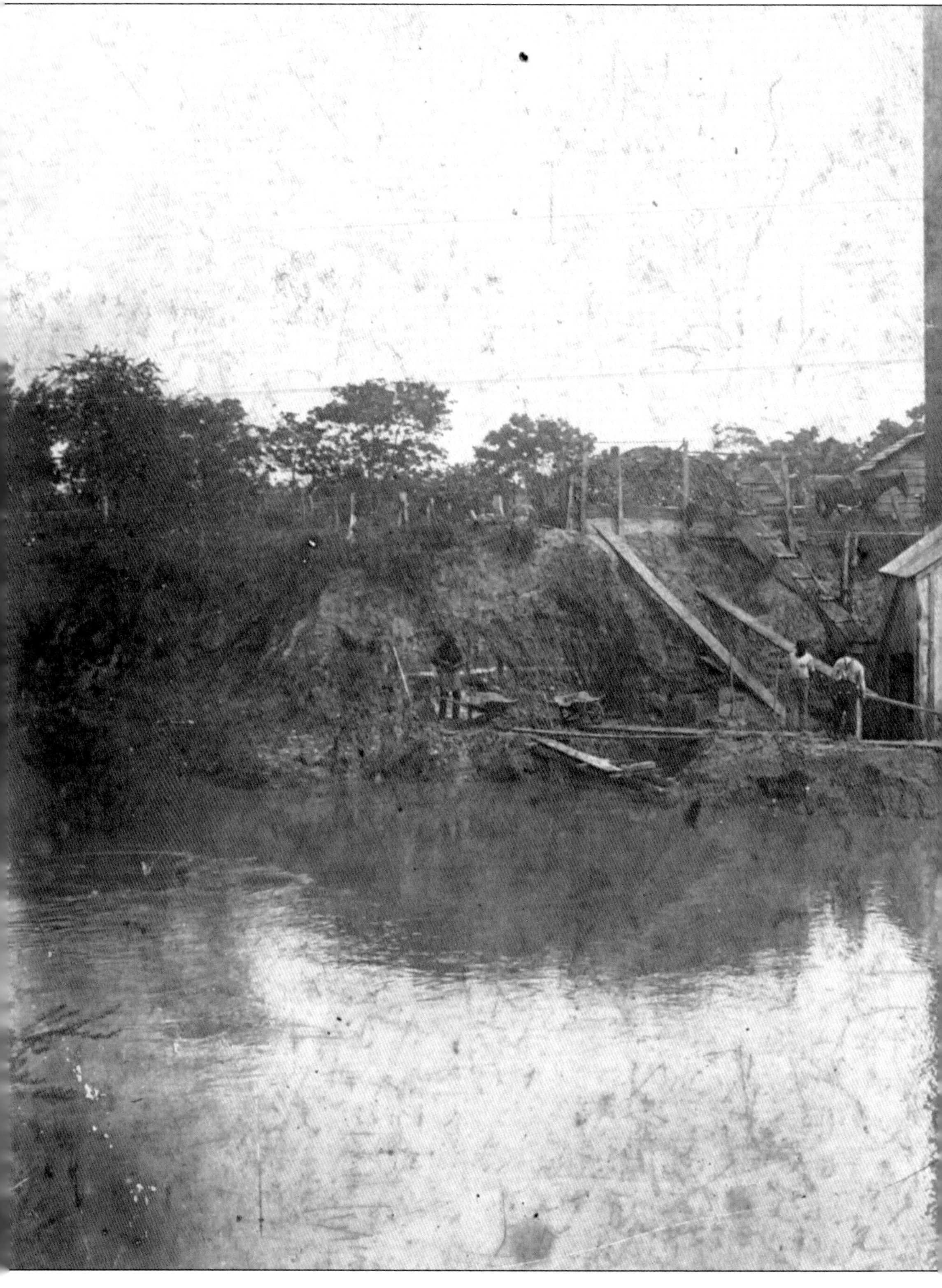

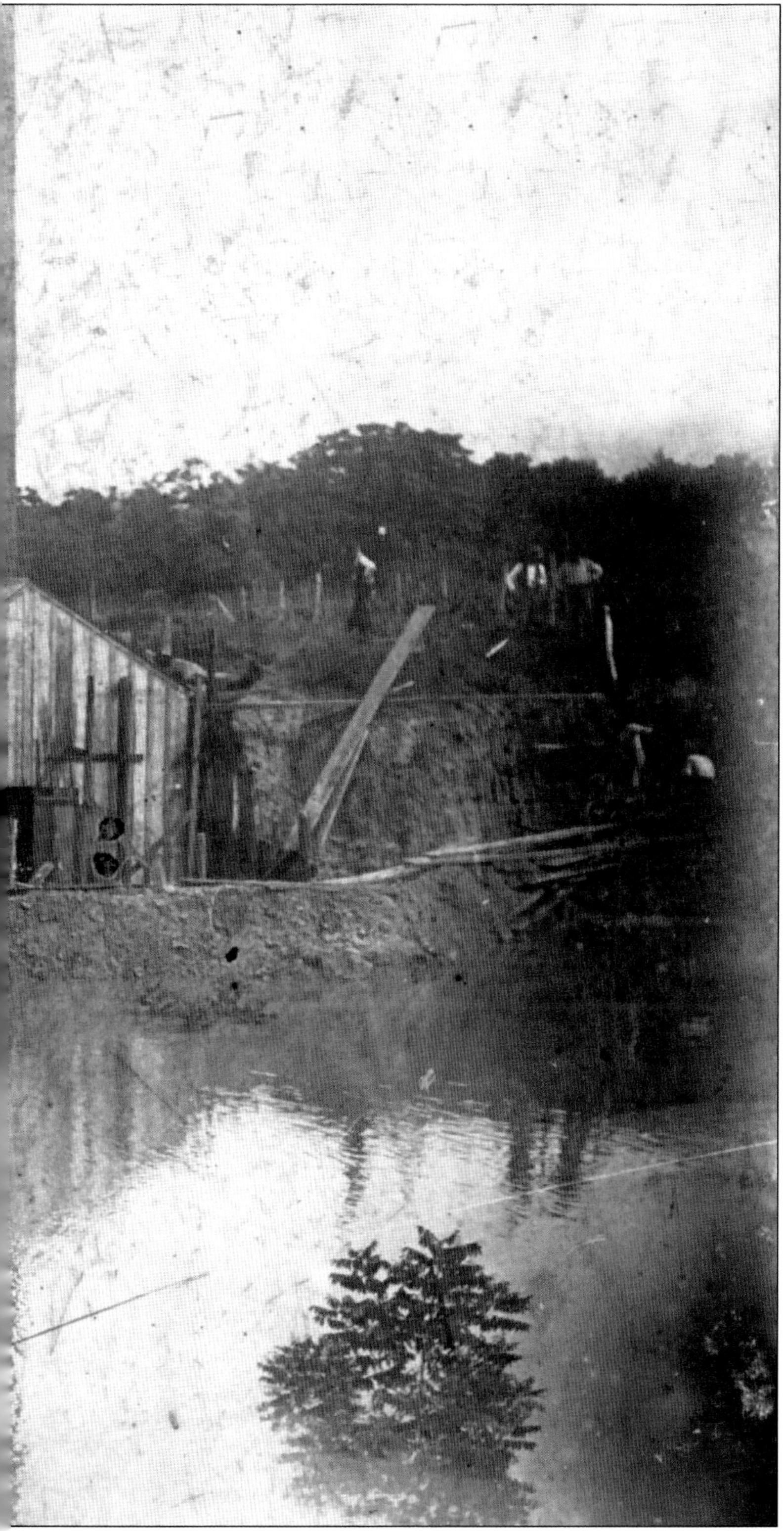

In this undated photograph, several men build a pumping station on the banks of the Brazos River, near what may be Richmond. A note in the margin describes how the water is being pumped from the river, and that it rose to the house in the center. Irrigation canals were established to help expand the agricultural economy in the region. Early explorers of the region left the land untamed, so the canal system did not exist when Austin's Colony was founded. Until the establishment of the canal network, settlers relied on the heavy rainfall of the lower Brazos River region for irrigation. (Courtesy of Fort Bend Museum.)

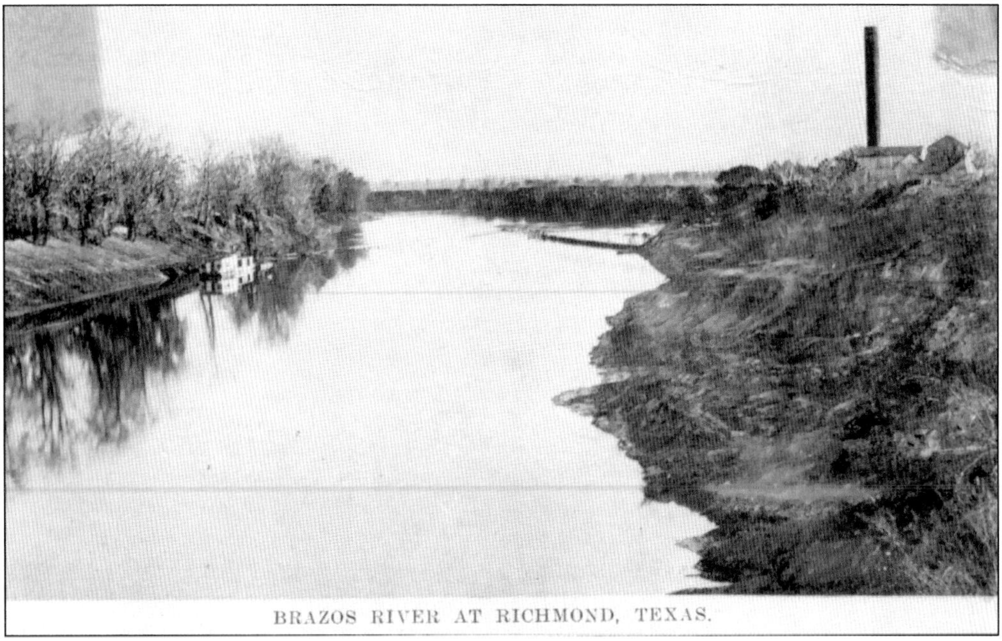


This postcard shows what may be the previously pictured pumping station. It appears wing dams may have been built across the river, although the photograph is not clear. Today, NRG Energy has a pump plant on the Brazos, located in a curve that looks very similar to this one. (Courtesy of Fort Bend Museum.)

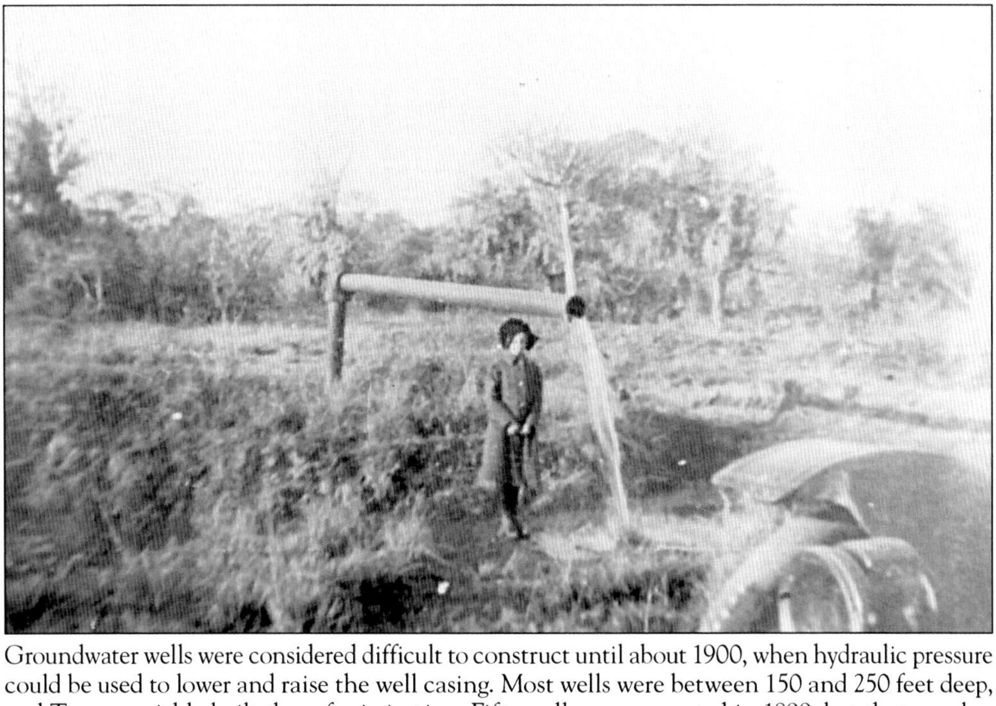

Groundwater wells were considered difficult to construct until about 1900, when hydraulic pressure could be used to lower and raise the well casing. Most wells were between 150 and 250 feet deep, and Texans quickly built them for irrigation. Fifty wells were reported in 1899, but that number had jumped to 1,500 by 1901. At the turn of the 20th century, a well with an eight-inch pipe was large enough to flood 200 acres of rice.

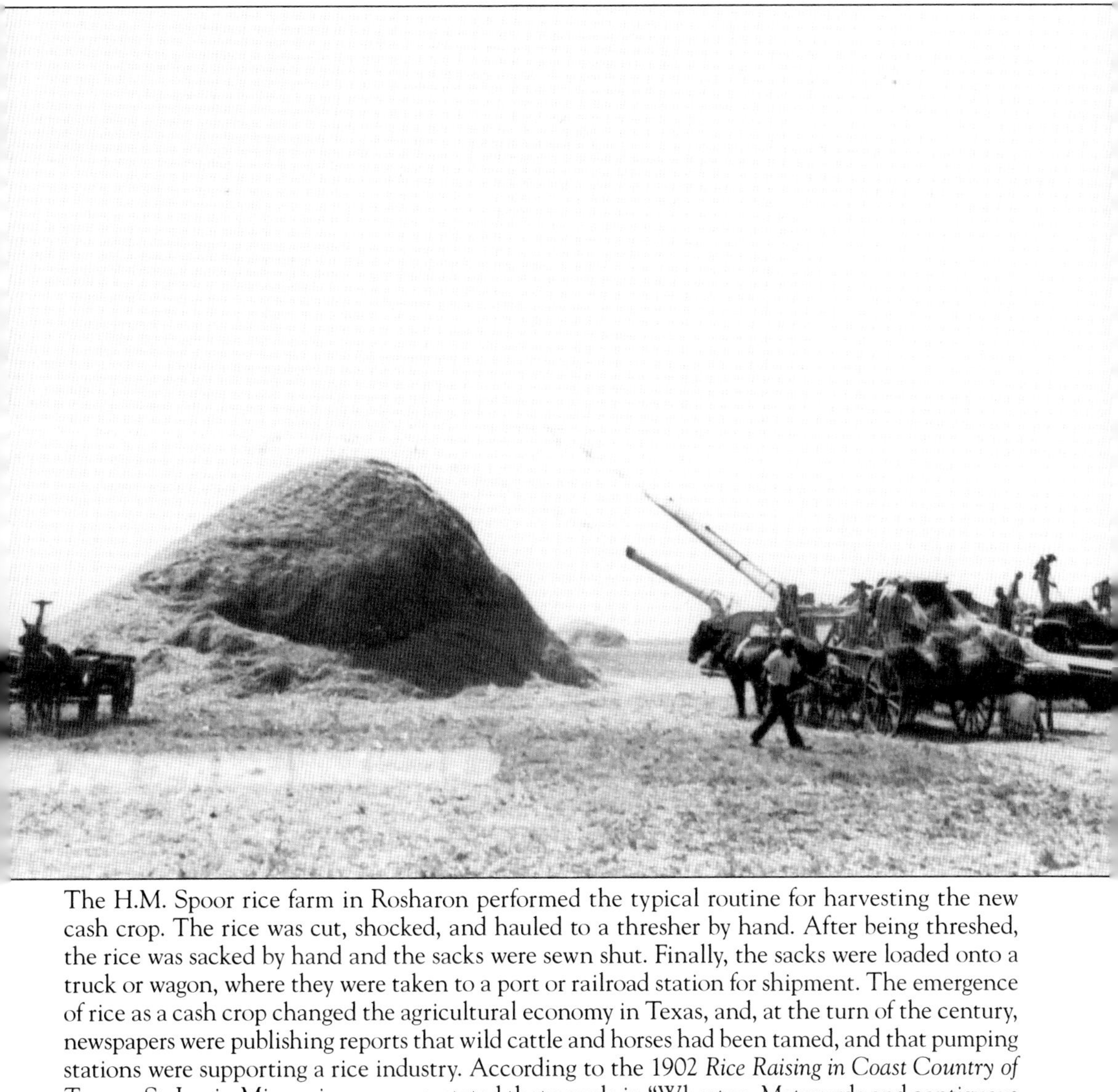

The H.M. Spoor rice farm in Rosharon performed the typical routine for harvesting the new cash crop. The rice was cut, shocked, and hauled to a thresher by hand. After being threshed, the rice was sacked by hand and the sacks were sewn shut. Finally, the sacks were loaded onto a truck or wagon, where they were taken to a port or railroad station for shipment. The emergence of rice as a cash crop changed the agricultural economy in Texas, and, at the turn of the century, newspapers were publishing reports that wild cattle and horses had been tamed, and that pumping stations were supporting a rice industry. According to the 1902 *Rice Raising in Coast Country of Texas*, a St. Louis, Missouri, newspaper stated that people in "Wharton, Matagorda and contiguous counties are more interested in agriculture development than winning sudden wealth by boring an oil gusher." The presence of canals and wells changed farming forever. Even some who had planted cotton and sugar turned to rice, because it was not dependent on "providence"—like crops that are dependent on rain.

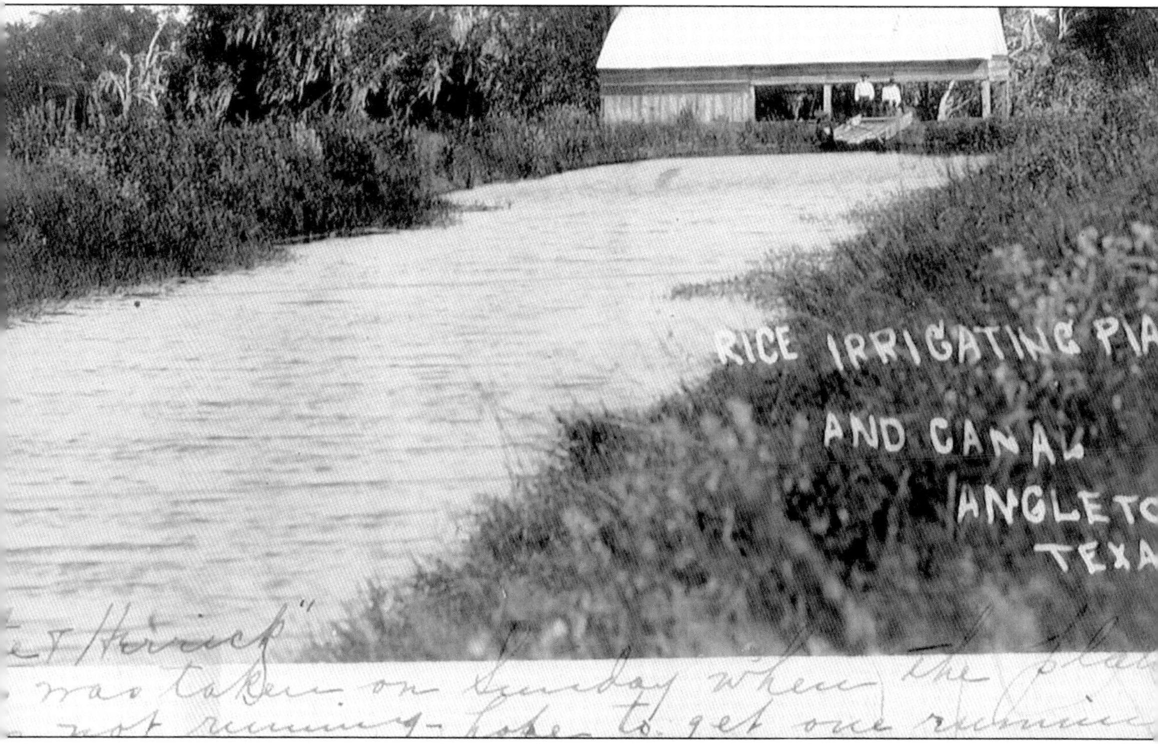


At the onset of the rice industry, travelers remarked that the irrigation canals of the Rice Belt were mind-boggling. In 1901, traveler James Kray described a scene of "pumping stations that throw immense volumes of water into irrigation channels for the rice fields. The streams from these pumping plants look like rivers, so great is the flow of wateries [*sic*] southwest of the oil region where the great development in farming is going on." He said people "were alive" because of the irrigation canals that made them able to farm. Farmers would send postcards to loved ones, describing life with the canal. This postcard shows an Angleton canal, and the handwritten note states that the picture was taken on a Sunday, when the plant was not running, and that the writer hoped to get another photograph with the plant running. Another person predicted that the Texas Rice Belt would have more wells than any other place on earth, and noted that it was already established as the "best agricultural belt in the United States."

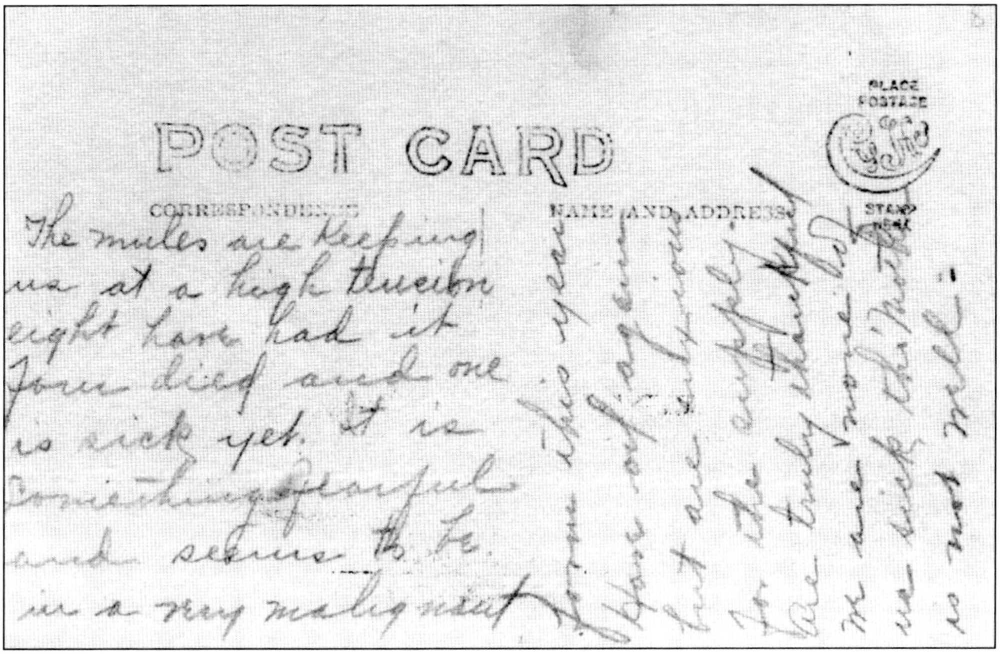


Despite the introduction of the canals, farming was still difficult. In this postcard, a person writes that, "The mules are keeping us at a high tension. Eight have had it. Four have died and one is sick yet. It is something fearful and seems to in a very malignant form this year. Have oil again but are anxious for the supply. Are truly thankful we are none of us sick tho [*sic*]. Mother is not well."

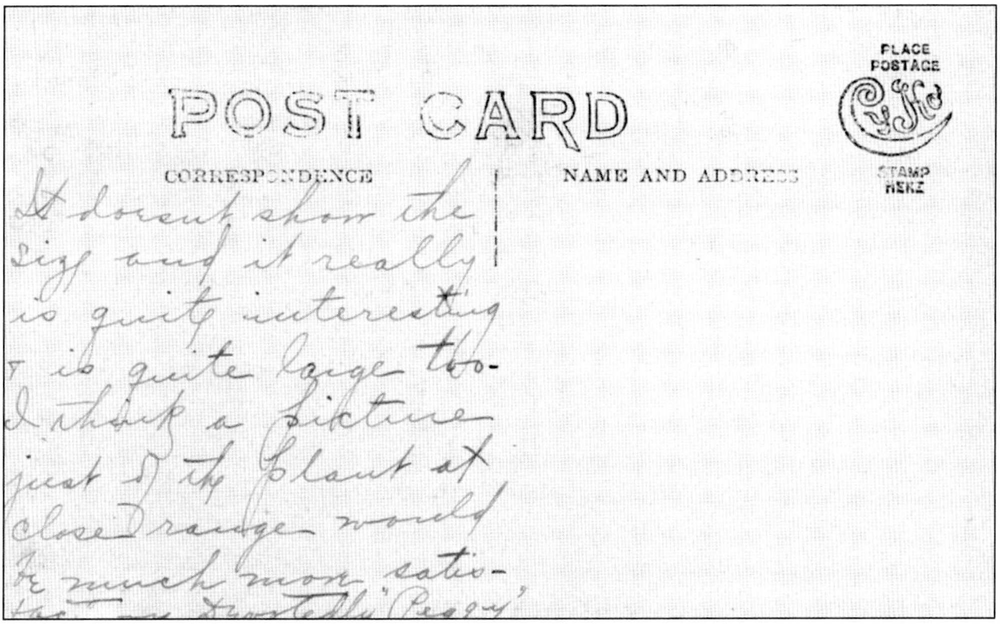


According to some travelers, the size of a pumping station could be remarkable. One woman, referring to her broken pumping station, wrote on this postcard that, "it doesn't show the size and it really quite interesting. I think that a picture just of the plant at close range would be much more satisfactory—Devotedly, 'Peggy.' "

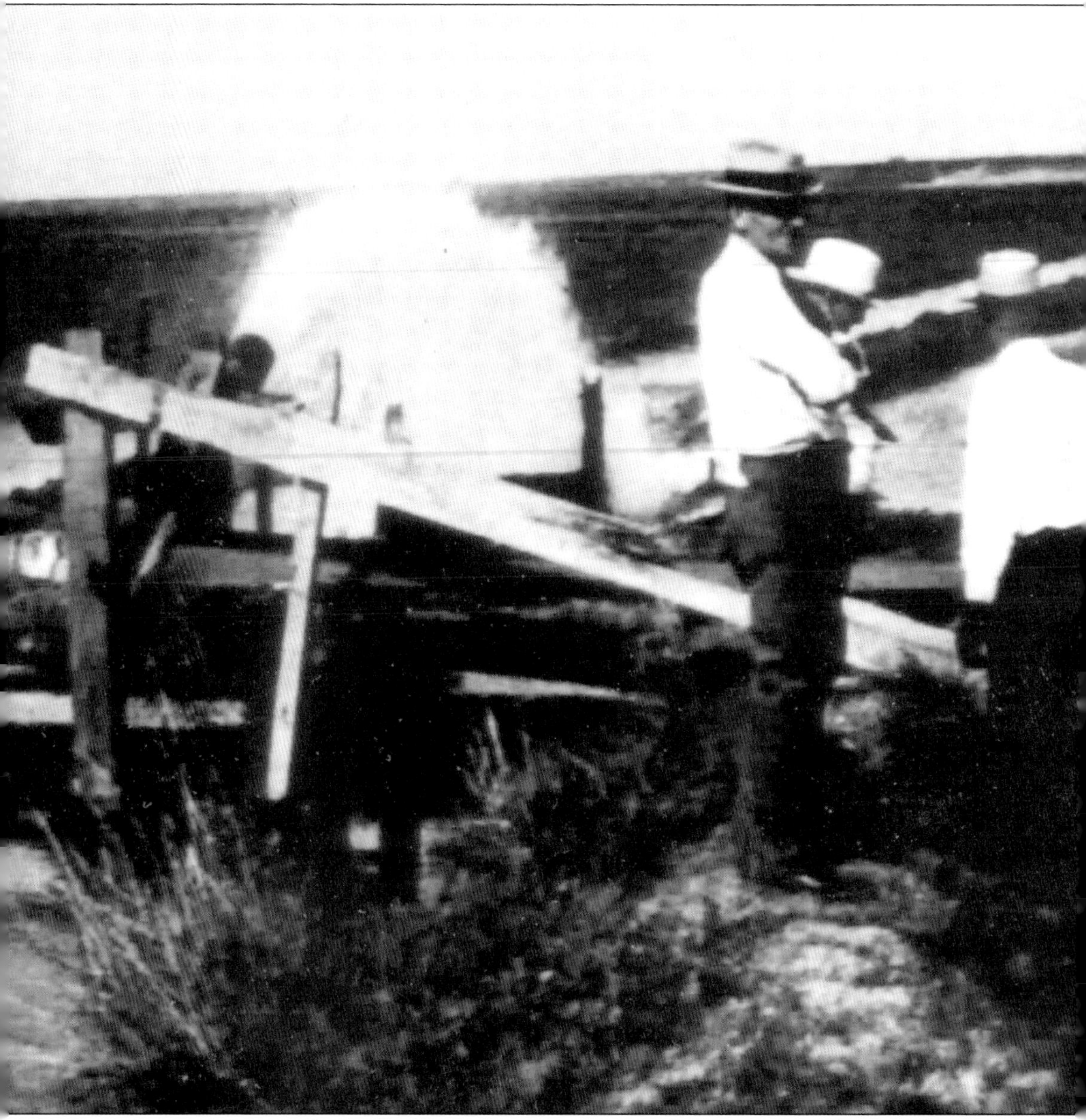

In this 1907 photograph, a pump irrigates a rice farm in Angleton. Pumping plants could produce 60,000 to 70,000 gallons of water per minute, while elevated canals, laterals, sublaterals, and distributing ditches could throw 700 gallons per minute. These canals would reach up to 20 miles long in 1900. Farmers could also create dams on creeks and use small pumps. The ability to produce water from the Brazos River and from groundwater wells made the area very attractive to farmers, and Angleton, Algoa, and Alvin were considered some of the most profitable rice areas in the Galveston, Fort Bend, and Brazoria triangle. The climate was also helpful, according to T.A. Haas of Brazoria County. He once reported that the gulf provided a dewy climate that kept rice growing even in a drought, and that a providence crop produced on 186 acres in Algoa yielded 30 barrels per acre. He sold the rice at $1 per barrel in Galveston and Houston. He also noted that the only reason he had a providence crop was because he could not get his wells started in time for the growing season.

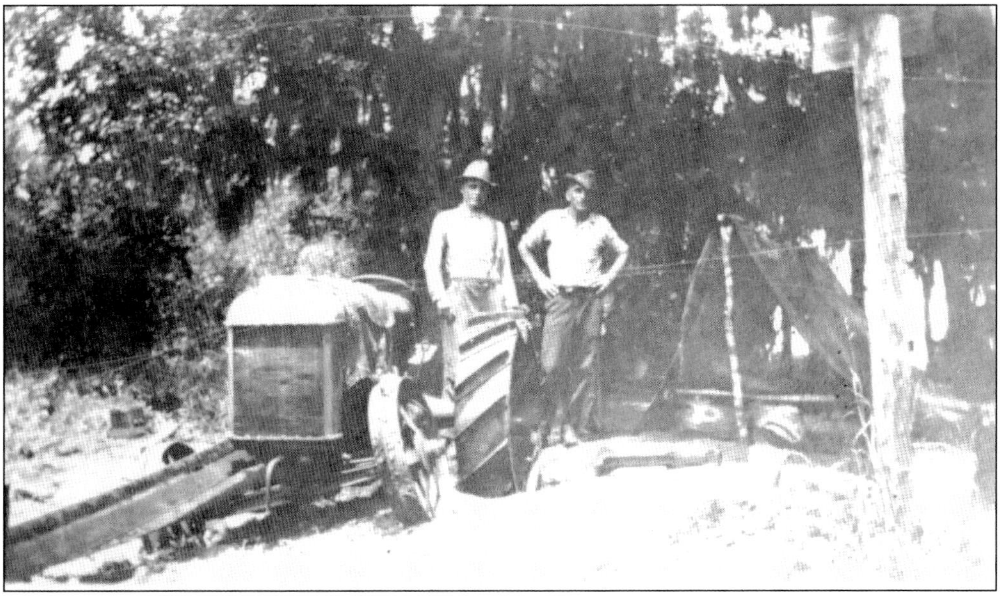

The engines and machinery used to create irrigation canals were a source of pride. As the rice industry emerged in Texas, it was routine for farmers to give details of their equipment to the public. Pictured here, Harbula and Joe Bulanek use an old Rumley tractor to pump water from the bayou into a canal to water rice. A tent can be seen in the background, as they had to stay with the tractor around the clock.

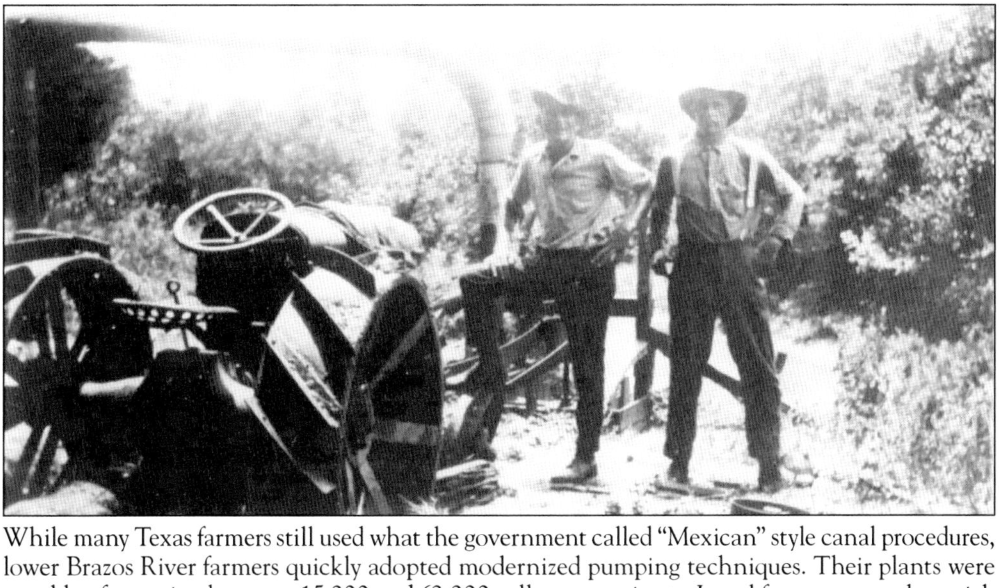

While many Texas farmers still used what the government called "Mexican" style canal procedures, lower Brazos River farmers quickly adopted modernized pumping techniques. Their plants were capable of pumping between 15,000 and 62,000 gallons per minute. Local farmers were also quick to adopt modern harvesting methods. Pictured here, Harbula and Joe Bulanek continue to use their Rumley tractor to pump water to their rice.

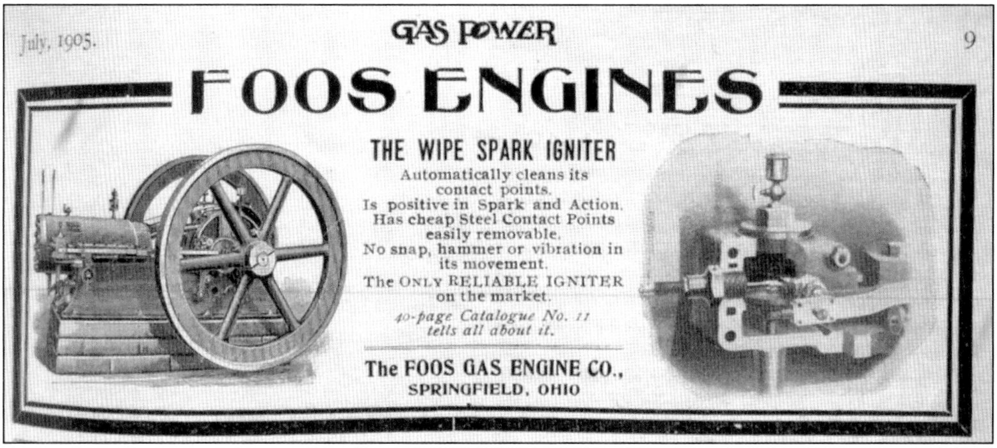


A 1902 federal government report about the Texas irrigation system notes that rice farmers purchased pumps and engines from four sources: Erie City, Foos, Morris, and custom pumps from a Mr. Baker of Angleton. Nine farms in Brazoria used these pumps to irrigate from 35 acres to 1,000 acres stretching from Fort Bend to Brazoria Counties. An advertisement for a Foos engine is pictured here.

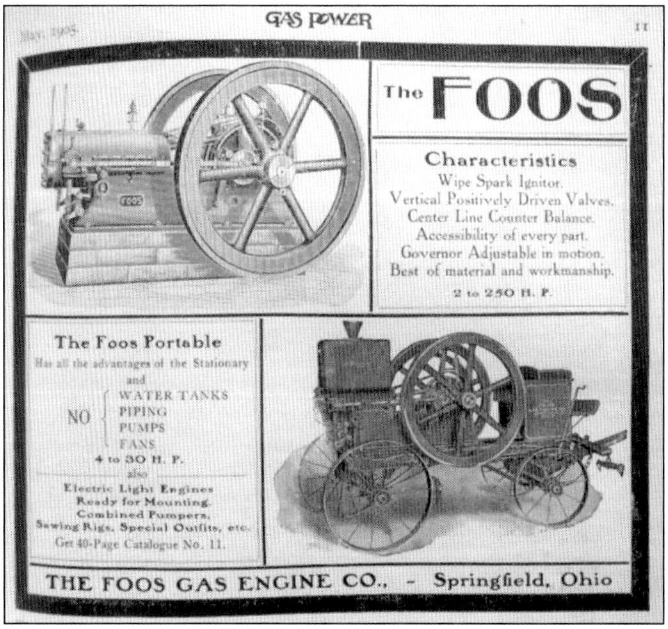


The engines used for pumping canals could also be adapted for farming and other everyday uses. The Foos Gas Engine Co. specialized in gas and oil engines, as did the other brands used by farmers. While farmers appeared to have an endless supply of water thanks to these devices, they also had to keep an inventory of gas and oil on hand to keep their equipment running. An advertisement from 1905, promoting several models of Foos engines, is pictured here.

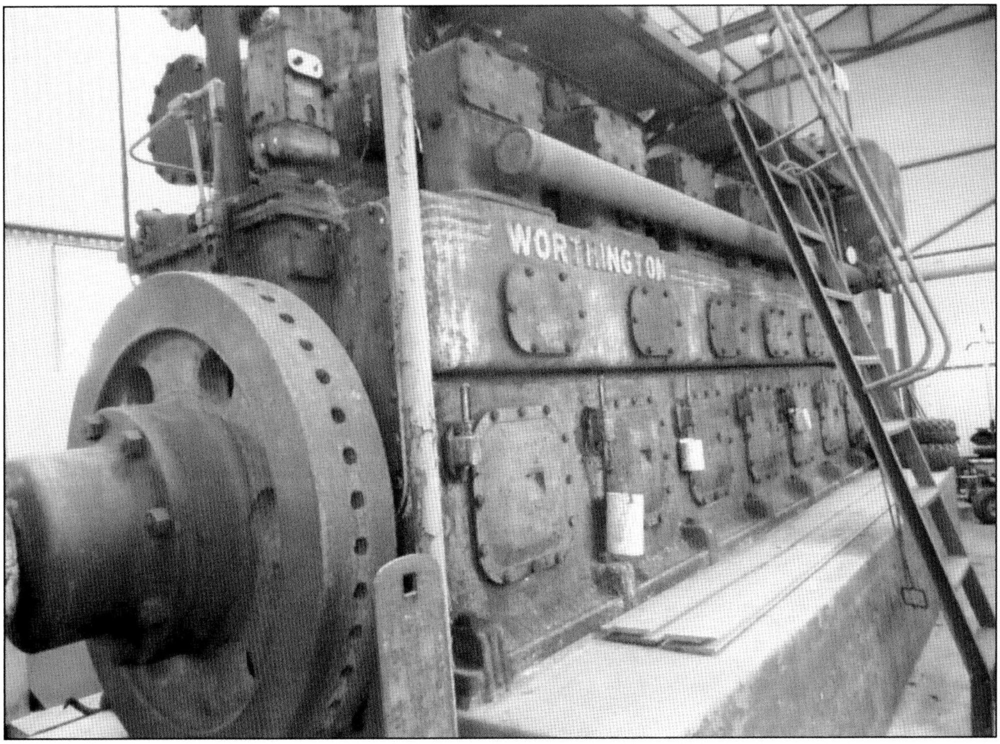

The Gulf Coast Water Authority (GCWA) used a Worthington engine for many years. This engine used a Philadelphia gear drive, and sat on a large concrete slab. The GCWA installed electric pumps in 1946, and installed the gas engine in 1965. The Worthington did not work as well as the electric pumps, however, and the GCWA stopped using the engine. A Johnson pump was connected to the Worthington engine, capable of pumping 100,000 gallons per minute. This vertical rotating pump was shipped from Pasadena, California, while the Worthington engine came from King of Prussia, Pennsylvania. A river flood in 1991 led the staff to use the engine one last time, but it has stood idle since. (Both photographs by Lora-Marie Bernard.)

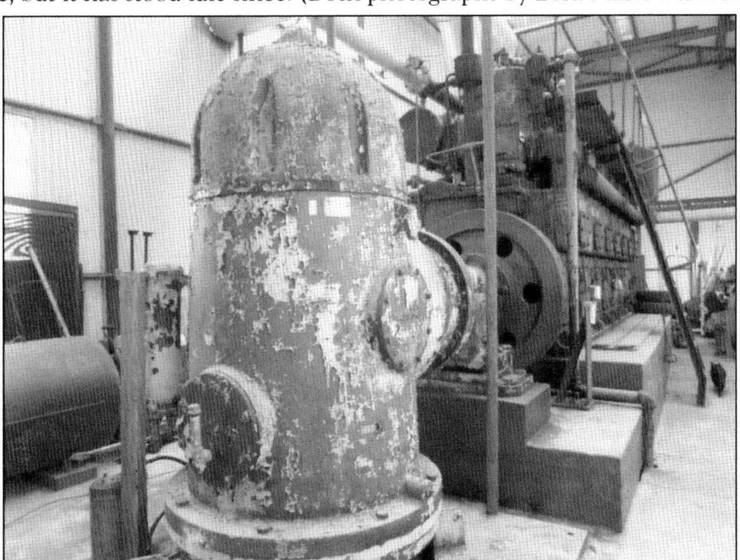

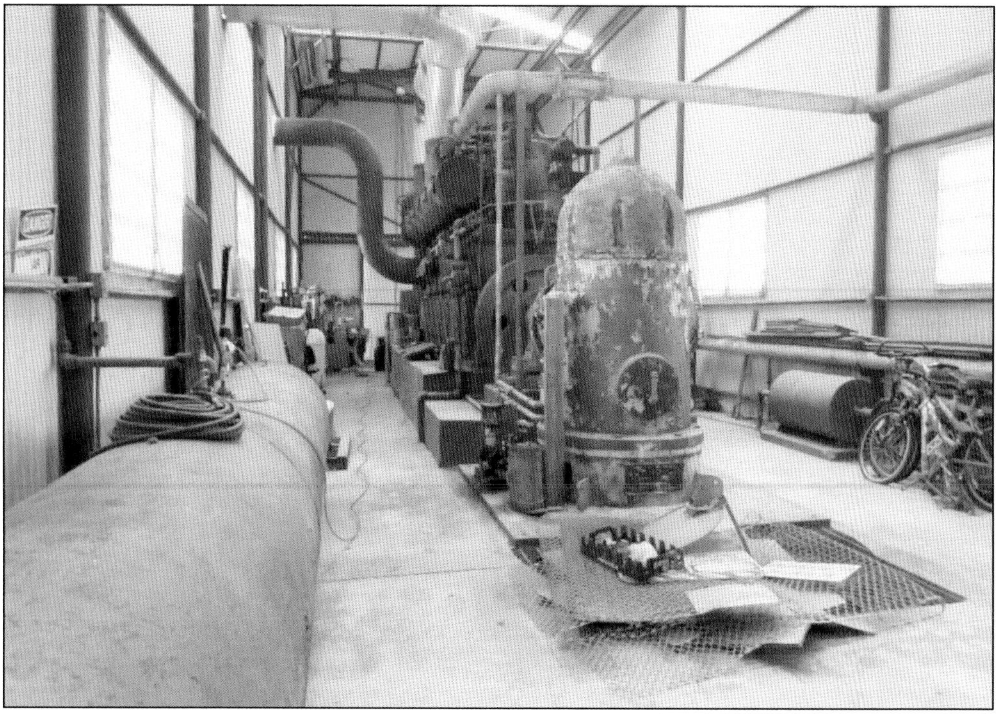

This engine room sports a 210-pound air pressure system that once supported the Worthington engine. The GCWA considered demolishing or dismantling the engine room, but eventually decided against it due to the difficulty of removing the equipment. The room now serves as storage for a variety of items. (Photograph by Lora-Marie Bernard.)

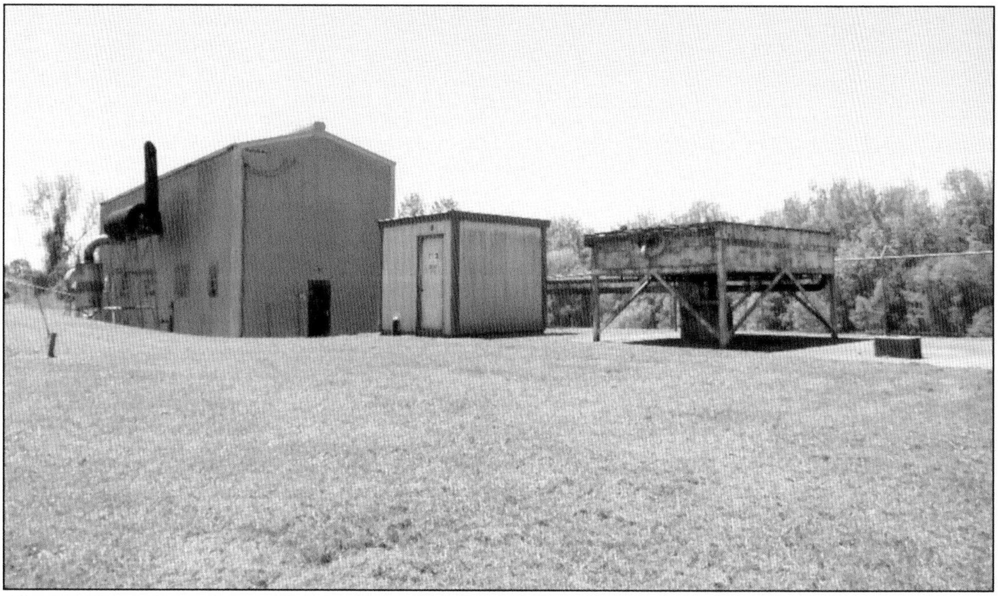

The Gulf Coast Water Authority originally used gas engines at its Shannon pump station. The engines and pump arrived by truck, and were used to pump water from the Brazos River into Jones Creek. The GCWA uses electric engines now, and the gas engine room serves as a reminder of the organization's history. (Photograph by Lora-Marie Bernard.)

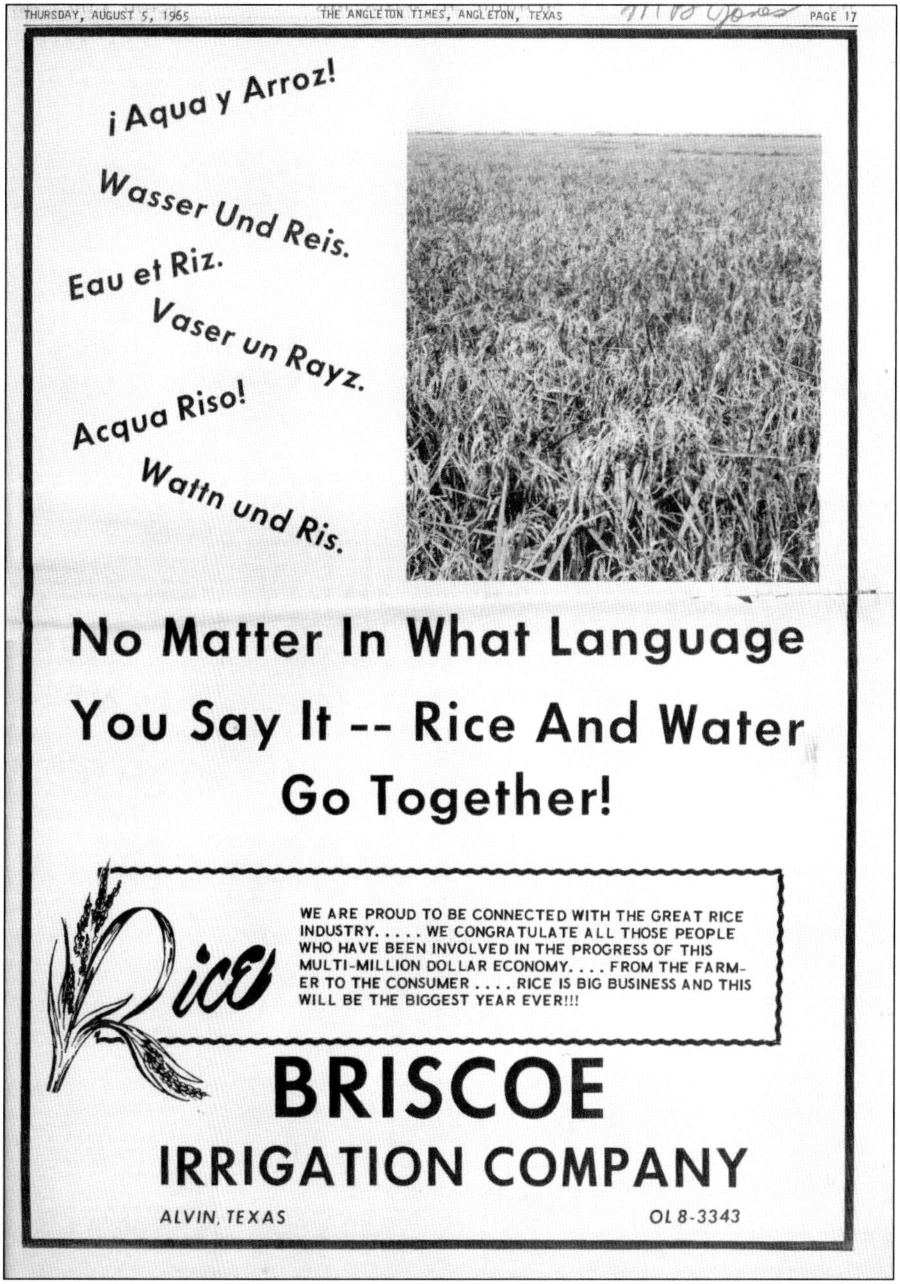


Efforts to promote rice farming in the early 1900s worked well, and rice fueled the economy of the lower Brazos River by the 1960s. Most of the rice grown was exported, which meant that the deepwater ports were as important to farmers as the canals that irrigated their crops. The pictured advertisement, taken from a special section of the *Angleton Times* in 1965, demonstrates the importance placed on the relationship between water management and the rice crop. Founded in the 1940s, the Briscoe Irrigation Company was built on the Brazos River near Arcola. Within a year, the company was supplying irrigation water to the area. Eventually, Briscoe Irrigation would be a major supplier to industries, such as Monsanto in Chocolate Bayou, and the Industrial Water Company. Briscoe Irrigation's system runs from the river, through Alvin, and on to Galveston Bay.

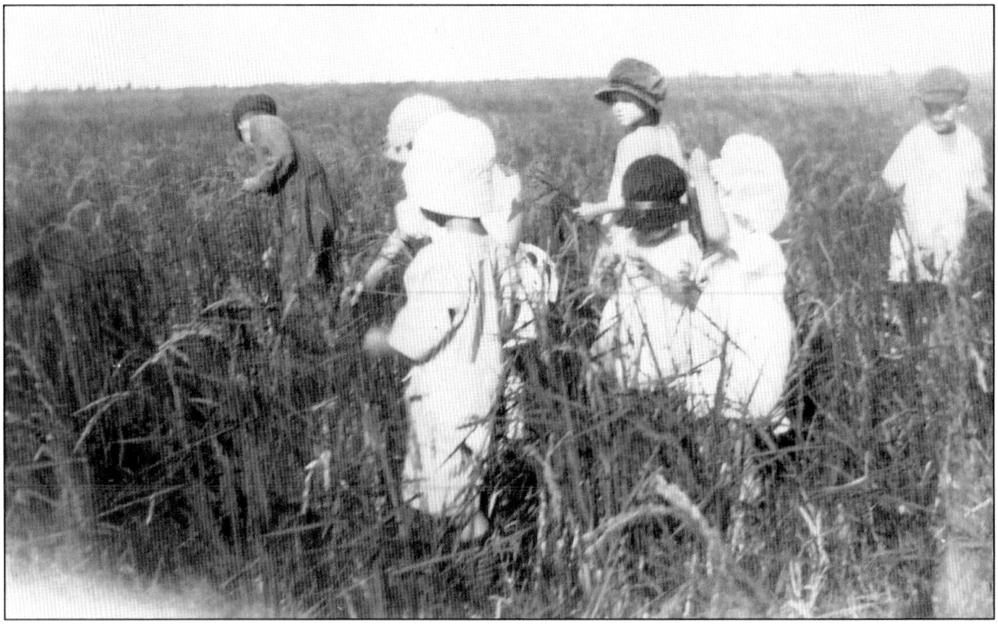

From an early age, Brazoria children were taught about the importance of rice in the community. They were taken to rice farms and allowed to roam in the fields after irrigation was drained, as seen in this photograph taken at Citrus Grove. The practice of teaching children about the benefits of rice continue today, with several rice associations providing elementary-level curriculums that form a comprehensive look at the crop. Some curriculums teach that the irrigation benefits wildlife, while others focus on farming methods or the nutritional benefits of rice.

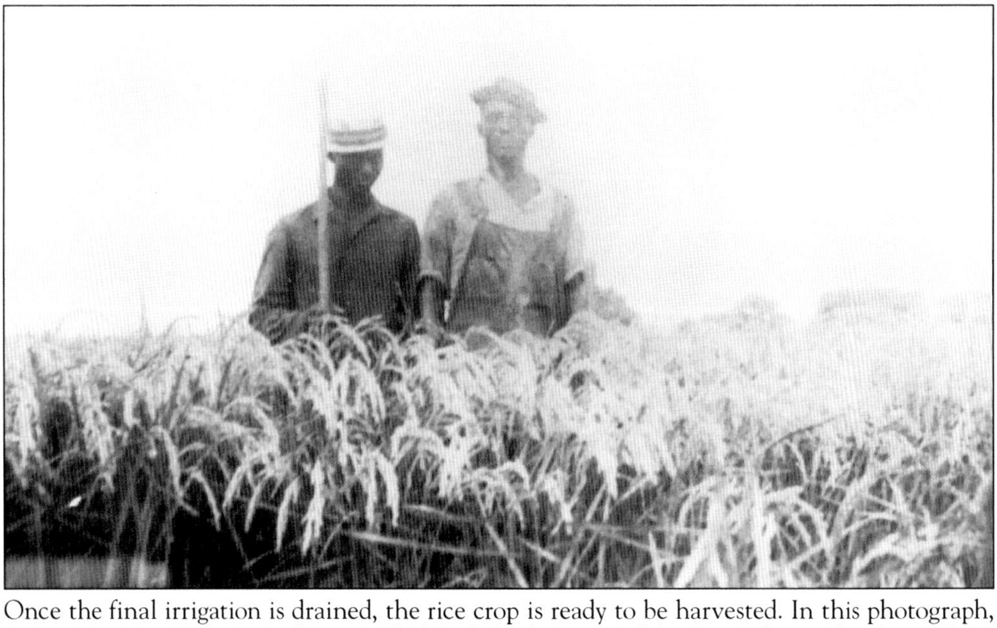

Once the final irrigation is drained, the rice crop is ready to be harvested. In this photograph, two men prepare to harvest their crop by hand. At the onset of the rice industry, the cheap Texas land was heavily promoted as providing a high return on investment. One account from R.M. Cash, secretary of the Texas Land and Rice Co., stated that he would rent an acre of land along the Brazoria Rice and Irrigation canal for $15 to $18 an acre.

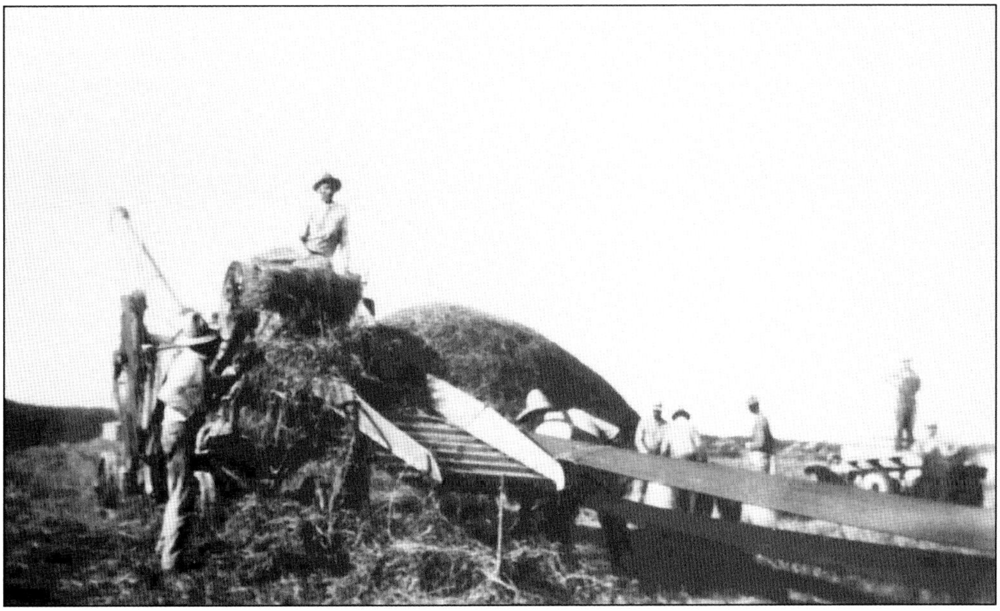

While the introduction of modern equipment made farming rice less labor-intensive than sugar, additional labor was still needed during harvesting. During World War II, farmers on the lower Brazos found cheap labor by using German prisoners of war. These men learned the rice culture, and performed all of the functions of the field.

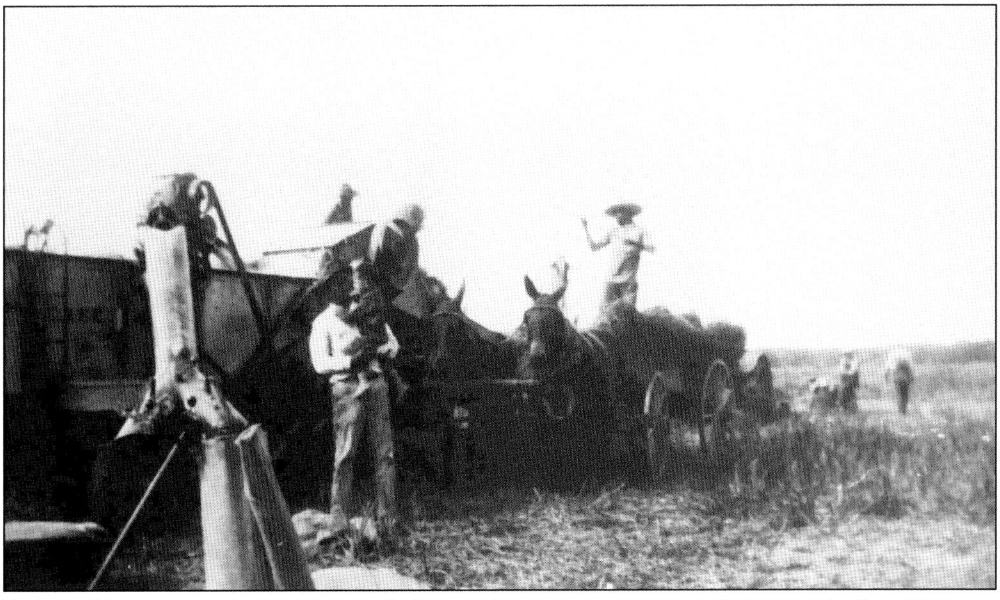

Early field equipment was either pulled by mule teams or by straw-fed steam boilers. Tractors were not used in the region until after World War II. In this photograph, German prisoners of war work in the fields with a mule team. One of the prisoners can be seen holding a small child, though it is not known why.

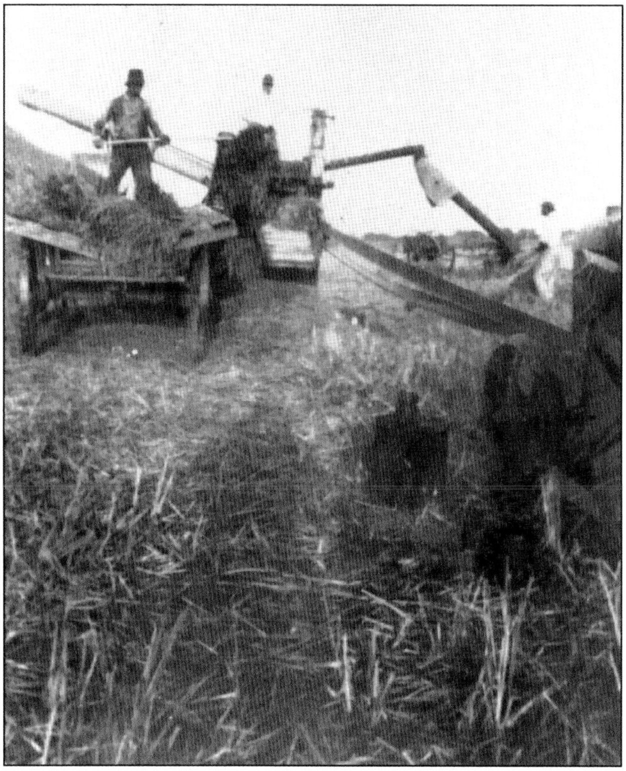

This photograph shows rice being loaded into the thresher by German POWs. Rice straw was promoted as being better than other types of straw, and was sold as readily as the grain. In addition to rice straw being sold as a better feed than prairie hay, it was also claimed that cheap, low-grade rice was better for hogs, horses, and cattle than corn or oats.

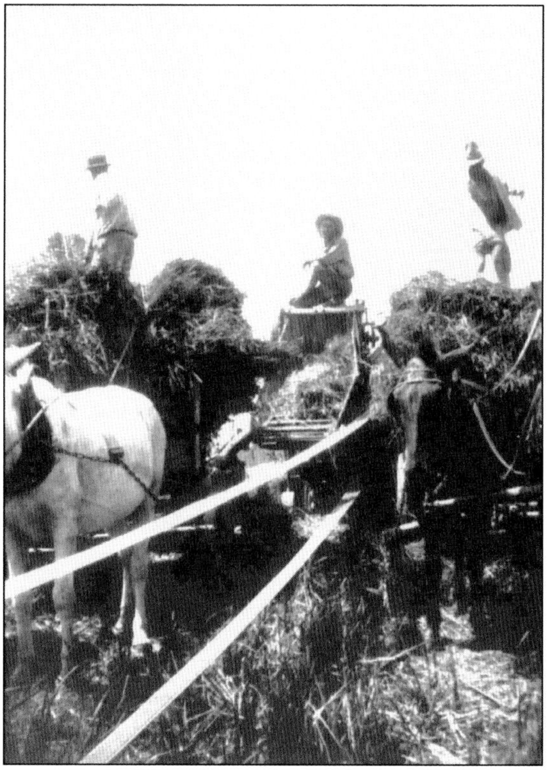

Even in the early days of the Texas rice industry, farmers failed to underestimate the reduction in labor that the crop would provide. The trade publication *Texas Farm and Ranch* once predicted that Texas would become the greatest commercial rice producer in the country, noting that the state had created "the operation with the best labor-saving contrivances of the world."

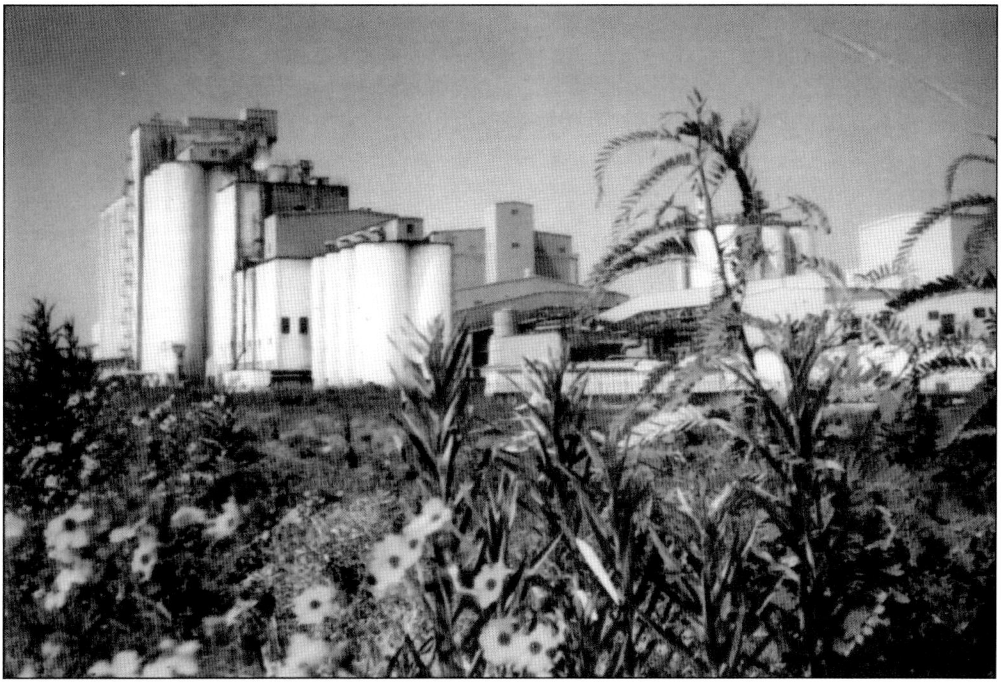

In the first part of the 20th century, rice from the Rice Belt produced a profit of $30 per barrel—compared to the $12.50 netted by wheat from Kansas. South Carolina rice farmers could only harvest 10 acres because the river bottoms kept the crop too wet to use machinery, and the US government once reported that the average Chinese or Japanese rice farmer only planted 1 to 1.5 acres. Rice Belt farmers could cultivate hundreds of acres.

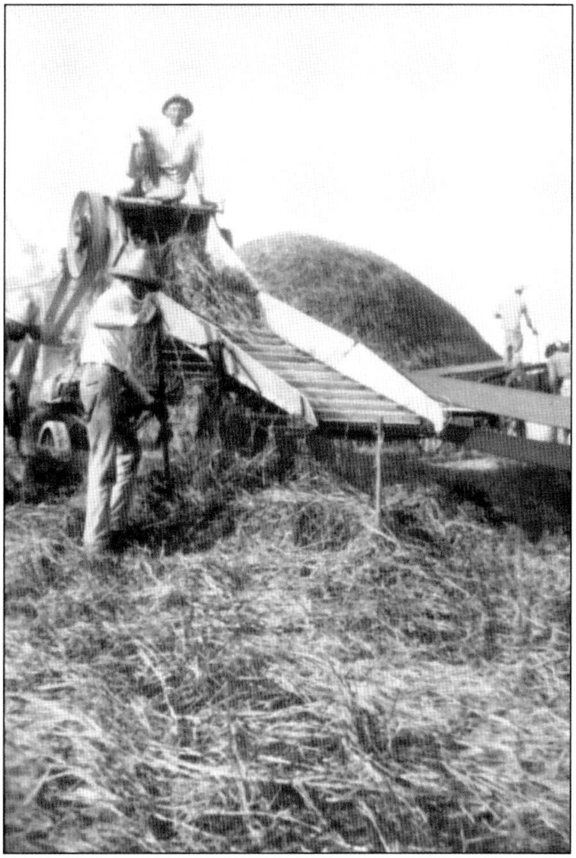

Rice farming held such promise that railroad executives were leaving the industry to farm. In 1902, Col. Charles B. Sloat reported that he would begin working for a 1,500-acre rice plantation near Rosenberg, because he would not let anything keep him from getting in on the ground floor of the new industry. In this c. 1930s photograph, laborers use machinery and equipment from the Peltier Farm in Danbury.

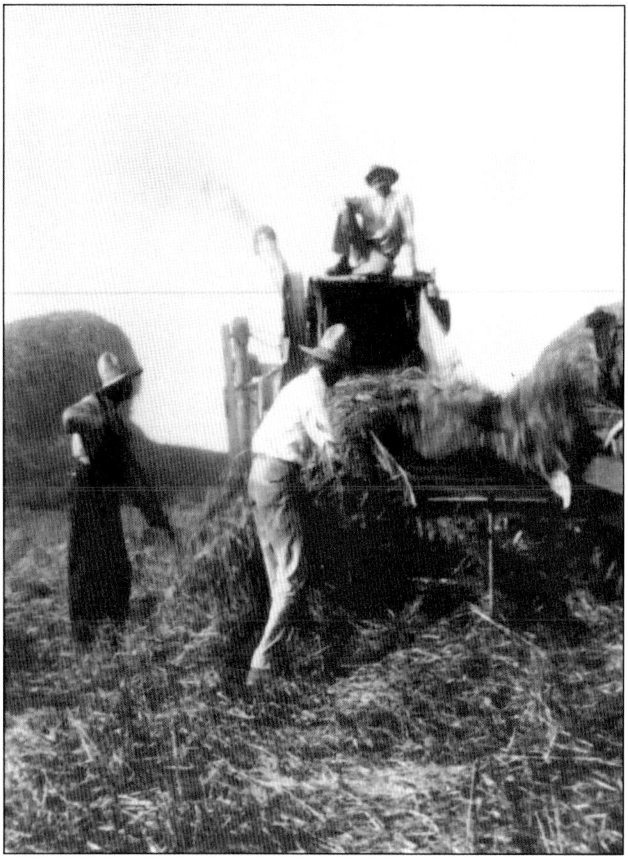

Mechanization meant that a farmer could plant and harvest 100 acres per laborer, with extra manpower brought on during the harvest. Exportation and the active promotion of rice to children and families caused an increase in demand, which farmers met without concern for overproduction or a decline in price. Rice was planted in April, May, and June, which gave nearly three months for harvesting the crop.

In 1945, Rice Belt production got an unexpected boost when a Brazoria company went to Kansas to purchase a rice dryer. The buyers observed the combine harvesters in the wheat fields and brought one back. They switched out the wheels for larger ones that kept it out of the mud, and readied the machine for work in Texas fields.

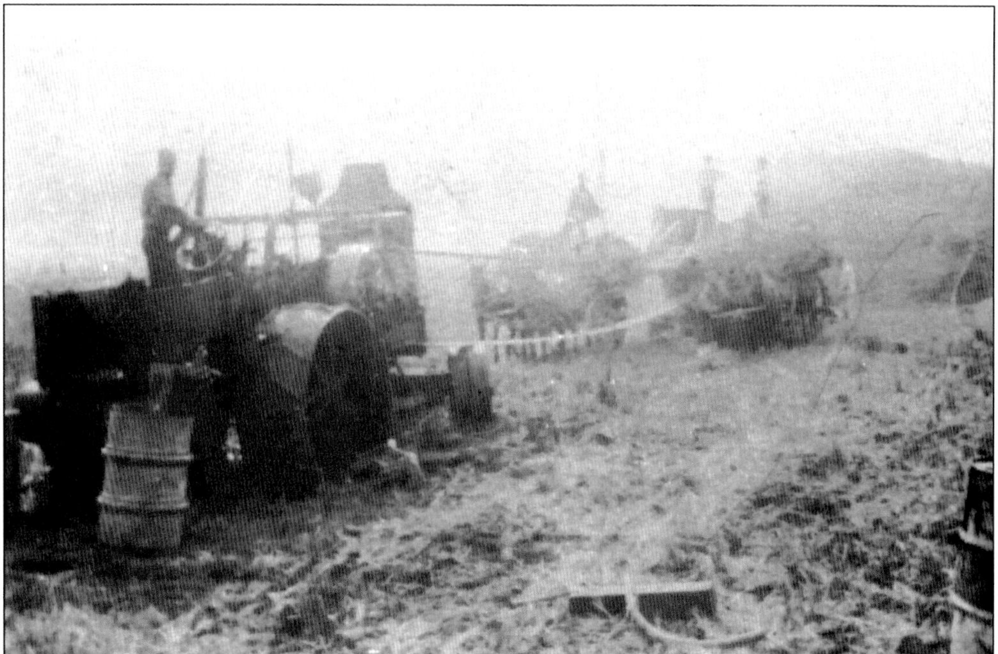

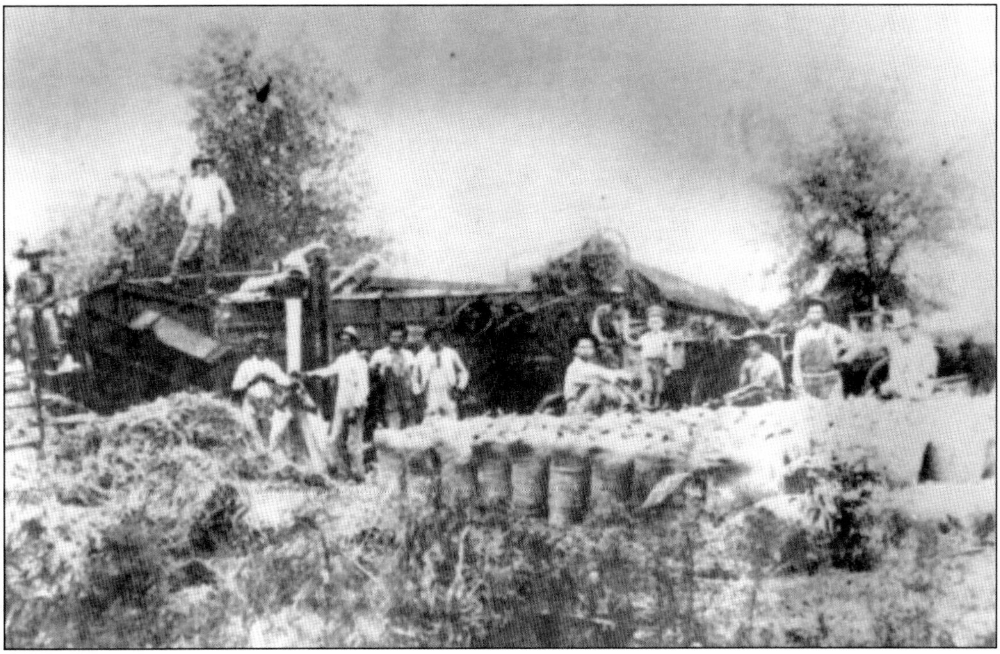

The spread of machine harvesting took decades, due to the complexity of rice harvesting. Once harvested and threshed, the rice needs to be dried. Because cutting takes place when the stalks are still moist, and the rice is immediately bagged for storage, the rice has to be cleaned and artificially dried later. This adds to harvesting time and costs more, which led most farmers to keep with traditional harvesting methods until about the mid-1950s. (Courtesy of Brazoria County Historical Commission.)

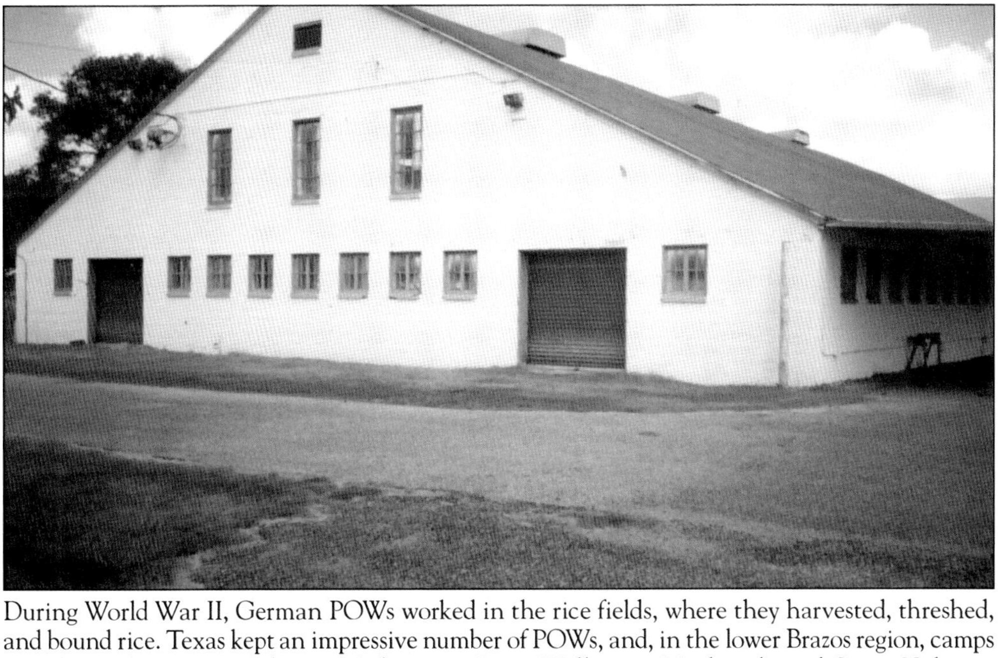

During World War II, German POWs worked in the rice fields, where they harvested, threshed, and bound rice. Texas kept an impressive number of POWs, and, in the lower Brazos region, camps were located at Fort Crockett in Galveston, Camp Wallace in Hitchcock, and Camp Hulen in Matagorda County.

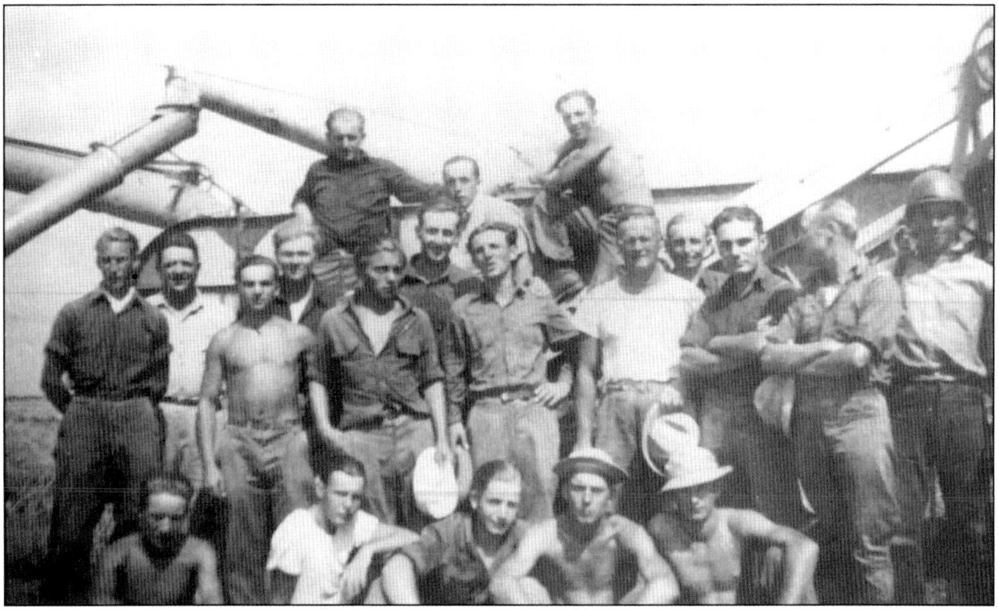

Because World War II required young men to leave farms, the federal government sent German POWs to work farms for $1.50 per day. These prisoners were paid 80¢ in canteen coupons, and were treated very differently from state prisoners or slaves. At camp, the prisoners had access to classes to teach them skills, and could even take correspondence classes at local universities. Both farmers and prisoners have recalled their time together fondly.

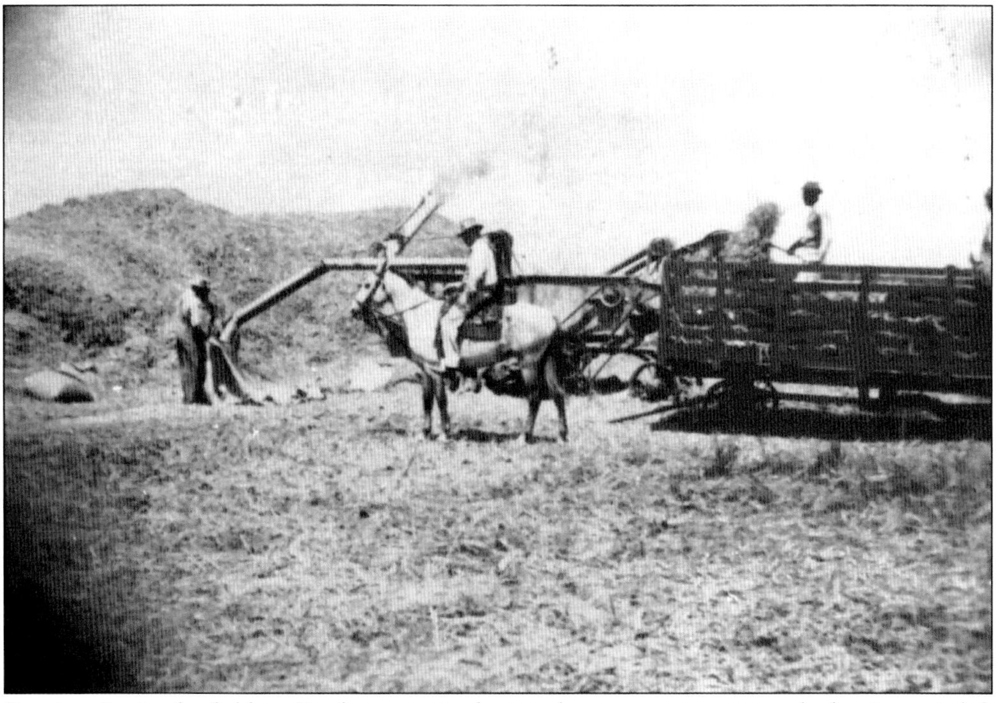

Bagging rice in the fields at Danbury required more than one person to catch the rice as it left the thresher. When a bag filled up, workers used a needle and twine to sew it shut. The rice was then thrown onto a cart and hauled away for drying.

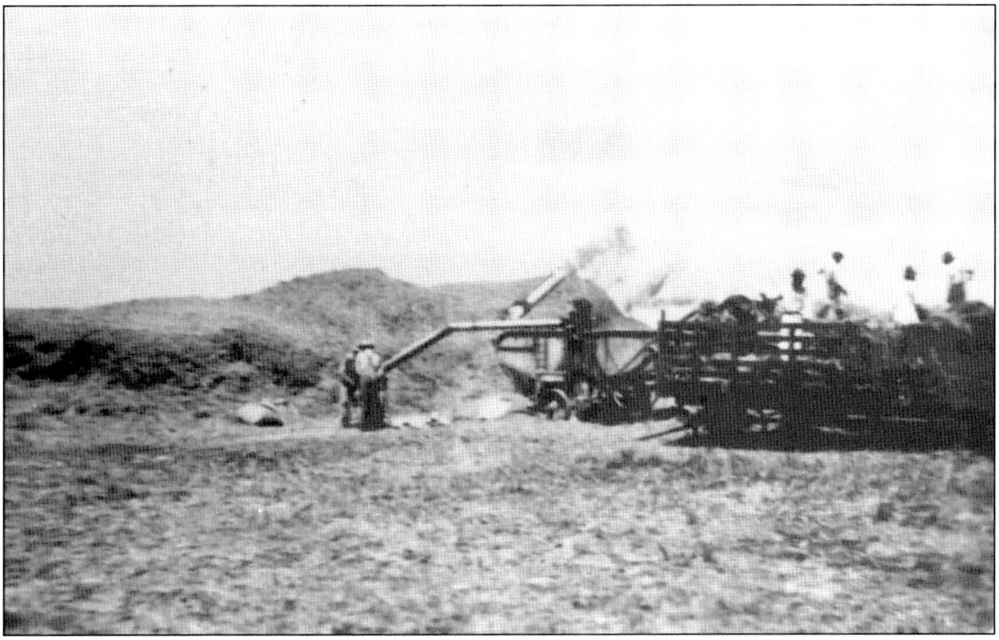

This photograph illustrates the entire rice harvesting process. The workers to the right have harvested the rice and are feeding stalks into the thresher. At the center, straw is thrown from the thresher into piles, while the workers to the left are collecting the rice into bags. Because this process produced more straw than rice, more workers were needed to feed the thresher than to collect the rice into bags.

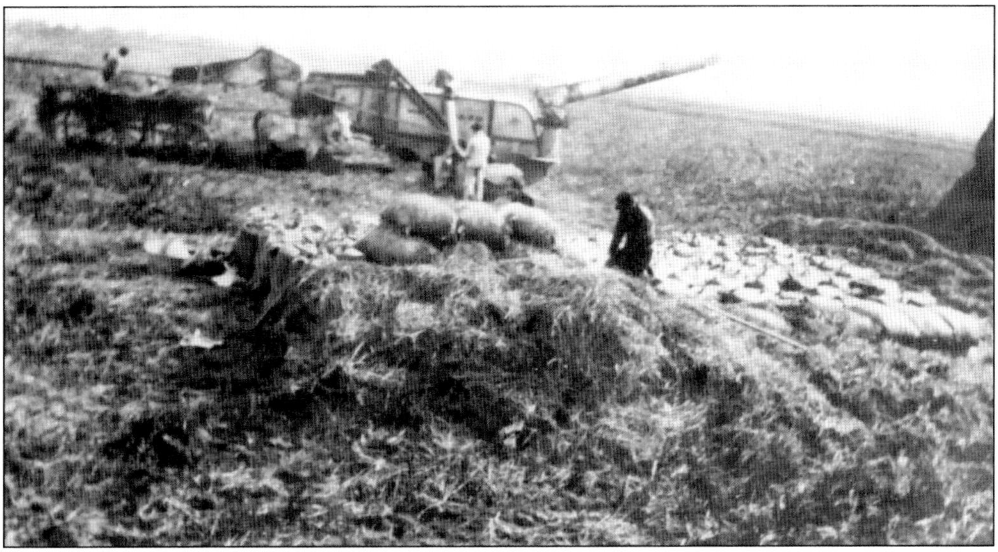

This photograph of a harvested field shows the combine and the mule drawn carts used in harvesting. Bags filled with rice are being prepared for transport at center, and the pile of discarded straw can be seen to the right. Transportation and cleanup was the most labor-intensive part of the process, as the field equipment that handles those aspects today was yet to be developed.

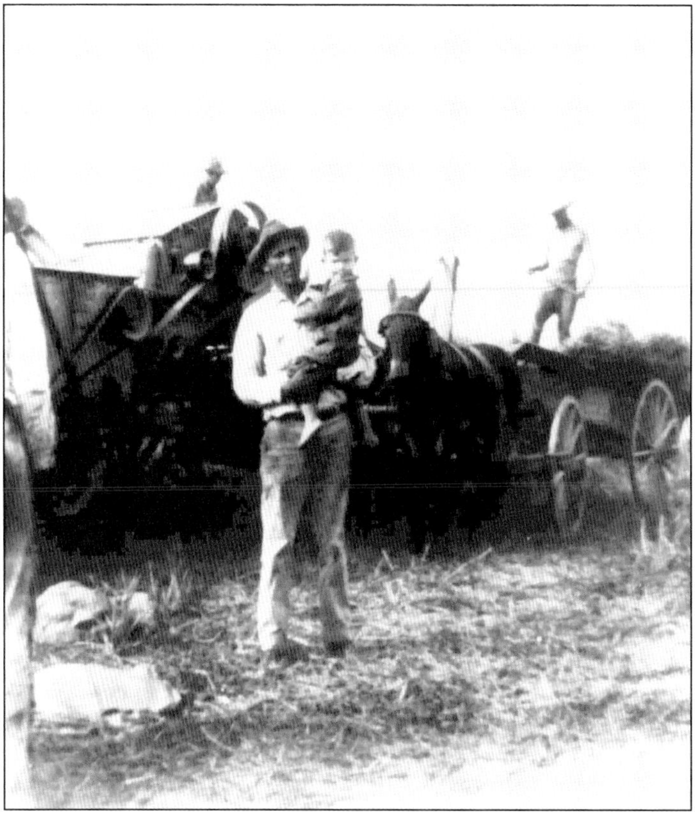

A German POW holds a young boy in the rice fields. Some accounts claim that the German POWs considered their time on the Texas farms as the grandest adventure of their lives. Stories tell of these soldiers reconnecting with local farmers after the war, and remaining in touch with them for the rest of their lives.

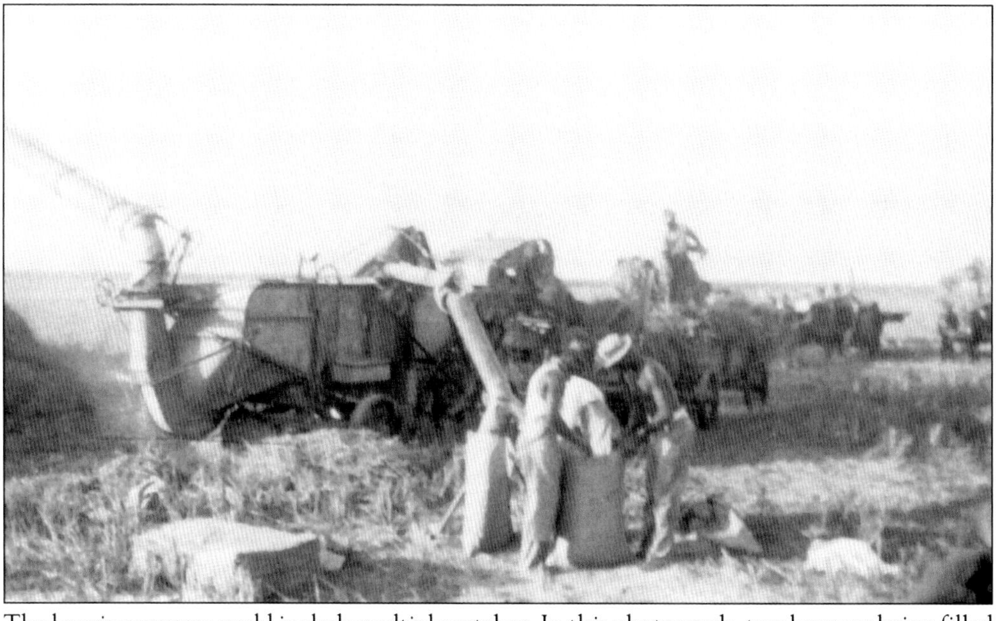

The bagging process could include multiple catches. In this photograph, two bags are being filled at a single time. This aided in the production, and illustrates how quickly the rice industry was advancing technologically. Advancements to agricultural equipment were considered critical to reducing labor costs and increasing a farmer's return on investment.

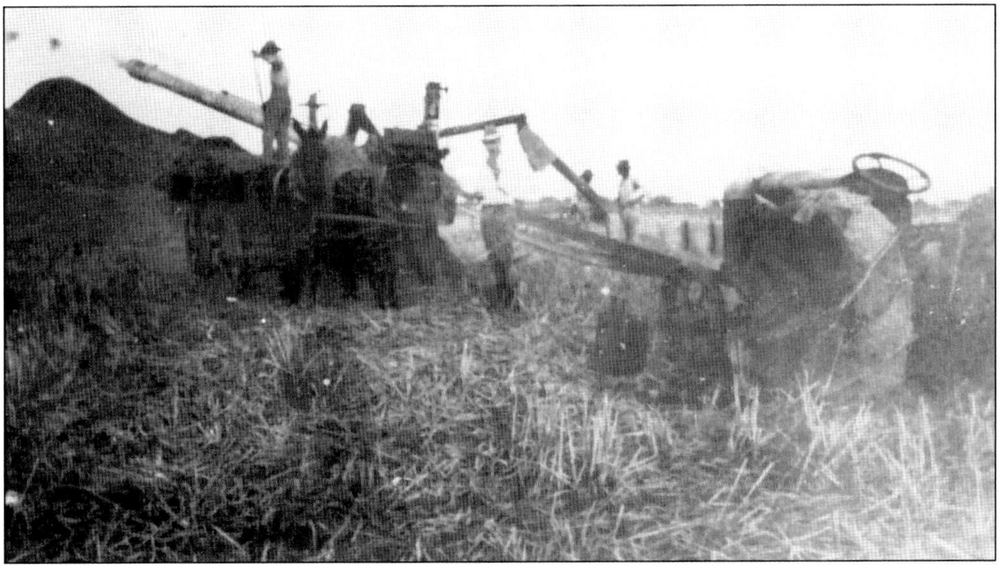

On December 19, 1901, the *Galveston Daily News* reported that more than 20 charters for rice corporations had been given in the Rice Belt that year. It also stated that "a large number" of charters were given to oil companies that intended to also grow rice, and that "a few" corporations planned to irrigate rice, but not grow it. In this photograph, workers separate rice in a Brazoria rice field.

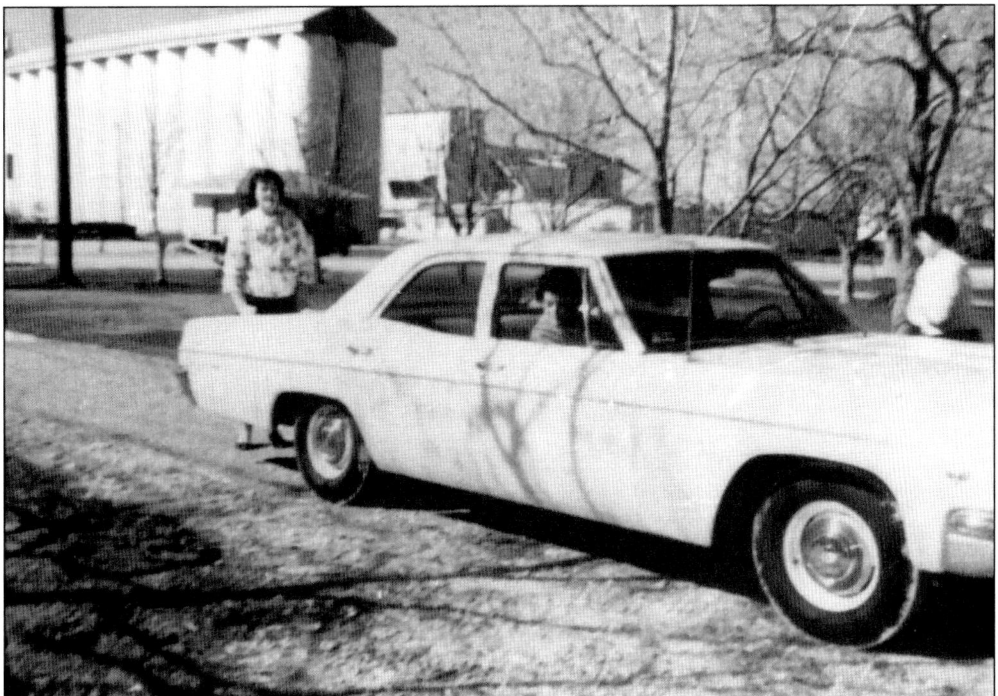

After combine harvesting became commonplace, drying shocks of rice was no longer required. Instead, rice was dried in a dryer. Rice drying could be done with an individual dryer, but commercial dryers were often used because some would clean the rice as well. The Danbury rice dryer can be seen in the background of this photograph, taken in Danbury in the 1960s.

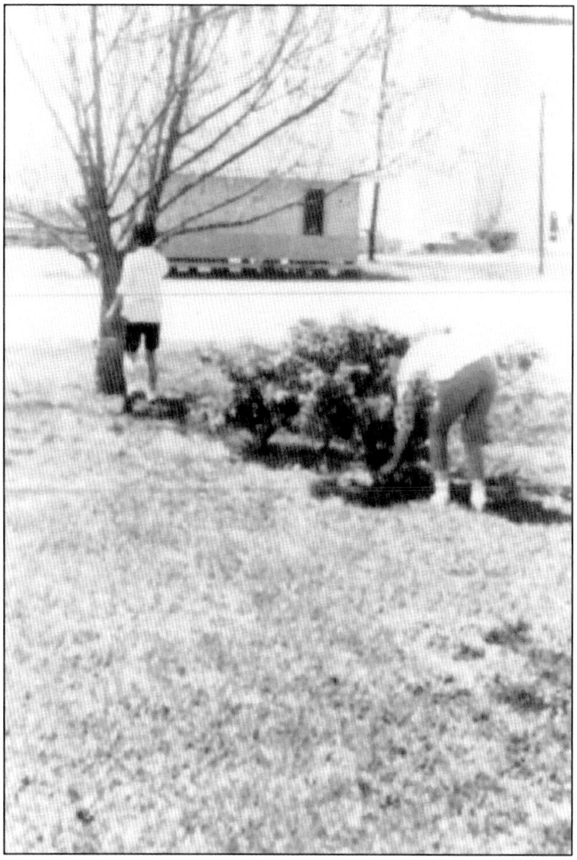

When wet rice was stored for longer than 24 hours, the farmer ran the risk of heat damage. This resulted in dark brown kernels that lessened the quality and price of milled rice, so the process of artificial drying was introduced. The women in this photograph are working on the landscaping outside of the Danbury commercial dryer. The company's office can be seen in the distance.

On October 28, 1967, a train derailed near the dryer at Danbury and caught fire. The fire spread, sparking a community-wide disaster. The entire rice drying and storage facility burned to the ground, leaving Danbury residents stunned for weeks as they battled with lingering smoke.

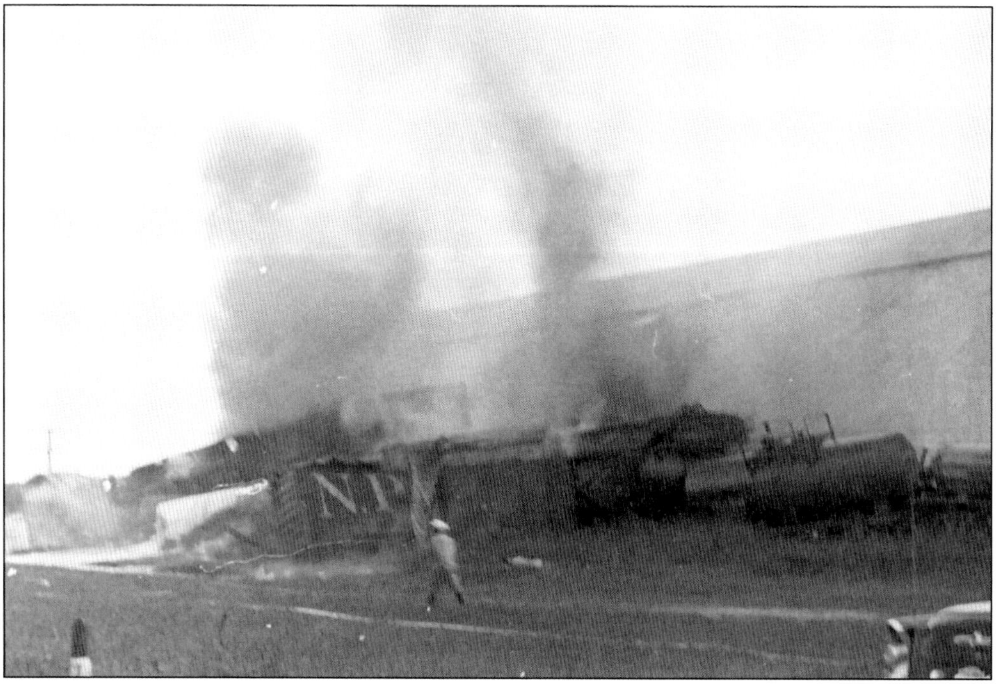

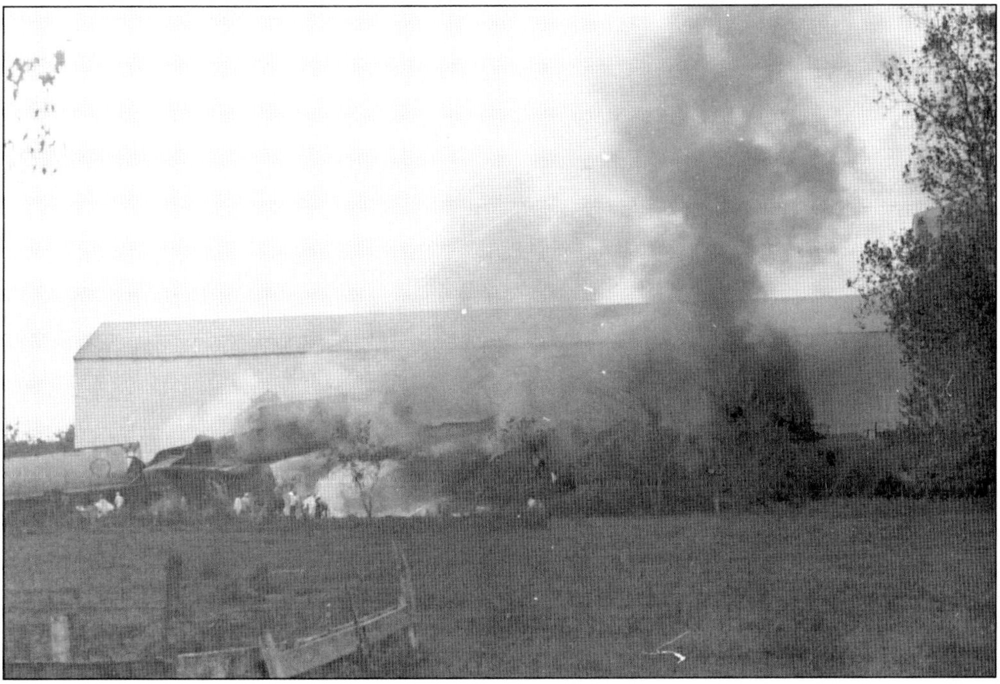

The Danbury fire burned for 13 days, leaving firefighters "tried by fire," according to the *Brazosport Facts*. About 40,000 barrels of rice were ruined for human consumption, but Laddie Korenok, the dryer manger, hoped to salvage the rice for animal feed. The rice was valued at $320,000, while the value of the rice dryer was estimated at $300,000.

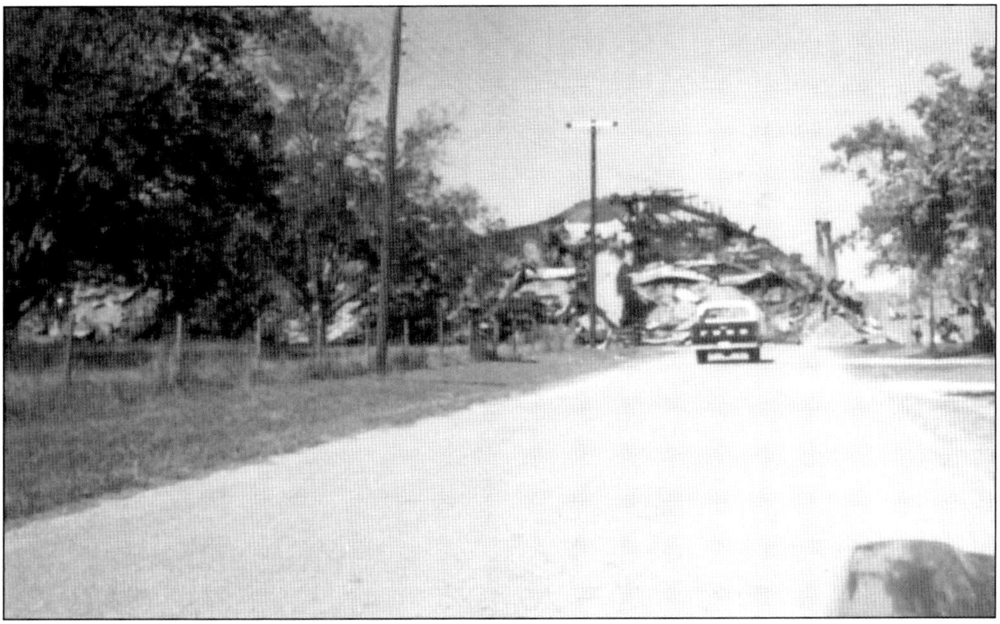

After the fire, 35 volunteer firefighters continued to monitor the dryer as it smoldered. Some were given time off from their jobs to help, while others stood watch during the morning and evening. The fire department chief told the local newspaper that he never heard from the railroad company. The efforts made to put out the fire eventually left Danbury residents with a water shortage.

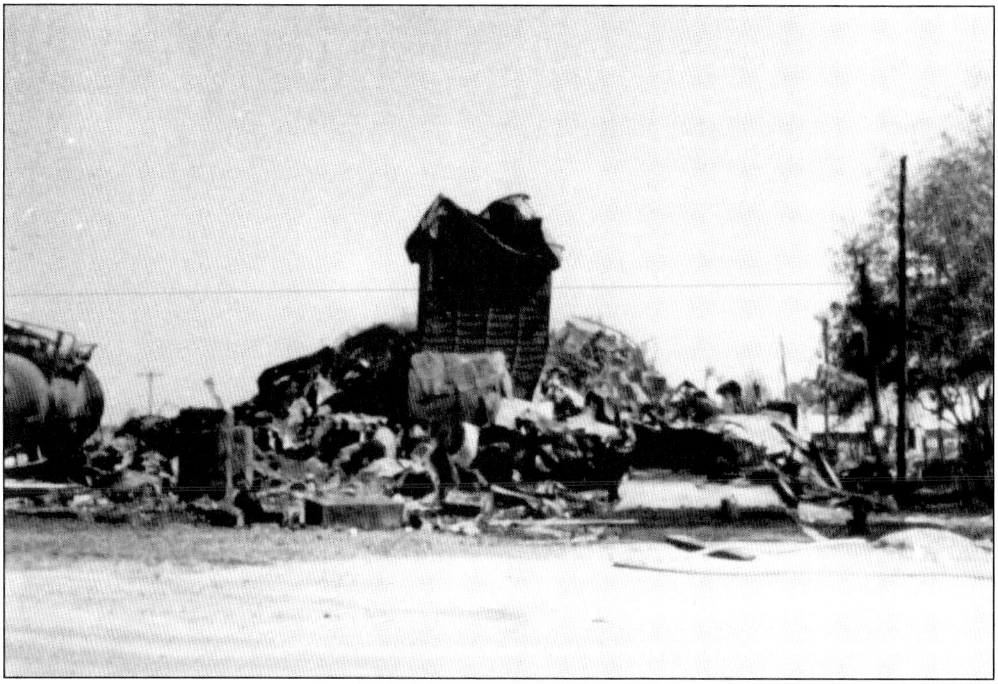

Dryer manager Laddie Korenok intended to collect a payout from his insurance company for the losses. After the fire, smoldering rice had to be trucked out of town, because it was creating an acrid smoke that was upsetting the residents. Some women complained they could not hang their laundry outside because of the particles. The rice that had been saved was stacked near the railroad.

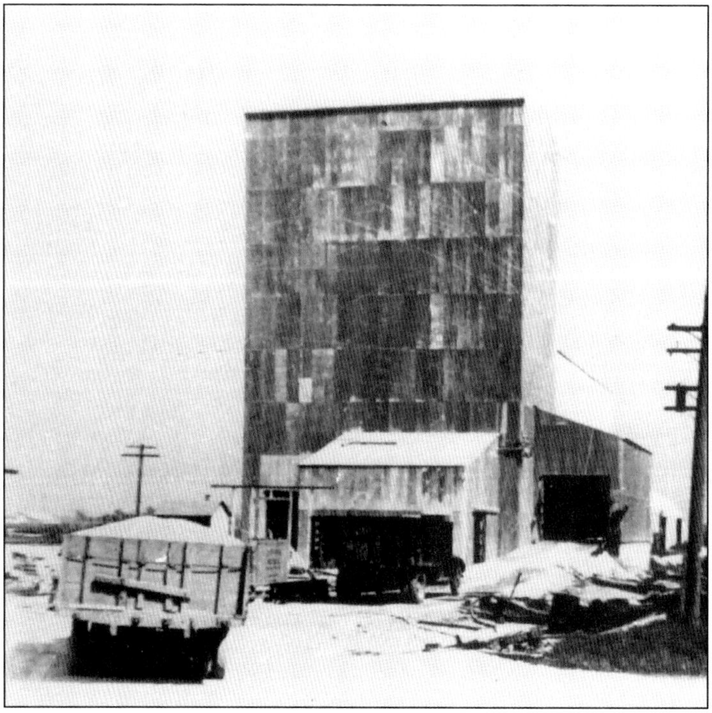

The first load of rice was delivered to the Danbury dryer in 1965, and it was a cause for celebration in the town. A commercial dryer was able to handle greater volume than individual farms, and it helped to modernize the local rice industry. Soon, trucks lined up to bring their rice in for storage.

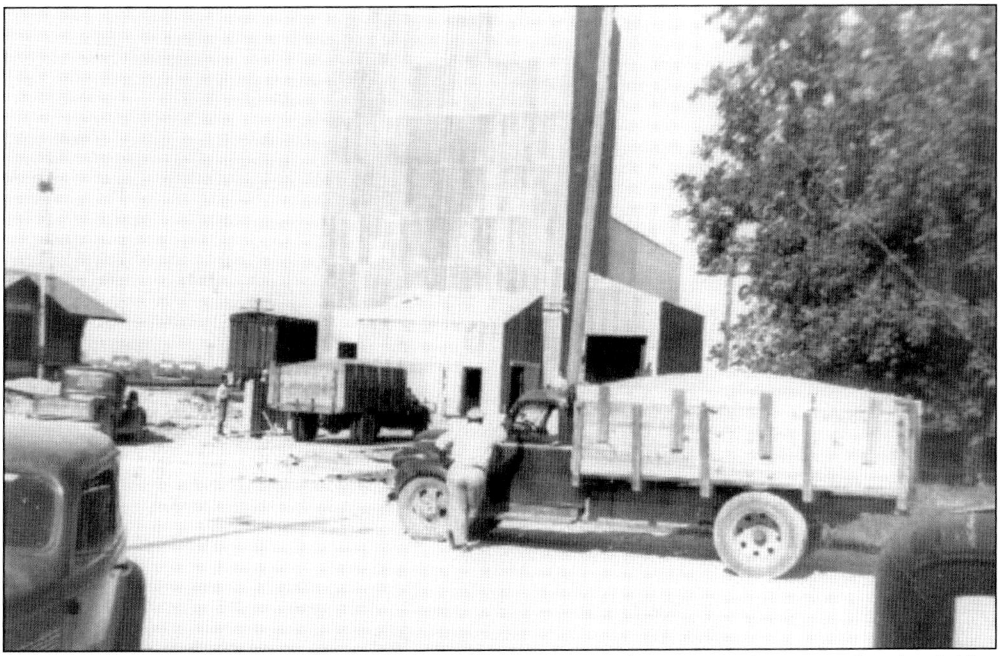

In this photograph, a line of trucks rings the Danbury rice dryer as it takes on its first load. Not only could the dryer clean and dry rice, the nearby rail station meant the rice could be quickly shipped as well. These hopes were dashed just a few years later, however, when a train derailment set the entire building on fire in 1967.

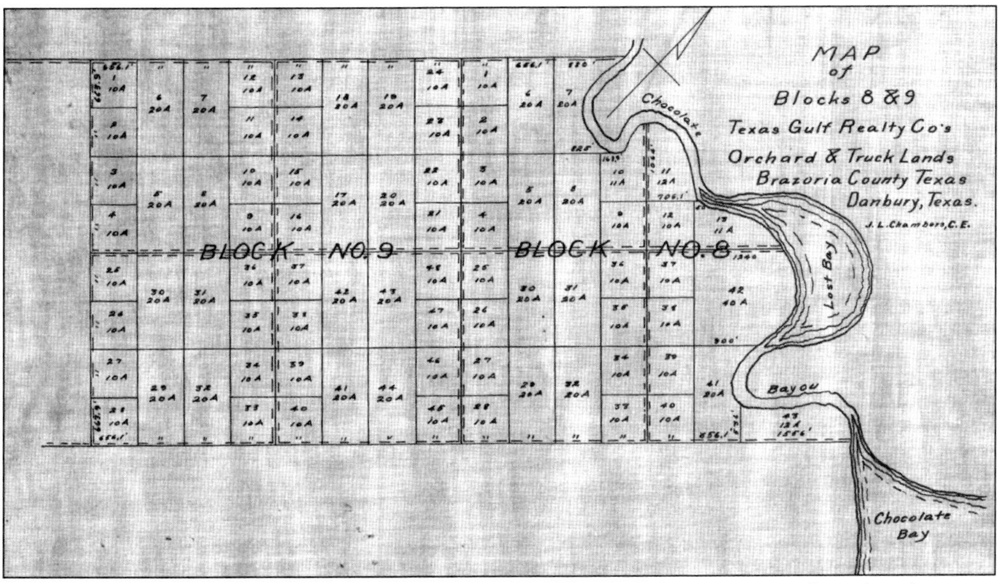


Danbury, a small community outside Angleton, was a hub for rice, crops, and cattle. The town flourished when the proliferation of farm trucks and overland transportation began to overtake river transport. Situated on Chocolate Bay, Danbury proved a good alternative to Galveston, and docks were built to accommodate the trucks while local rail provided further overland transport. This undated map from the Texas Gulf Realty Co. illustrates various tracts of land in town.

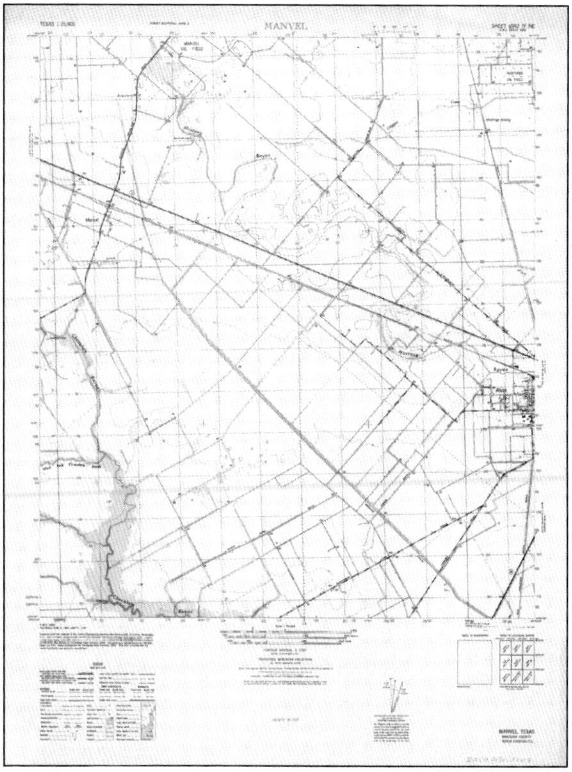


In 1955, the town of Manvel was known for its oil field and gas wells, but the American Canal also ran through it. The American Canal was a division of the American Rice Association and is today operated by the Gulf Coast Water Authority as Canal A. Manvel maintains a unique position in the canal system, as all three of the major canals run through it.

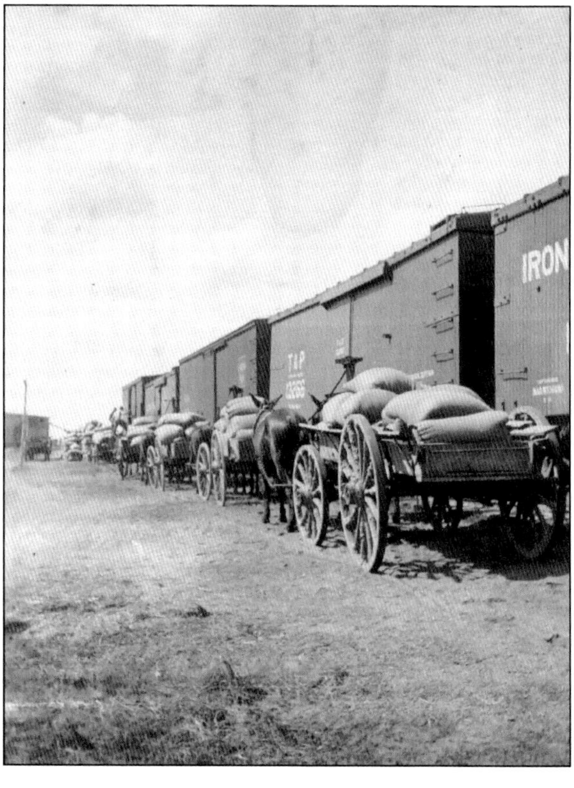


In this undated photograph, bags of crops are being hauled to the railroad by mule-drawn wagons. Railroads vied for crop transportation business in the same way that landings did during the days of Austin's Colony. At the onset of the industry, rice was recorded as paying four times as much as cotton, making it the most profitable commodity handled by the railroads.

Camp Wallace can be seen in the upper right of this 1943 map from the Army Corps of Engineers. This was the Naval Air Station during World War II, and it relied on well water from Alta Loma. The government sold the site in 1949, and for a while, farmers stored rice in it. The site was used by various businesses and was sold repeatedly before eventually being demolished when it sustained damage during Hurricane Carla in 1961.

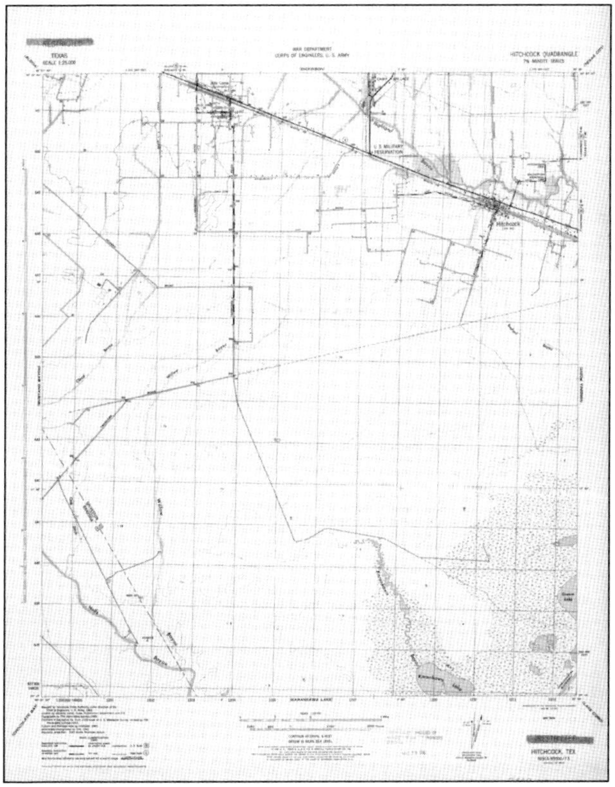


Similar to the work of the men who pumped water out of the bayou and into the irrigation canals, harvesting rice was a long process that often required a camp to be set up in the field. Here, men are seen resting near their tents in one of these "rice harvest camps."

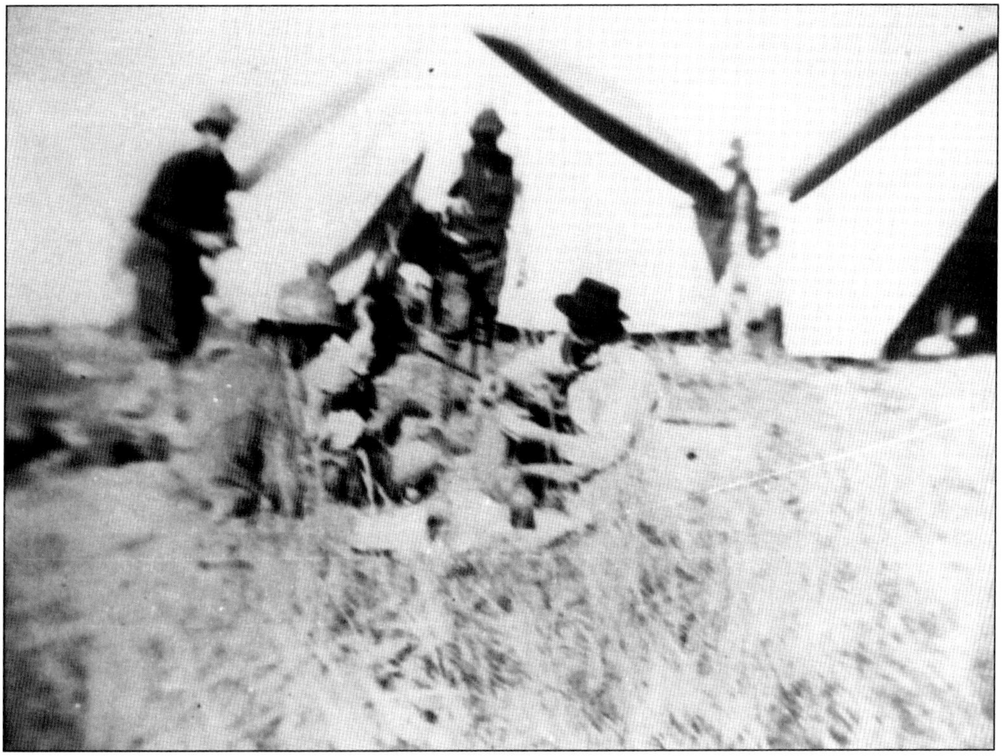

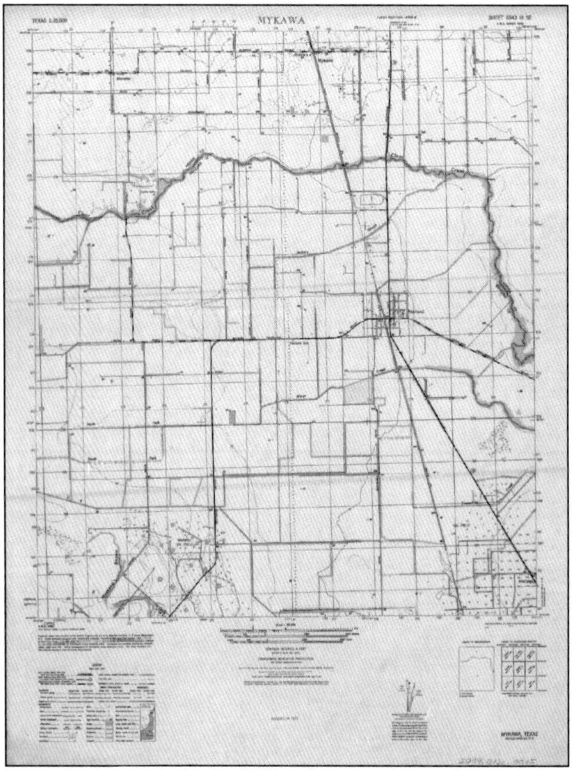


In 1904, the Houston Chamber of Commerce asked Japanese farmers to discuss rice production with them. The visiting farmers brought seed with them, and this Japanese seed increased local production from 18 to 34 barrels per acre. One of these men, Shinpie Mykawa, even died in the fields while planting rice. The local farmers were so impressed with Mykawa that they named their community after him.

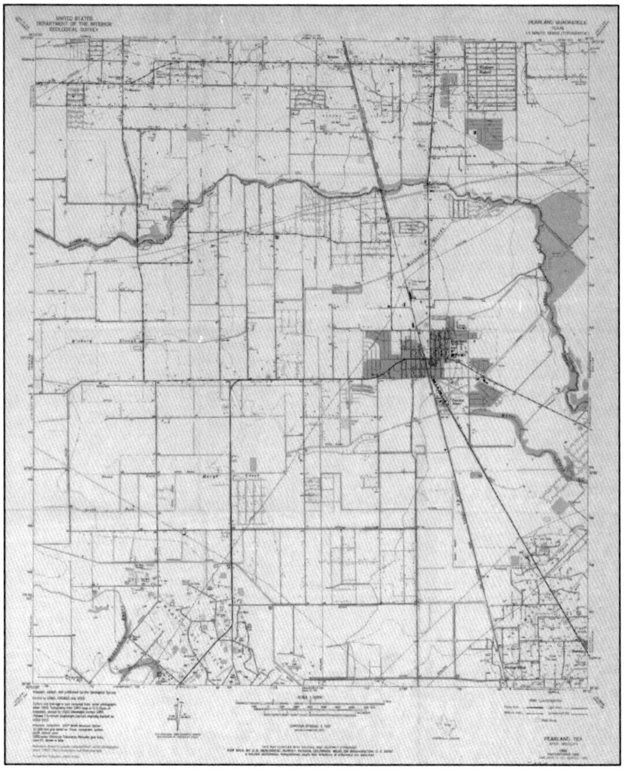

In this 1969 map by the US Geological Survey, Pearland can be seen as a designated urban area. The map documents the airport and the high school, and also marks a pump house, pump, and a canal that diverts water from Clear Creek to the city. There is also a ditch and levee that runs from the creek to the community.

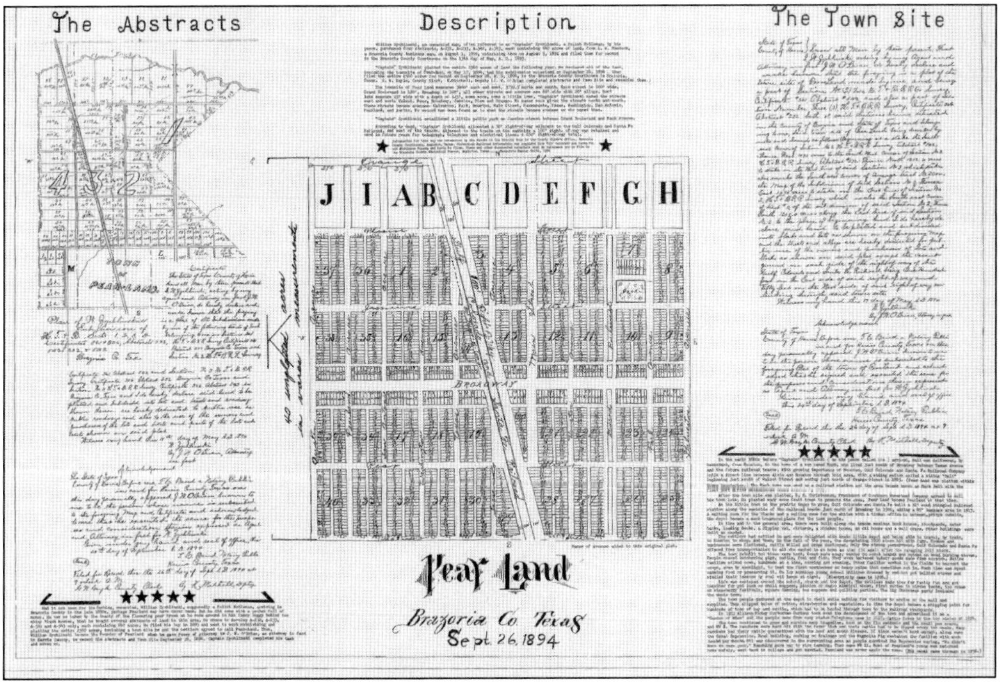


This is a copy of the original plot for Pearland, with notes written by Margurite Massey Smith in 1994. She writes that William Zychlinski, a Polish nobleman, was so enchanted with the pear trees that grew wild here that he bought several land abstracts in 1893 and platted them to build the town. Smith also notes that the Brazoria canal arrived in 1934 and that ranching gave way to rice farming after the freeze of 1924.

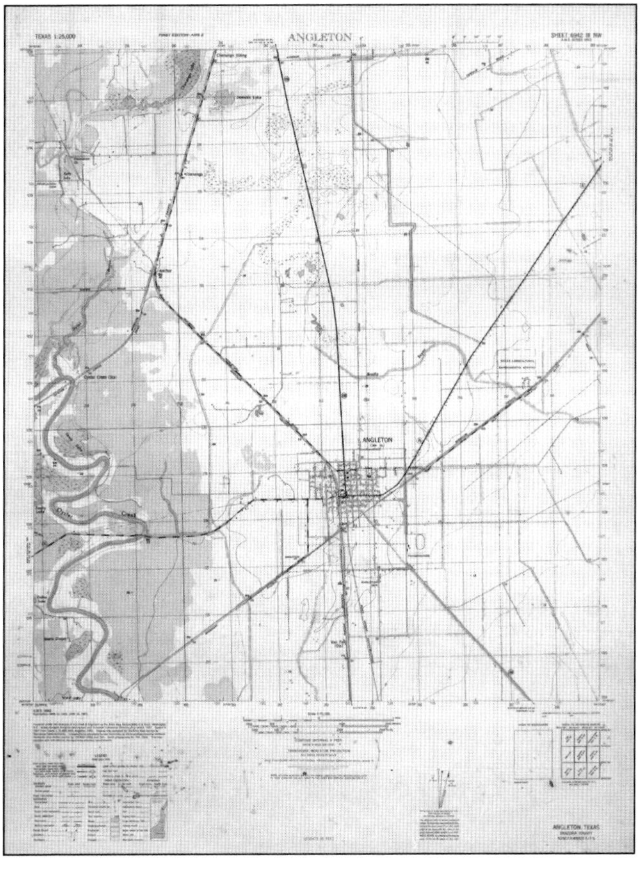


The Texas Agricultural Experiment Station can be seen to the northeast of Angleton in this map from 1943. The station still stands as part of the Texas Agricultural Extension Agency. The agency dates from 1888, and by 1894 its first field office had opened in Beeville. Today, field stations operate throughout Texas, testing ways to strengthen and adapt crops.

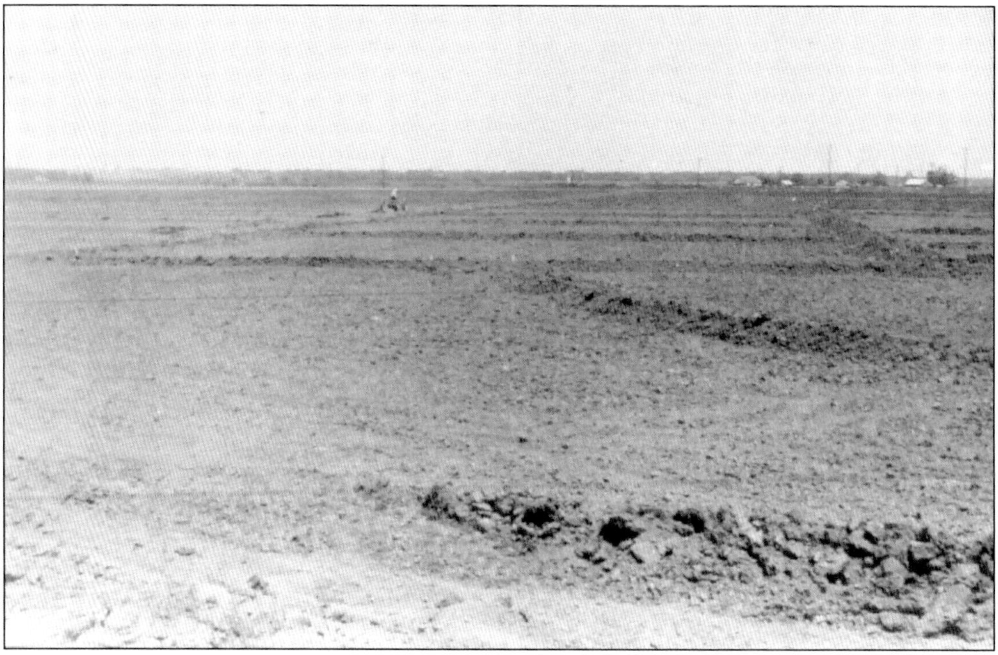

Crop experiments were an important part of the Rice Belt's development. These tests began around the turn of the 20th century at the Texas Agricultural Experiment Station in Angleton. The belt was a good candidate for these tests because rice lands should be level and have a smooth soil surface, although this is not absolutely necessary.

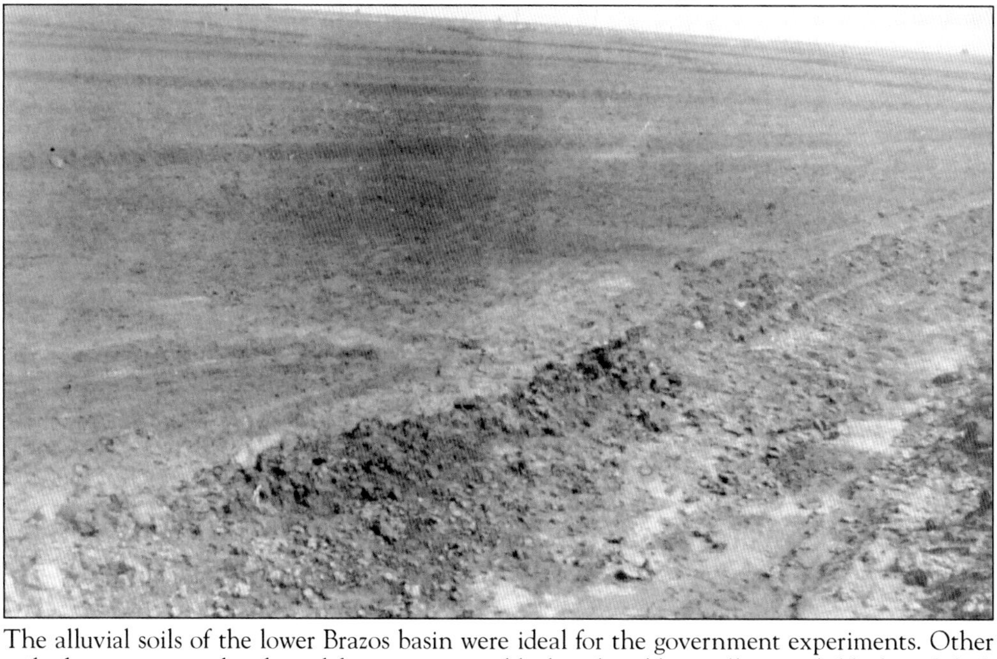

The alluvial soils of the lower Brazos basin were ideal for the government experiments. Other soils that were considered good for testing were black soil and hogwallow, with black and dark sandy loam being the best. Farmers said that either soil should sit upon firm clay subsoil. Test farmers would document the weather, soil conditions, and seed to determine how well a variety of rice would do in the Rice Belt.

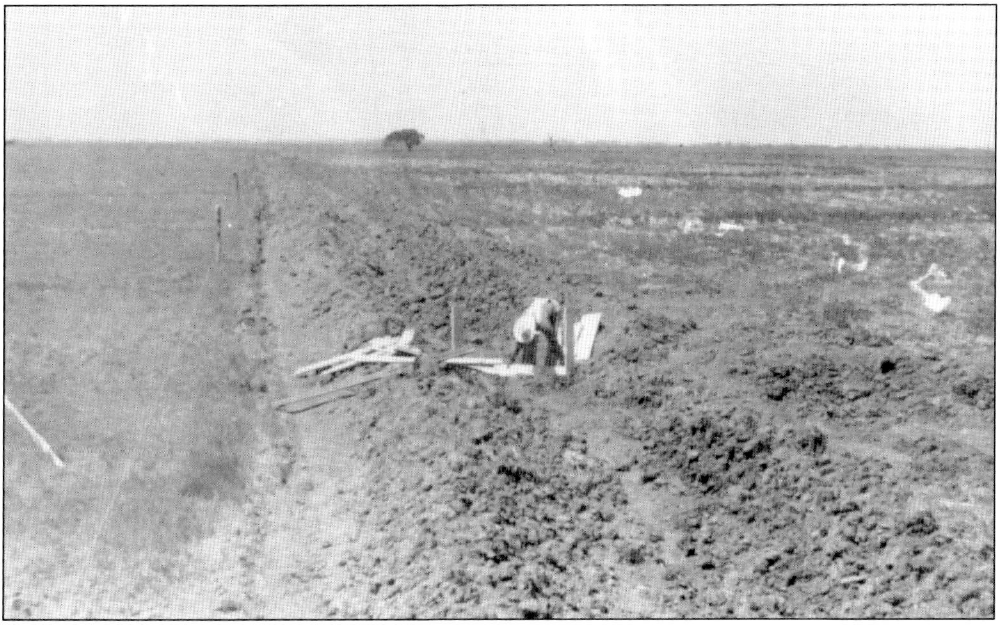

Irrigation levees are built at the Texas Experimental Station, and test farmers studied how to build canals and how the different types of canal affected crops. The idea of endless water changed the way farmers thought about the weather, and some farmers said that they were studying their well capacities, engines, and pumps instead of their almanacs. One farmer noted his trouble ended when his well met all of his water requirements.

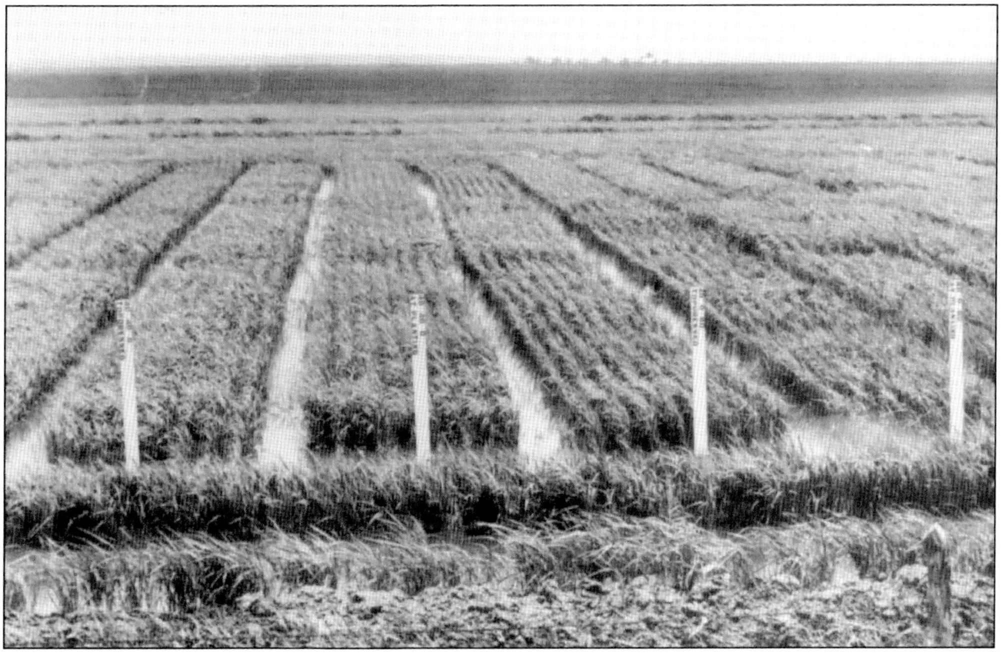

This photograph shows an experimental field being irrigated for testing purposes. The markers denote the type of crop in each row and other important details. The field stretches into the distance, illustrating the commitment that the station had to testing Texas crops and creating more hearty varieties that could withstand the climate.

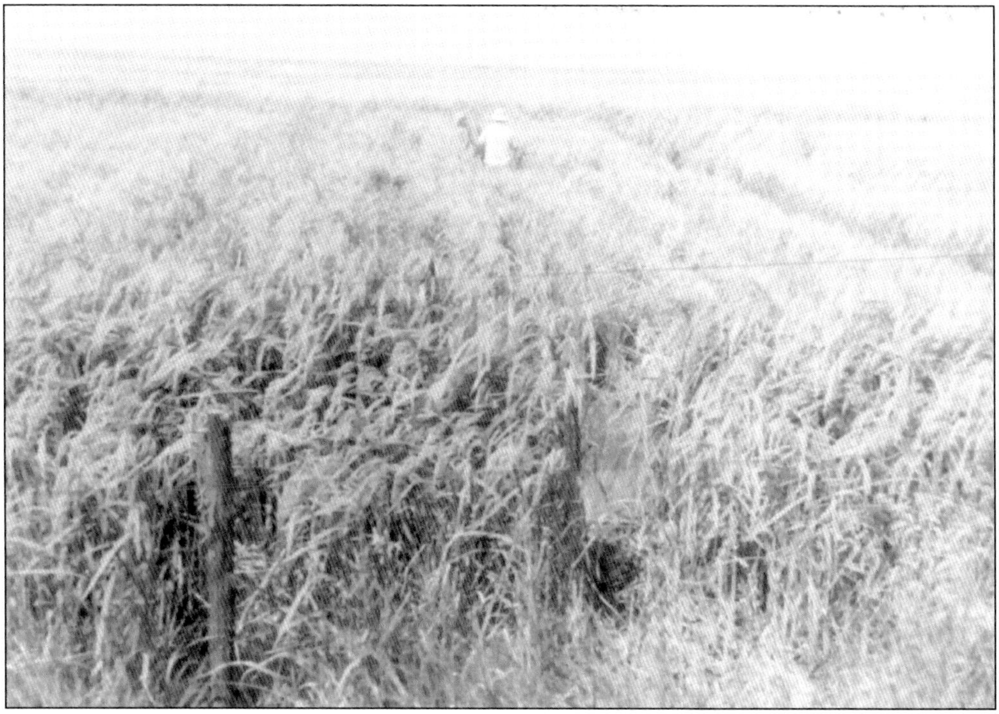

Records of the first experiments in Brazoria County date to the early 1900s, when a single worker maintained the fields. He recorded extensive details about the effects of the weather and noted how the area could swing between extreme drought and heavy rainfall.

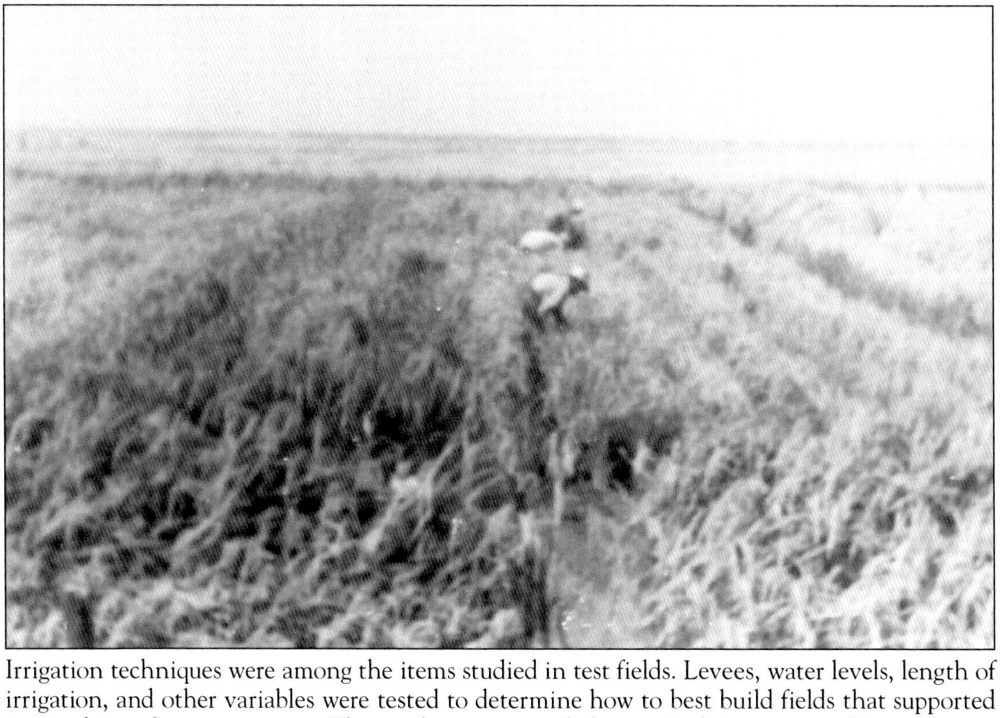

Irrigation techniques were among the items studied in test fields. Levees, water levels, length of irrigation, and other variables were tested to determine how to best build fields that supported rice and complementary crops. The results were recorded extensively in notes and journals.

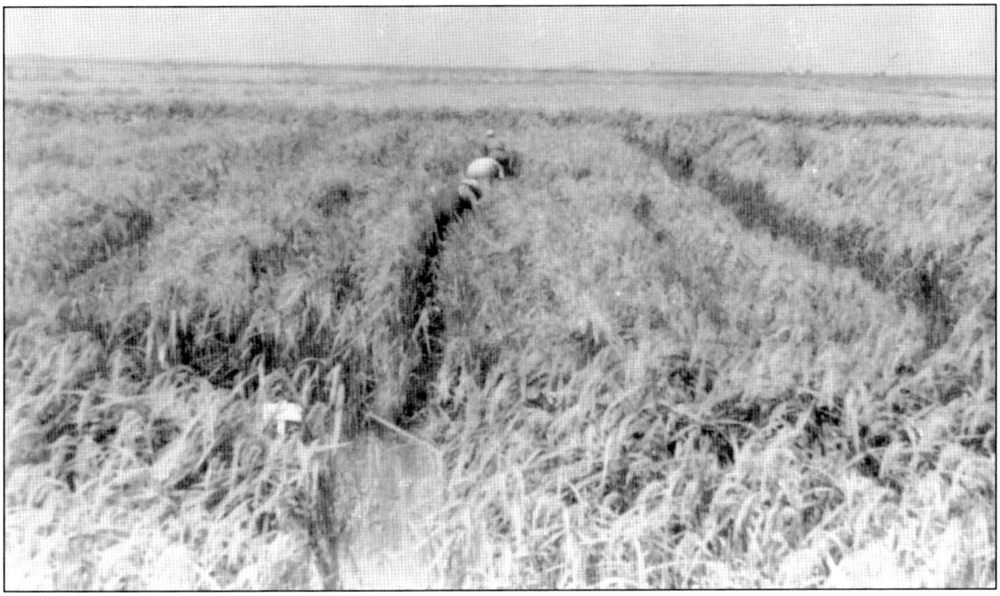

In this photograph, the test farmers at the Texas Agricultural Experiment Station in Angleton work cooperatively with rice breeders at the Beaumont station. Hundreds of varieties of rice were tested in the mid-20th century. Today, experimental stations are scattered throughout the state, where testing is still done on many crops.

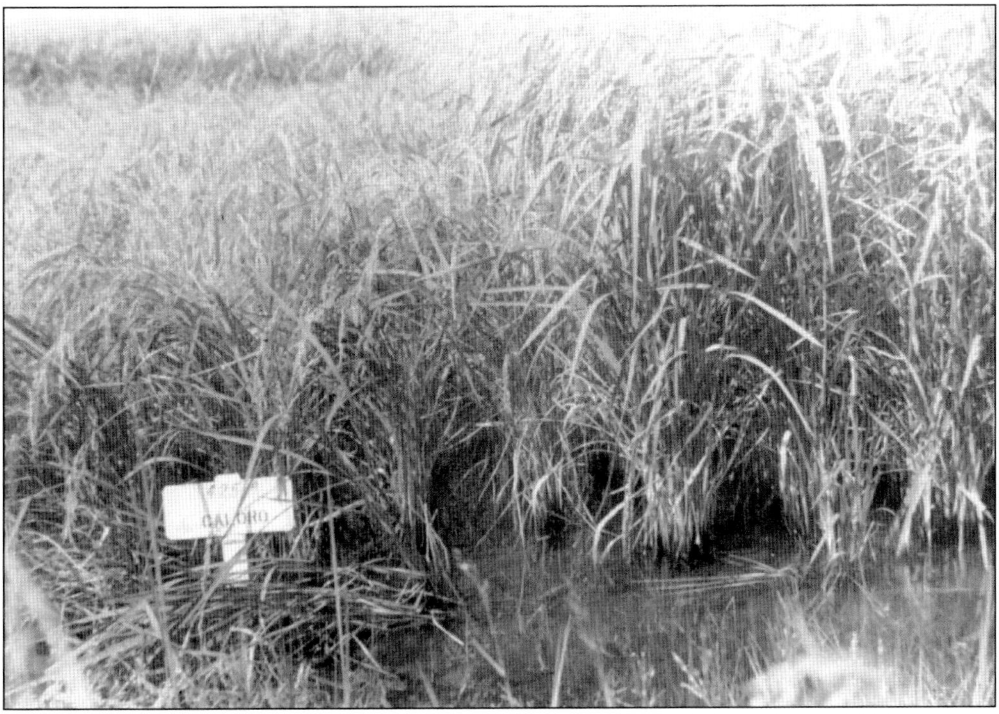

Cal Oro is being tested in the Angleton fields in this photograph from the mid-20th century. Cal Oro was a varietal from the Cal-Oro Rice Growers, a nonprofit business from California that incorporated in 1947. The experiments helped determine the best methods for growing rice, as well as for strengthening different varieties through crossbreeding.

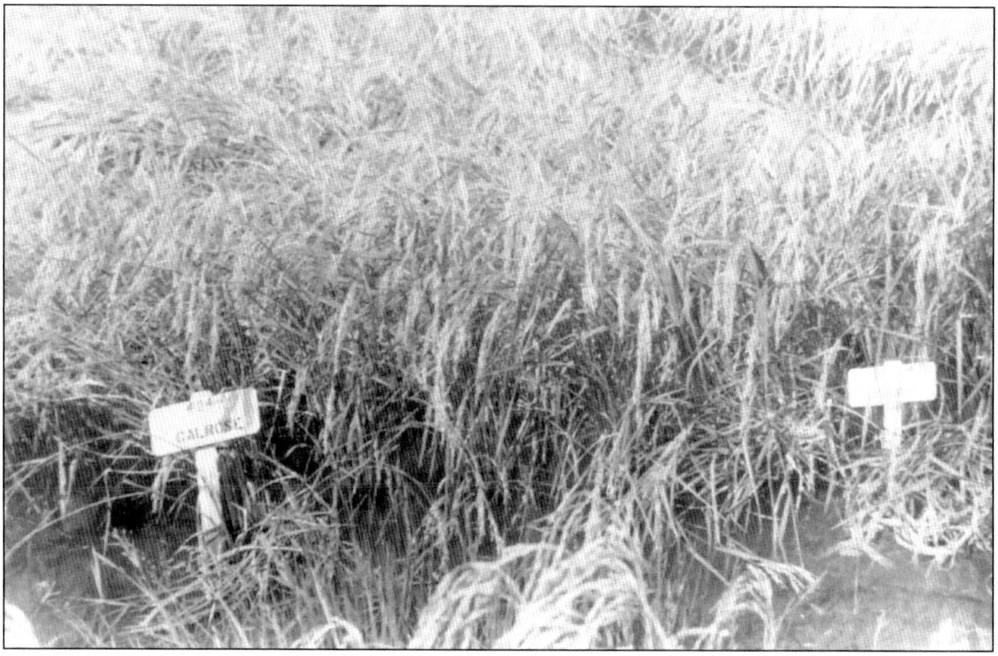

In addition Cal Oro, the station tested another rice varietal that is still being produced and cultivated. Calrose is a medium-grain rice that is popular in several grocery store chains, and is used in table dishes and Asian recipes. When cooked, Calrose rice gets soft and the grains stick together.

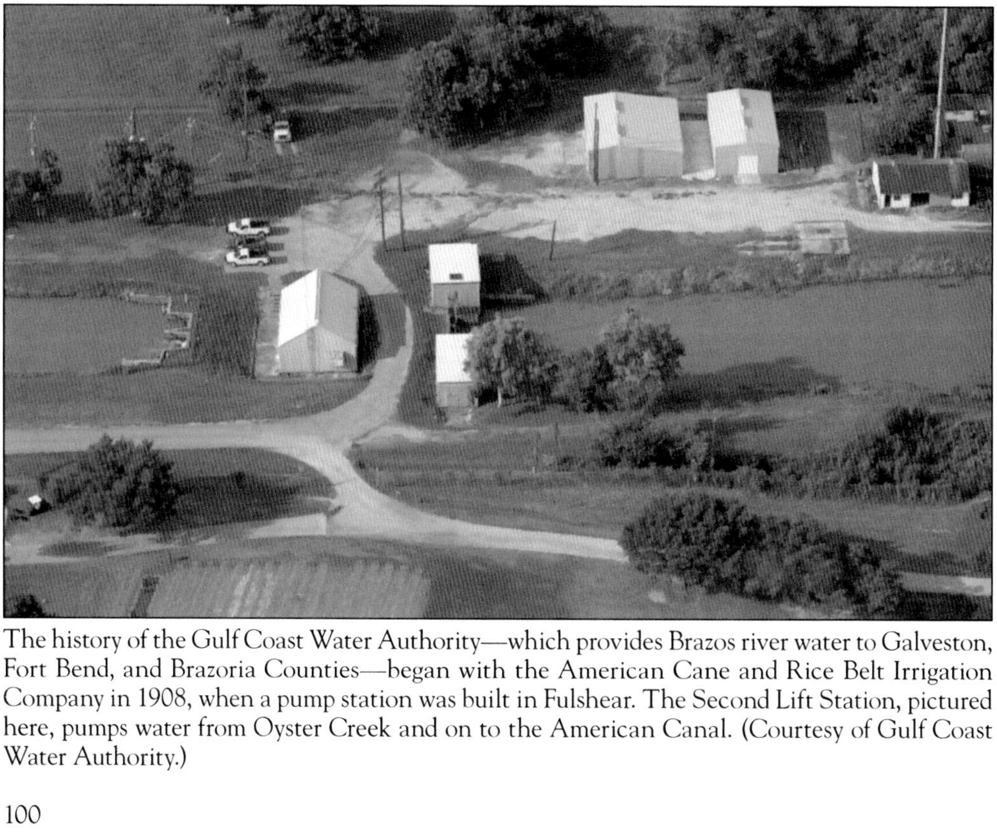

The history of the Gulf Coast Water Authority—which provides Brazos river water to Galveston, Fort Bend, and Brazoria Counties—began with the American Cane and Rice Belt Irrigation Company in 1908, when a pump station was built in Fulshear. The Second Lift Station, pictured here, pumps water from Oyster Creek and on to the American Canal. (Courtesy of Gulf Coast Water Authority.)

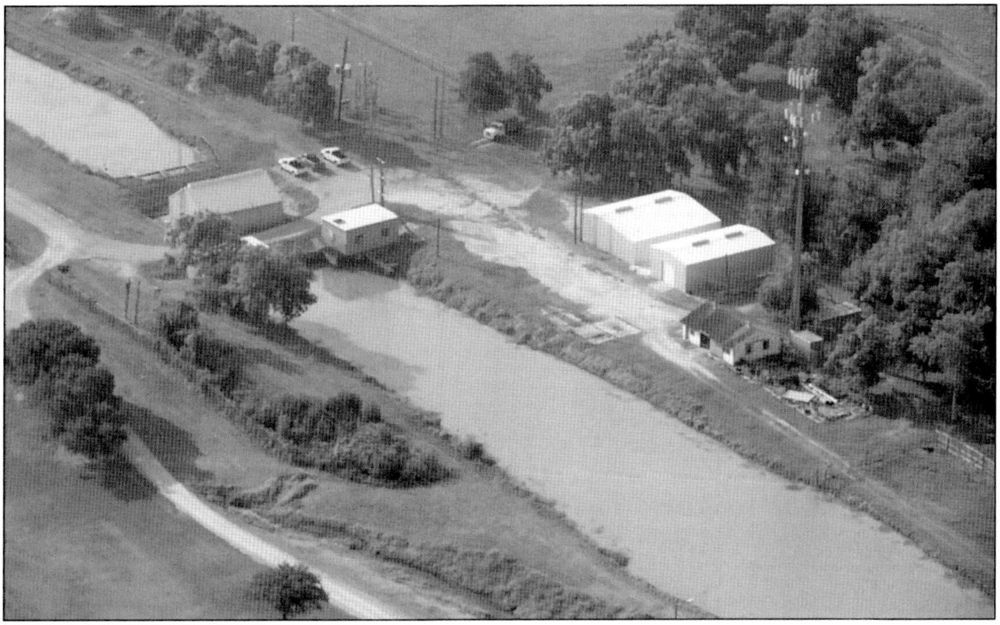

The old Second Lift Station was shut down in 1931 and replaced by a new station in Sugar Land. It had four pumps, which could produce a total of 223 million gallons of water per day, and allowed for water to travel from the east side of Fort Bend, along northern Brazoria County on Highway 6, south of Clear Creek, and east into Alvin using manmade canals. (Courtesy of Gulf Coast Water Authority.)

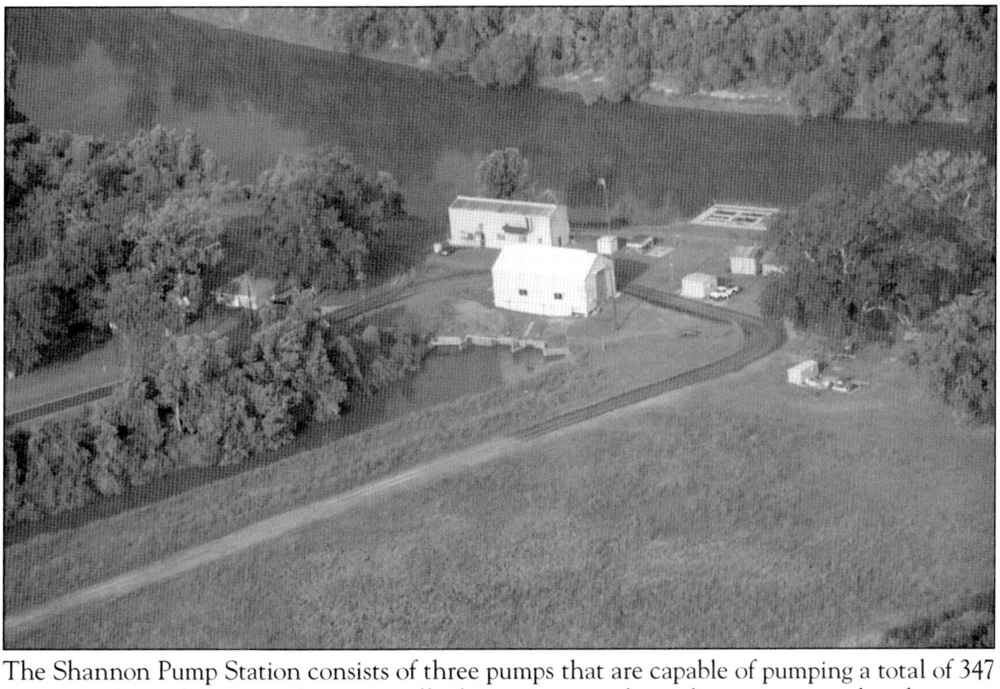

The Shannon Pump Station consists of three pumps that are capable of pumping a total of 347 million gallons of water per day. Originally the pumps were driven by steam power, but they were converted to electric power when the canal system was expanded in 1931. Pictured is a natural canal system, which flows from Jones and Oyster Creeks. (Courtesy of Gulf Coast Water Authority.)

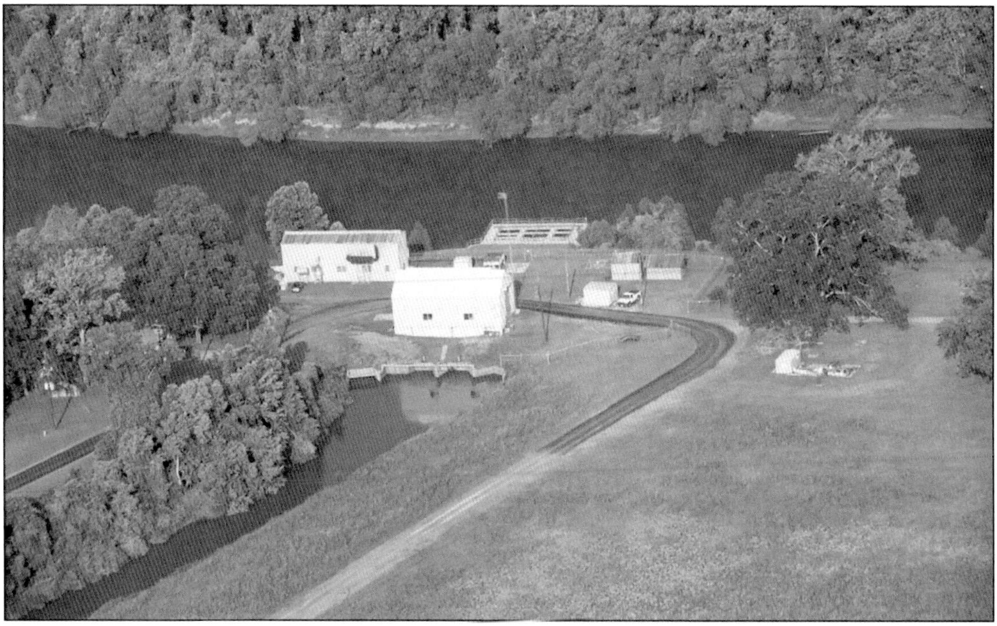

Further development of the Shannon and Second Lift canal systems, known as System A, continued in the early 1940s with the "New Extension" that linked them to Galveston County. The water authority began delivering Brazos River water to the City of Sugar Land, Fort Bend Water Control and Improvement District No. 2, and the Pecan Grove municipal utility district. Each area constructed its own water treatment plant. (Courtesy of Gulf Coast Water Authority.)

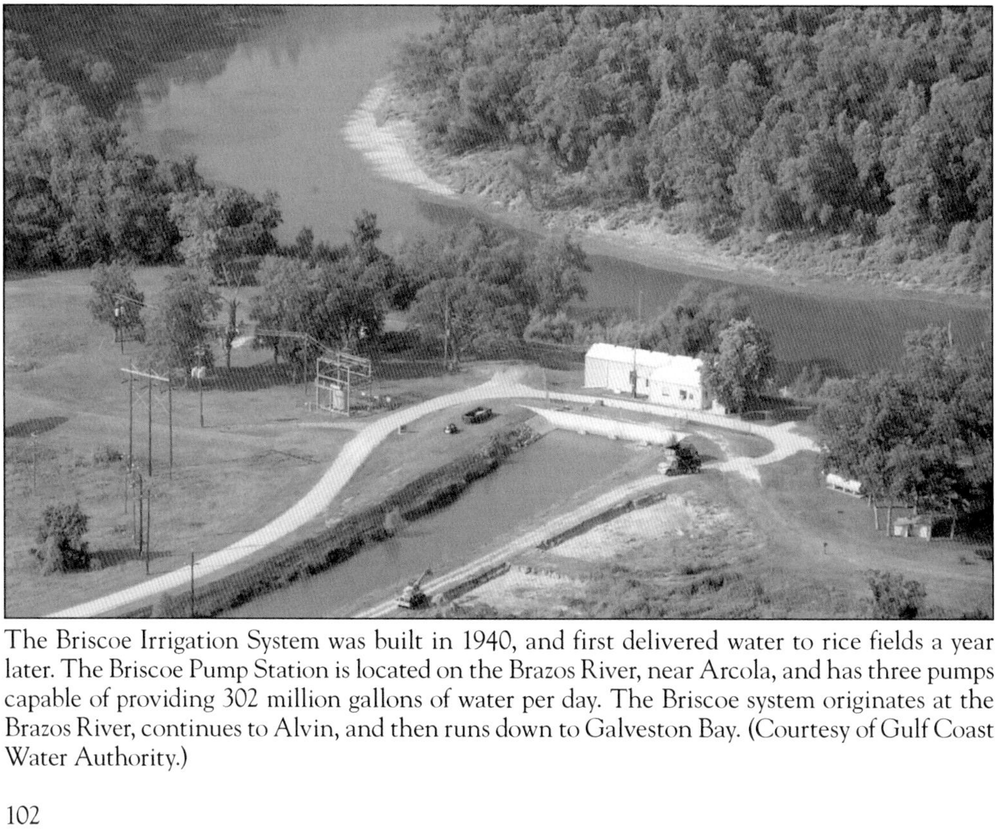

The Briscoe Irrigation System was built in 1940, and first delivered water to rice fields a year later. The Briscoe Pump Station is located on the Brazos River, near Arcola, and has three pumps capable of providing 302 million gallons of water per day. The Briscoe system originates at the Brazos River, continues to Alvin, and then runs down to Galveston Bay. (Courtesy of Gulf Coast Water Authority.)

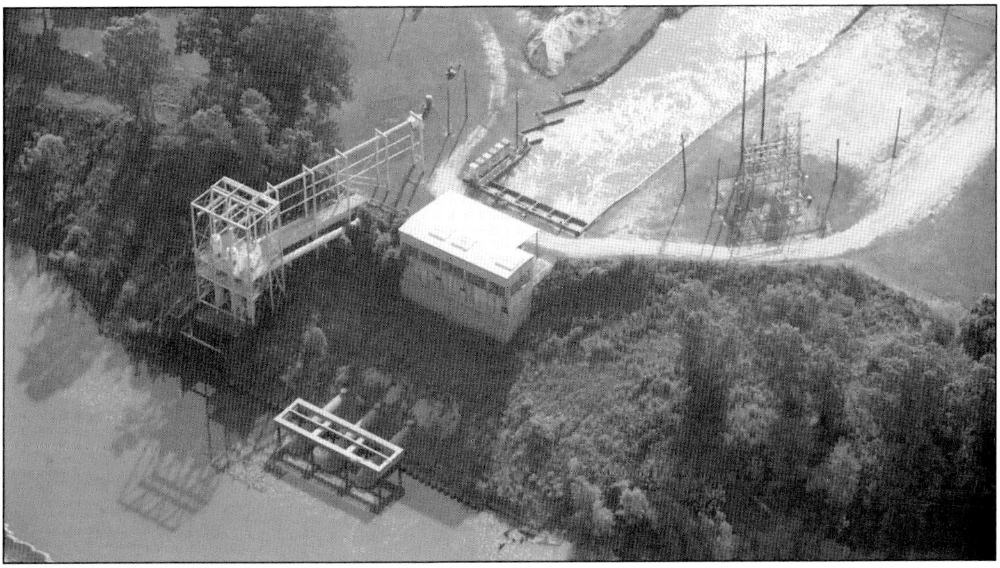

The Briscoe Irrigation Company grew in the mid-1940s, when it built canals and contracted to supply water to industries such as the Industrial Water Company in Texas City and Monsanto in Chocolate Bayou. For 20 years, it would be the only canal system to supply industrial areas. The Juliff Canal supplies two thirds of the local rice fields—15,000 to 16,000 acres—and is dormant during non-growing seasons. The pictured pump station was named after William May, who began working at the plant when he returned from World War I. When he died, the GCWA general manager, Ivan Langford, contacted the Guinness Book of World Records and attempted to have May recorded as the longest-serving employee of a single job. The book's producers were intrigued, but declined due to a lack of consistent employment records. (Both, courtesy of Gulf Coast Water Authority.)

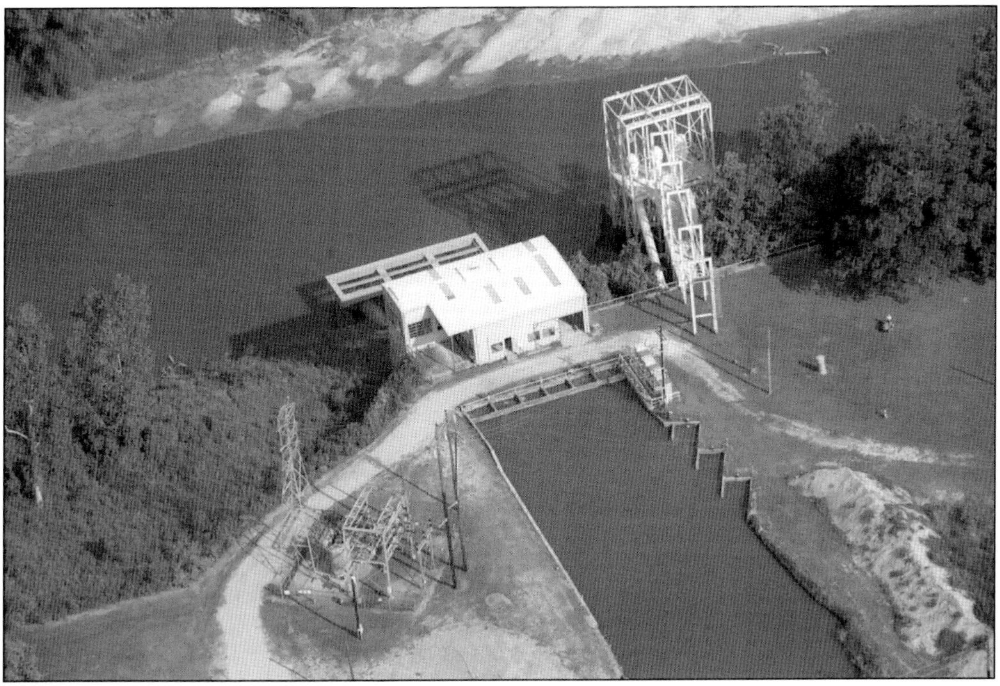

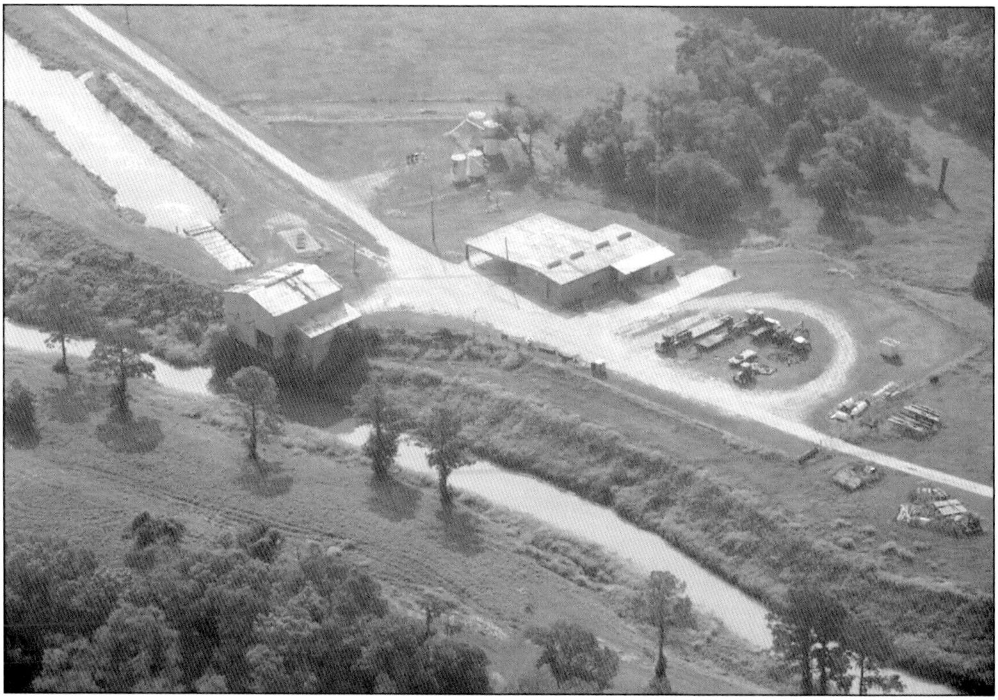

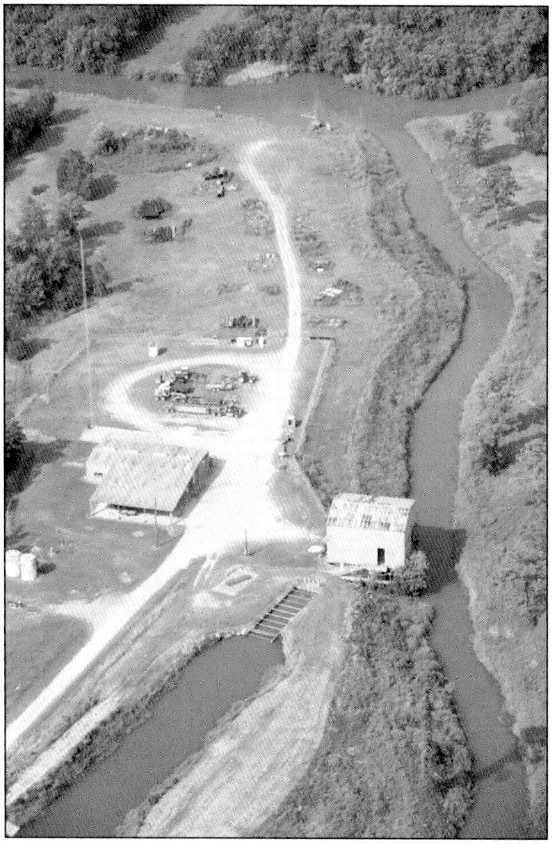

The local canal system has been known by several names, including the Cane and Rice Belt Irrigation Company, the Brazos Valley Irrigation Company, and the American Canal Company. In 1958, the American Canal Company's name was changed to the American Canal Company of Texas. The Brazos River Authority purchased the American Canal Company of Texas in March 1967 and the Briscoe Irrigation Company later that year, creating what became known as the Canal Division. In 1971, the Brazos River Authority purchased the Galveston System from the Industrial Water Company. In 1975, a lateral canal connected System A to System B, which provided a route to supply raw water to the Chocolate Bayou Company. (Both, courtesy of Gulf Coast Water Authority.)

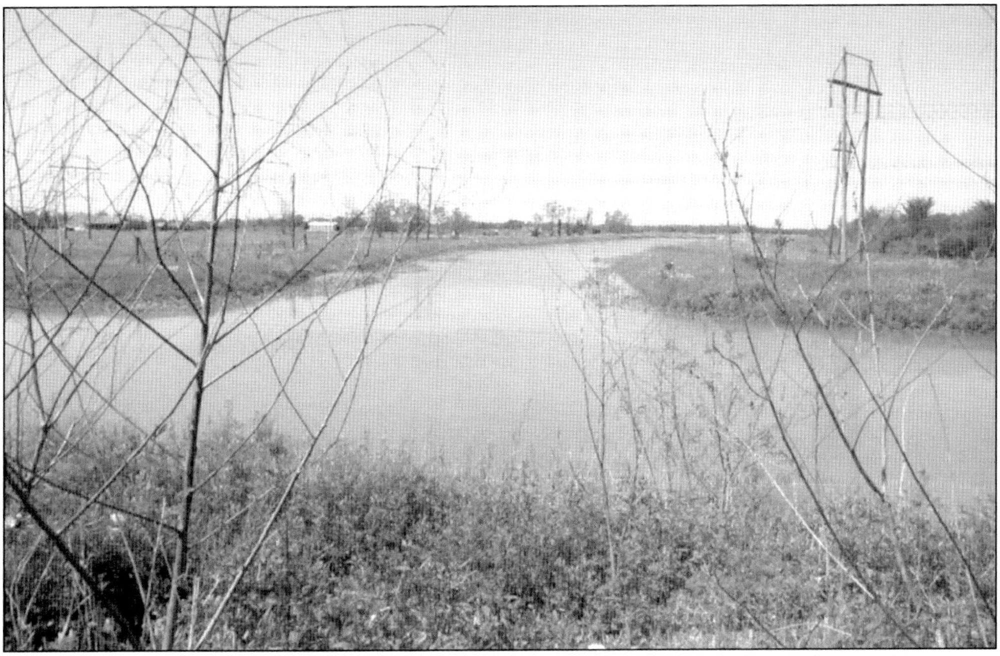

The Gulf Coast Water Authority created Canal G to move water to the Galveston Reservoir, while the reservoir in Texas City is fed by Canals A and B. These canals intersect in Santa Fe and travel along several farms. The water in these systems remains steady at depth of about eight feet. Canal G parallels State Highway 6 until it moves into Texas City, where it turns near State Highway 146 and the Texas City Municipal Golf Course. Canal G also travels northeast from Santa Fe, and moves into Texas City where it enters the reservoir. It leaves the reservoir through the Industrial Canal, which winds south to the Industrial Pump Station at FM 1765 and State Highway 146. (Both photographs by Lora-Marie Bernard.)

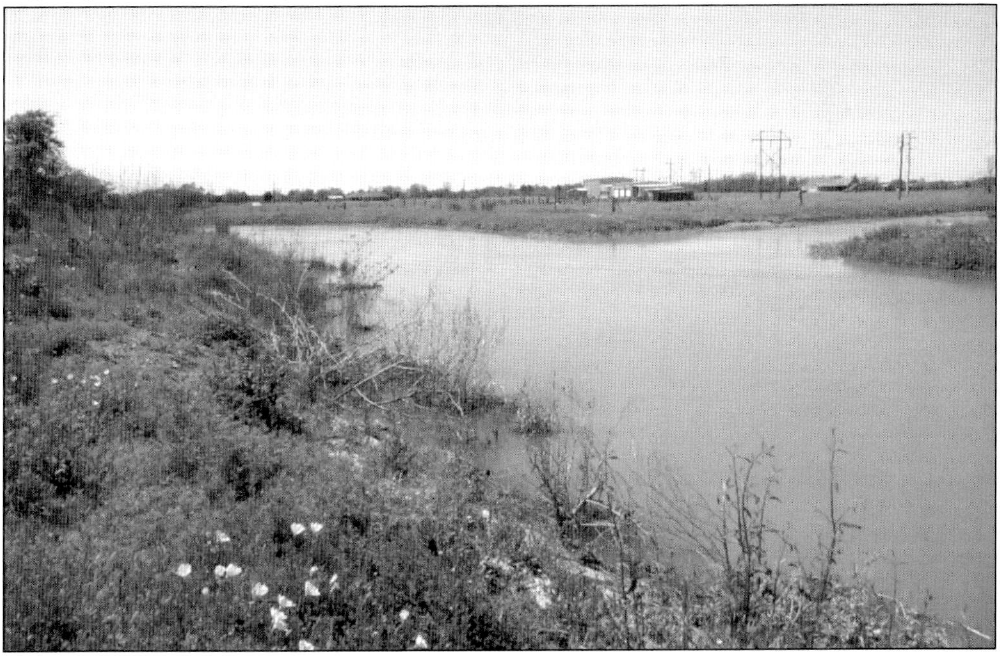

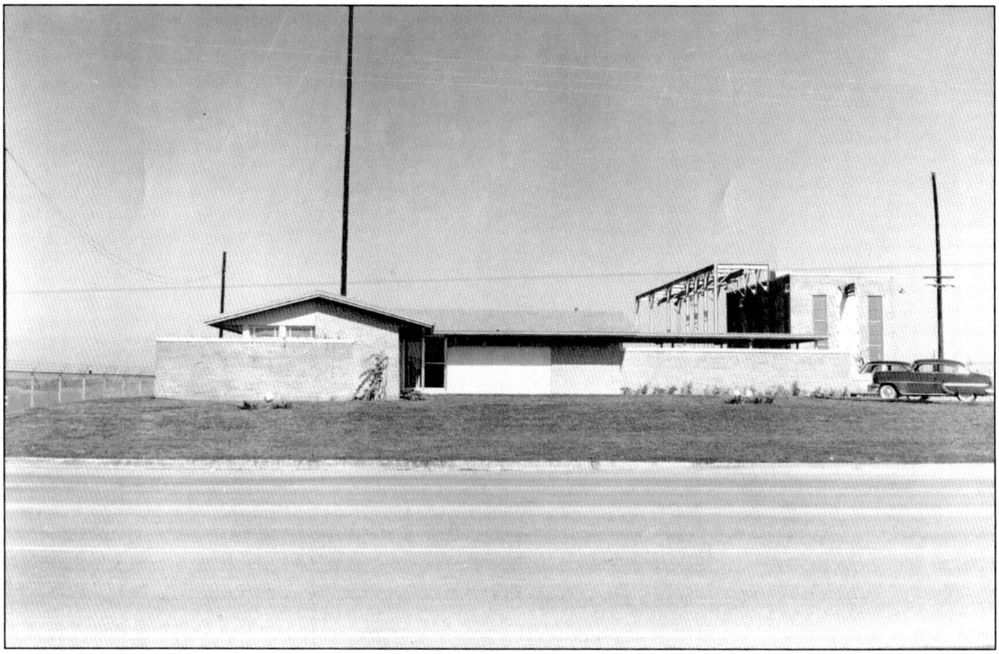

The Galveston County Water Authority purchased the Canal Division of the Brazos River Authority in July 1988. This allowed the GCWA to gain perpetual water rights to the waters of the Brazos River. In 1989, the authority changed its name to Gulf Coast Water Authority. The board of directors represents customers in Brazoria, Fort Bend, and Galveston Counties, and meets at the GCWA headquarters in Texas City each month to consider the needs of residents, farmers, and industry. The headquarters, pictured here in the latter part of the 1900s, is located across the road from the Dow Chemical plant near State Highway 146. (Both, courtesy of Gulf Coast Water Authority.)

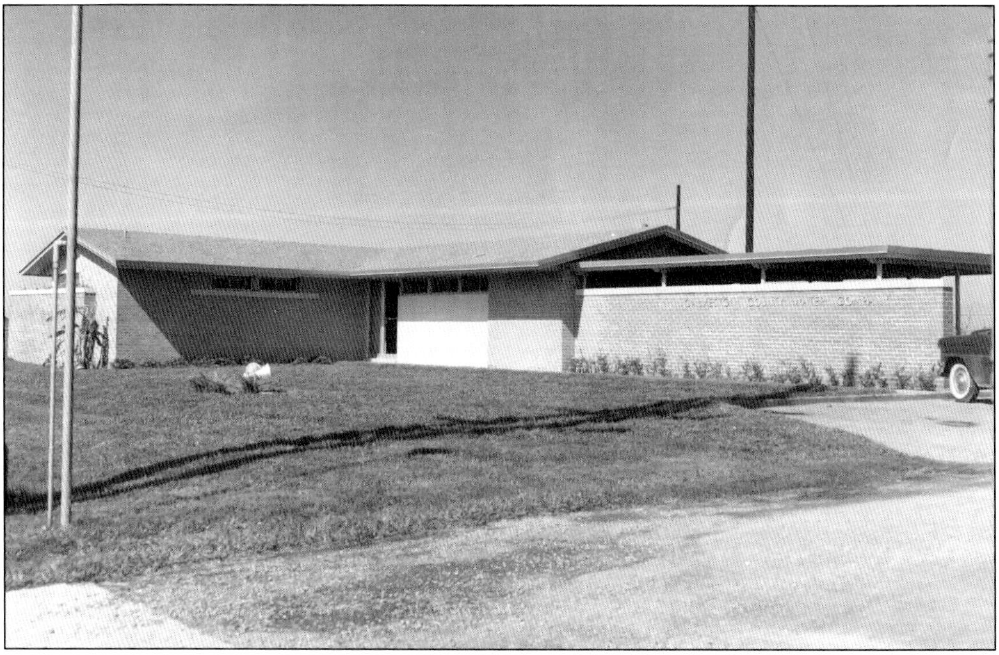

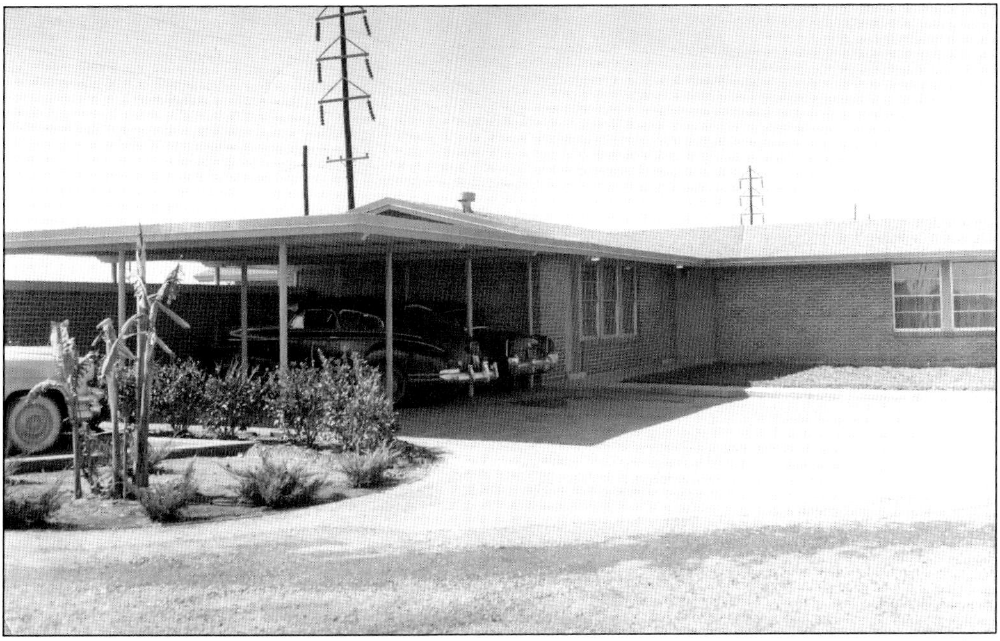

The Gulf Coast Water Authority headquarters is also the site of the industrial pump station that feeds water to Texas City petrochemical companies. The Texas legislature created the Gulf Coast Water Authority in 1965 to provide water for agricultural, industrial, and municipal purposes within its service area. (Courtesy of Gulf Coast Water Authority.)

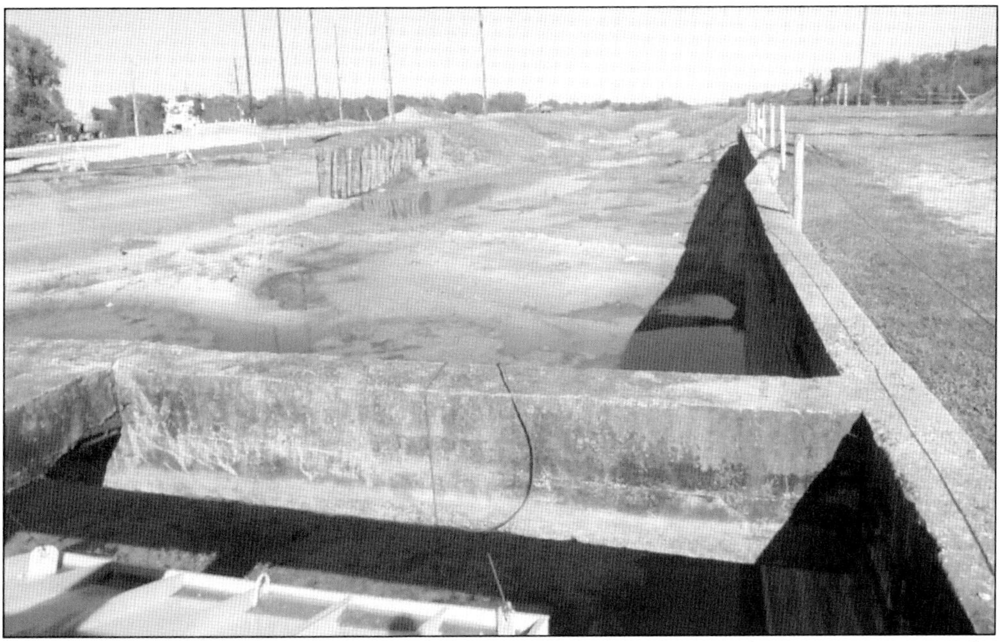

The Juliff Canal serves rice farmers through the Gulf Coast Water Authority. At one time, the GCWA supplied water to almost 20,000 acres of rice farms within the tri-county area, but staff now anticipate watering only about 3,000 acres. The canal sits dry whenever rice farmers are not raising a crop, but it is dry in this photograph because the water level of the Brazos is too low for pumping. (Photograph by Lora-Marie Bernard.)

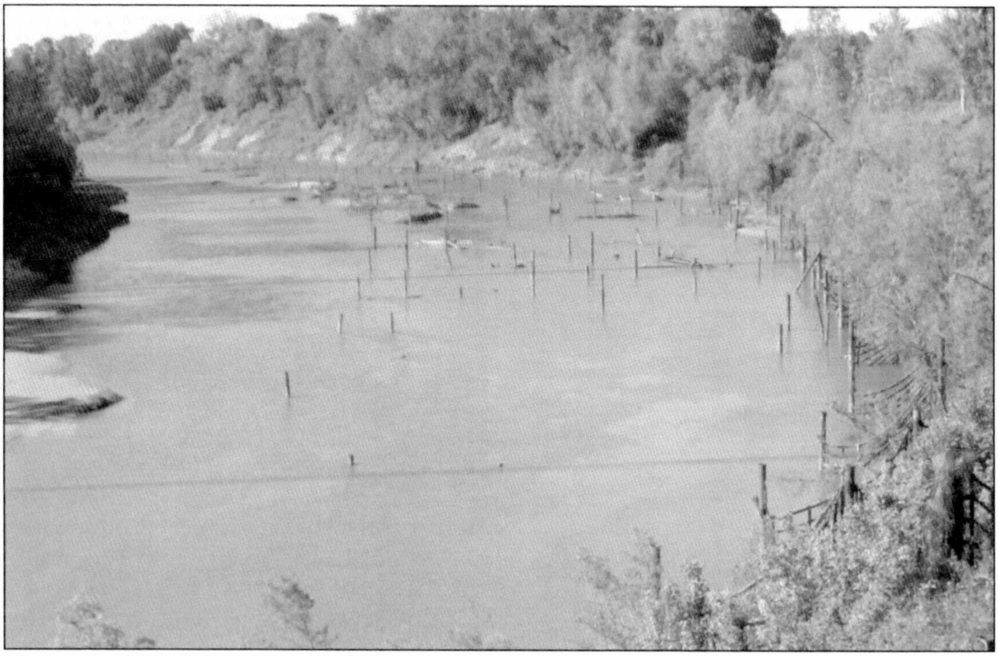

The Brazos River enters a wide bend at the Juliff Pump Station, which makes it unwieldy most of the time. In 1957, a raging flood eroded much of the bank seen on the left above. Several bulkheads were built over the years to try to stop this erosion, the remnants of which have been visible since the river level declined in the millennium drought. Under normal conditions, the Brazos River covers the three pumps (pictured below) that transfer river water into the Juliff Canal, but now grass and weeds encroach upon them. Directly beneath the pumps, the river is about 10 feet deep, but—just a few feet from the pumps—a person can now walk across the bend where sections of the bed resemble sandbars. (Both photographs by Lora-Marie Bernard.)

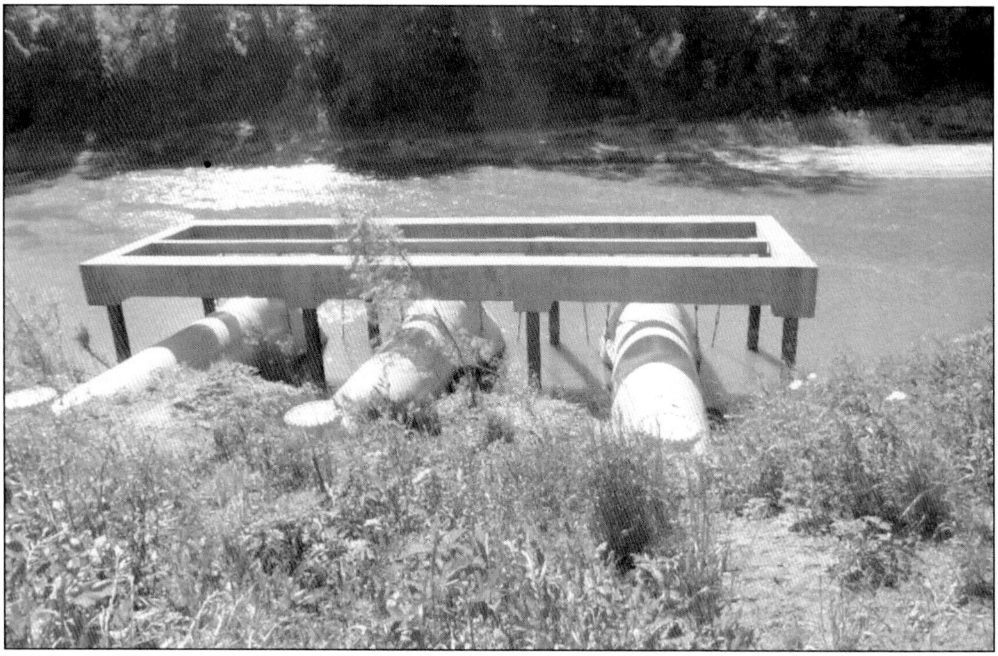

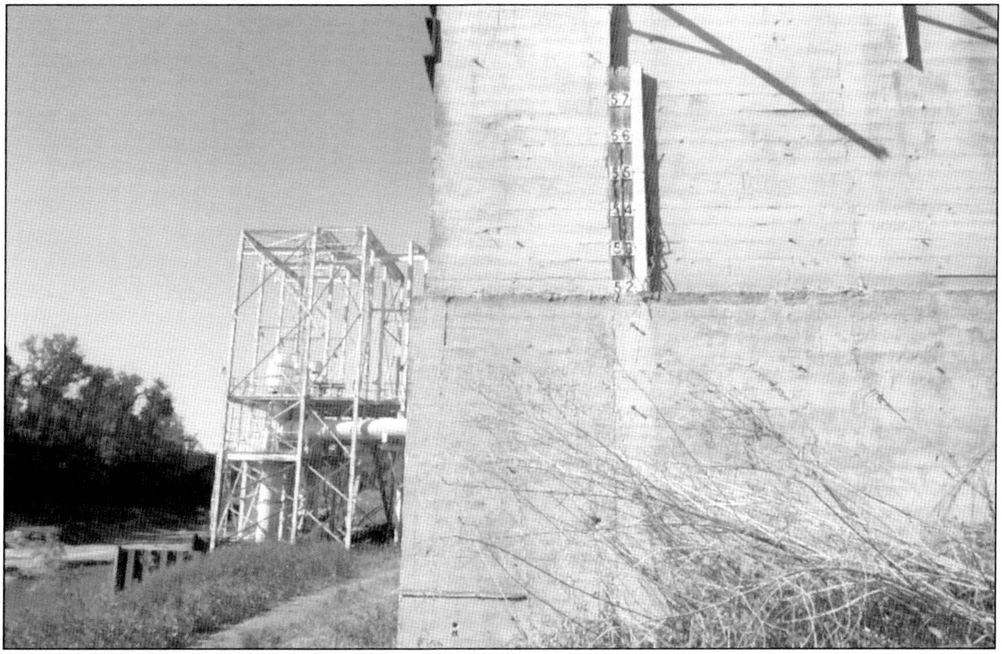

For the first time since 1945, water authorities have stopped supplying rice farmers with irrigation from the river. If the river were pumped under 2014 levels and conditions, it would be completely dry within a week. The above photograph of the exterior of the Juliff Pump Station shows how high the Brazos River is normally. Under normal conditions, the water would rise about 25 feet over the exposed pipes to the left. Instead, the water is so low that the banks and bed are dry enough to walk on. A sign on the corner of the building shows that it is common for the river to rise 57 feet above its bed. (Both photographs by Lora-Marie Bernard.)

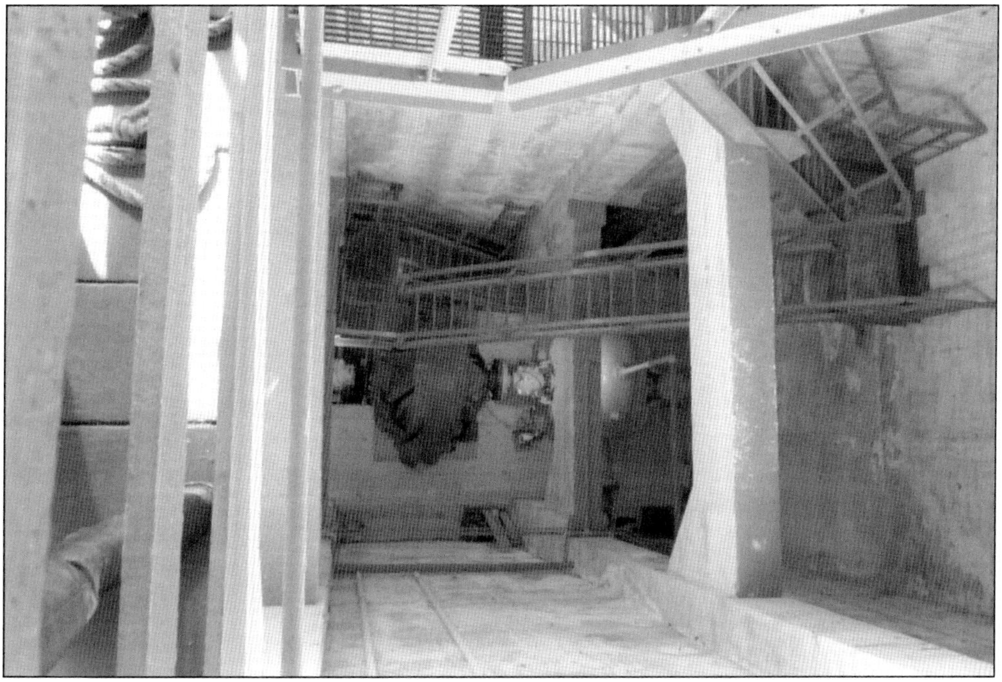

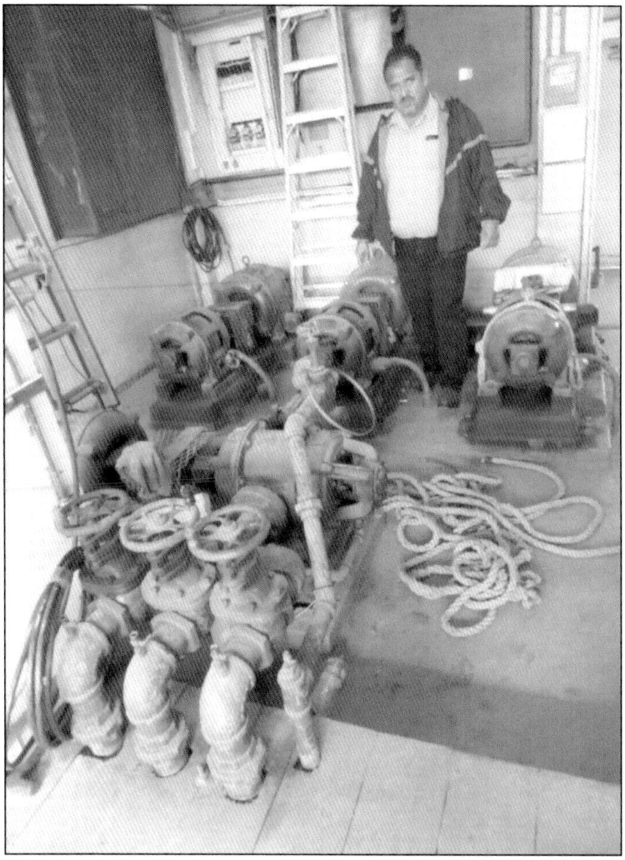

Originally, three exciters were used to create pressure in the river, which pushed water toward the pumps. When the pressure reached 15 pounds, the water pumps were turned on and the exciters were turned off. Plant manager William May, who worked at the Juliff station for 66 years, knew how to operate these original exciters with exact precision. May passed away in 2011, at the age of 92, and the station was renamed in his honor. A modern plant office is being built near May's old home to house state-of-the-art computerized equipment and allow for remote operation of the station. The original exciters, and other pieces of equipment that May operated, will be kept on site as historical demonstration pieces. (Both photographs by Lora-Marie Bernard.)

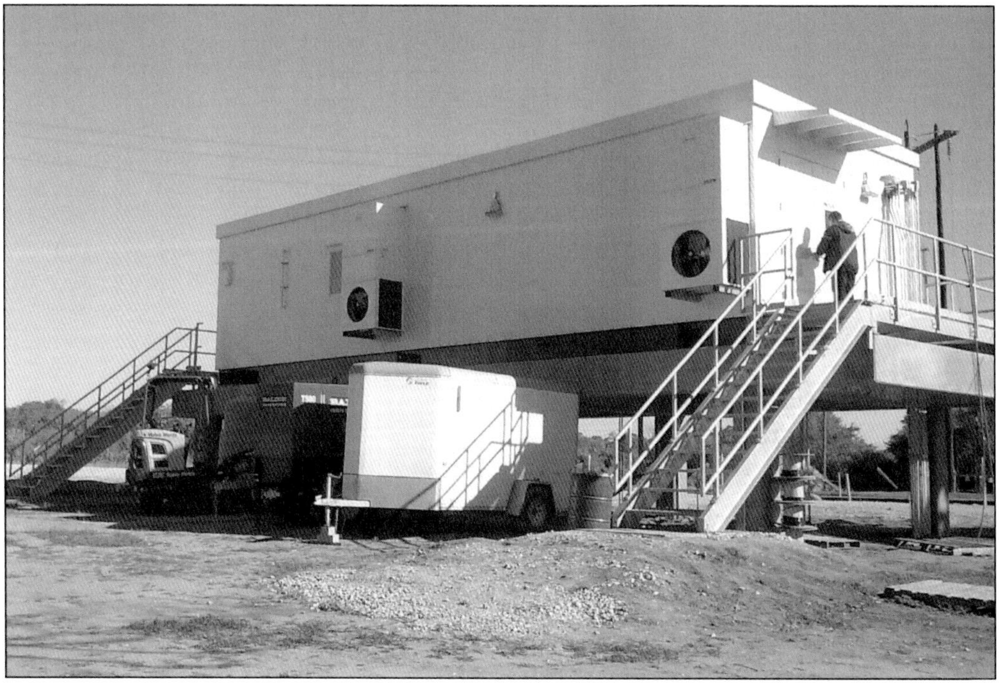

Since the pump station is not operating, it is undergoing renovations. The pictured elevator does not operate, but, when it did, only William May could use it. Gear switches from the Electric Machinery Company in Minnesota were among the original equipment that May operated daily. He remained at the station for days at a time to monitor the weather and the equipment, and even slept alone in the pump house during Hurricane Ike in 2008. At one point during that night, debris flew in off the river and broke a window. He climbed the stairwells and a ladder to repair the damage, since the elevator was not working. He was 84 years old at the time. (Both photographs by Lora-Marie Bernard.)

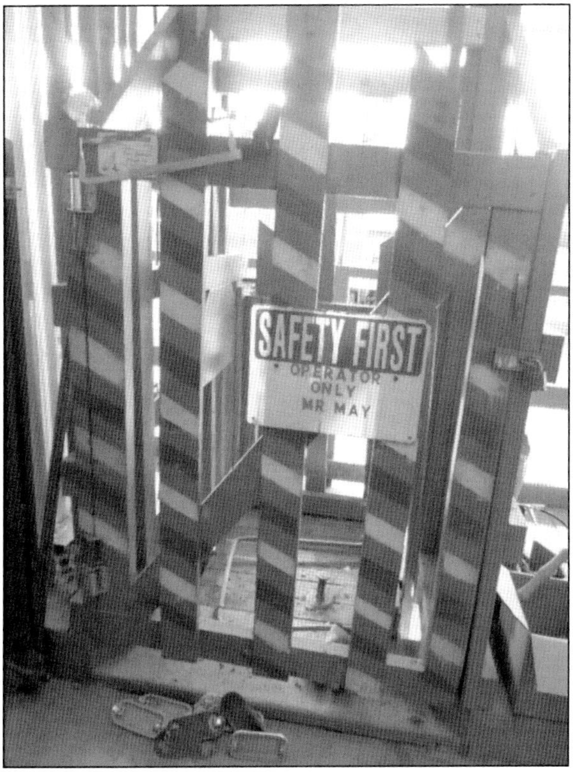


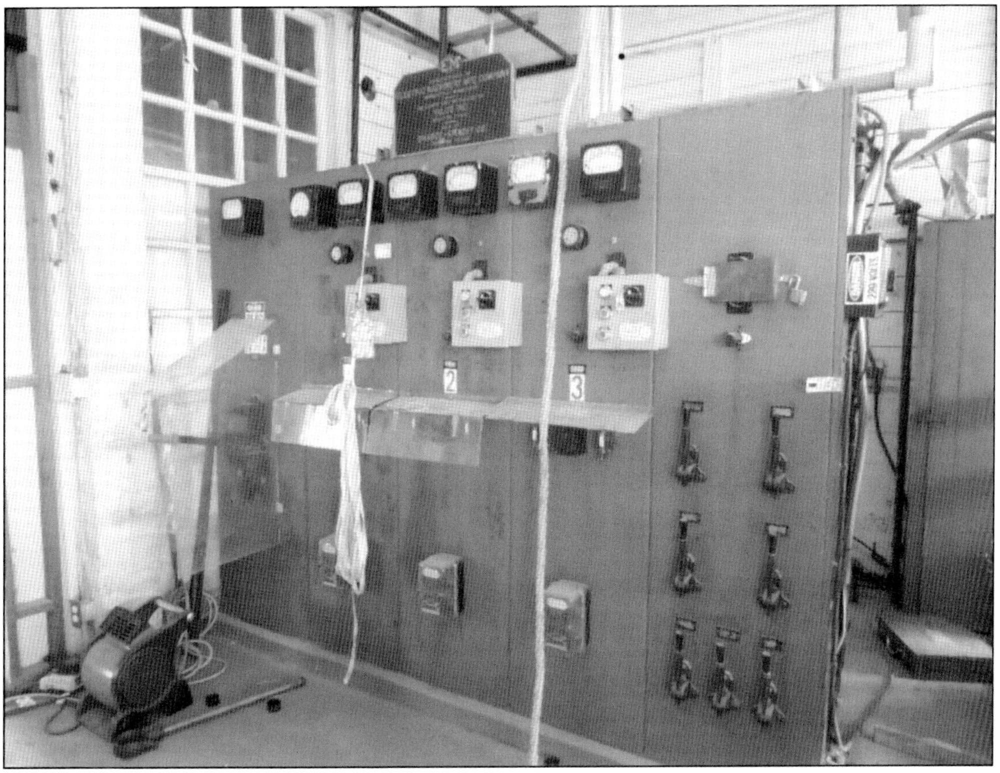

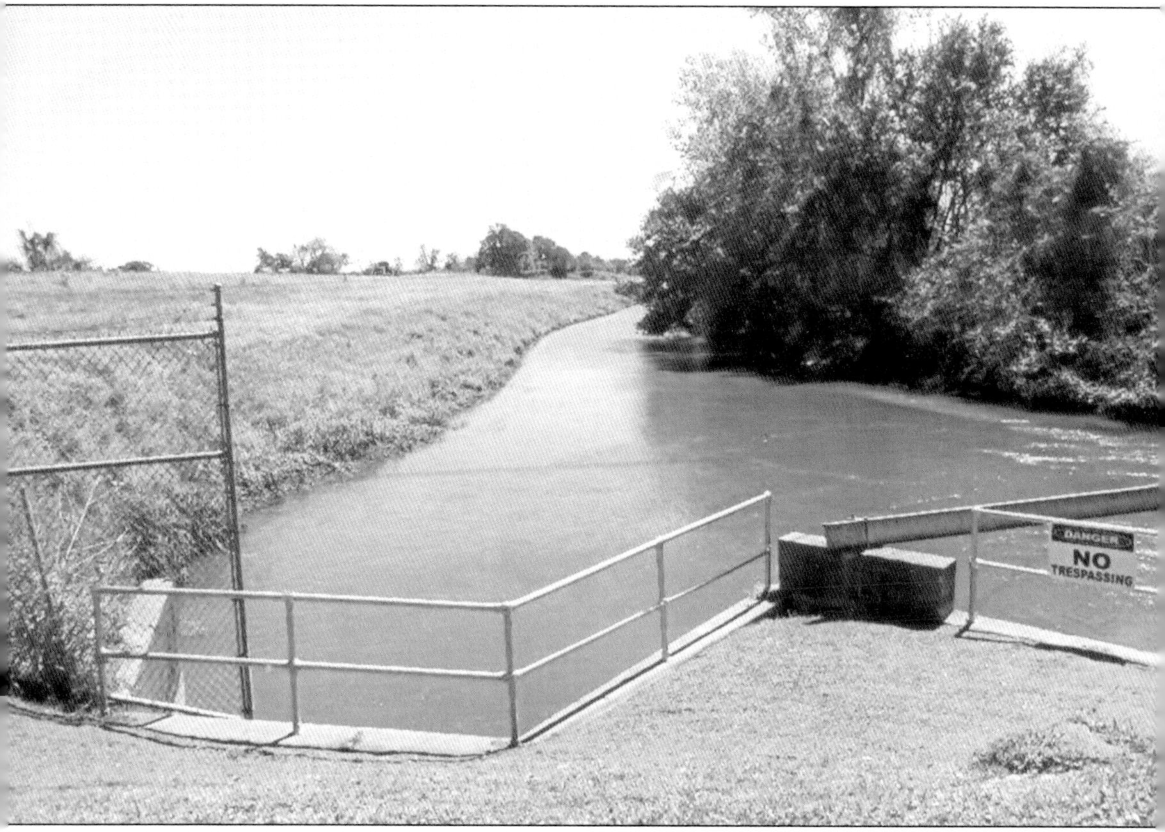


Mules dredged Jones Creek when the Shannon Pump Station was built. According to Joe Crow, an early plant manager, men drove the mules as they dragged Fresno scrapers. Fresno scrapers were used to build dams from the 1800s to the early 1900s, and were like plows that stored the loose dirt in a trap until it could be emptied. A brick foundation was laid near the pump house as a base for the station's boiler, and coal was hauled overland so that the boiler could create steam for the pump engines. Crow said that the remnants of the foundation remained near the pump house for decades, along with the pipe that transferred steam into the station. The station diverts Jones Creek into Oyster Creek to supply municipalities and industry, but originally supplied irrigation to rice farmers. (Photograph by Lora-Marie Bernard.)

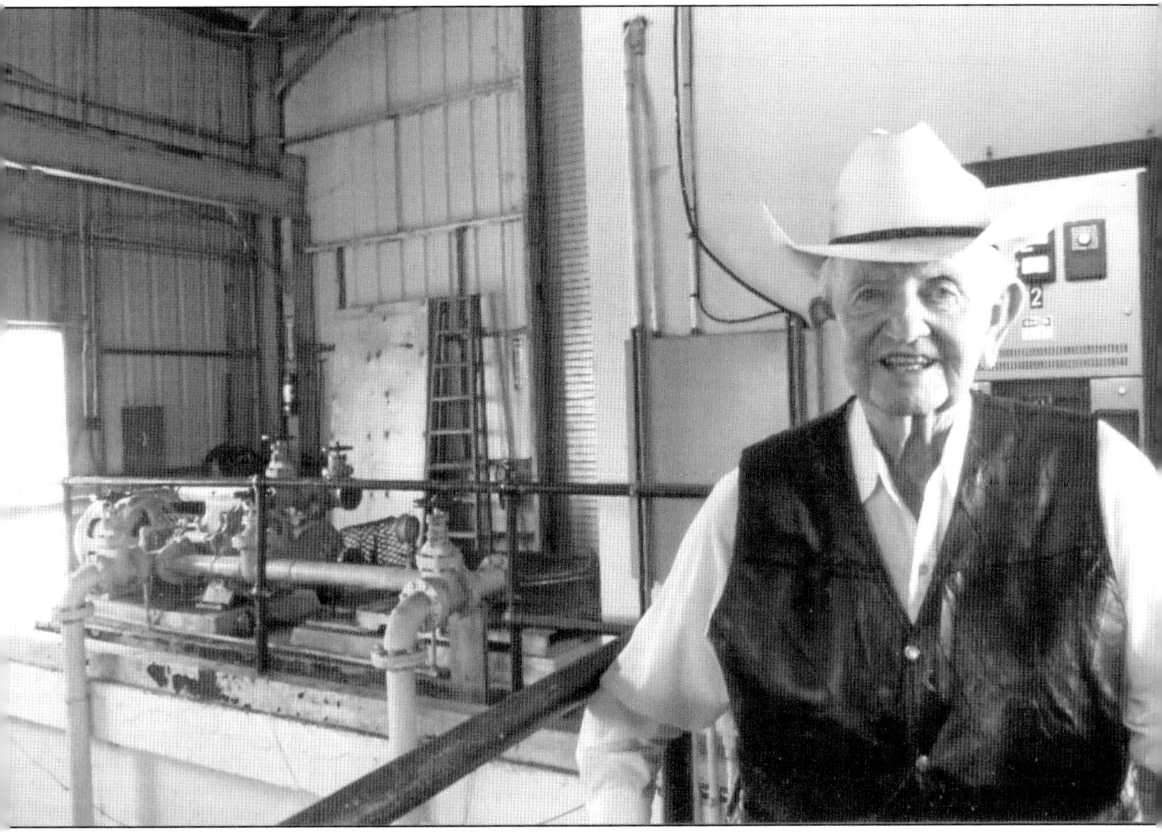

Joe Crow began working at the Shannon Pump Station in 1946, and was serving as the pump manager when he retired in 1990. He said that he applied with the American Canal Co. because it was a good job. He received $180 per month, a house to live in, and the company even paid his utilities. When he started as the night pumper he was given a small house, and was glad to move into the "bigger house" when he was promoted to head pumper. He raised his family at the pump station, and remained in the home until he retired. The job offered Crow an unexpected surprise when he was deputized during the Korean War. He was told the government feared the plant might be "blown up," and Deputy Crow carried a gun at work until the 1950s. Today, Crow still lives in the neighborhood, and staff members bring him to the pump station so he can "check on it" and visit. (Photograph by Lora-Marie Bernard.)

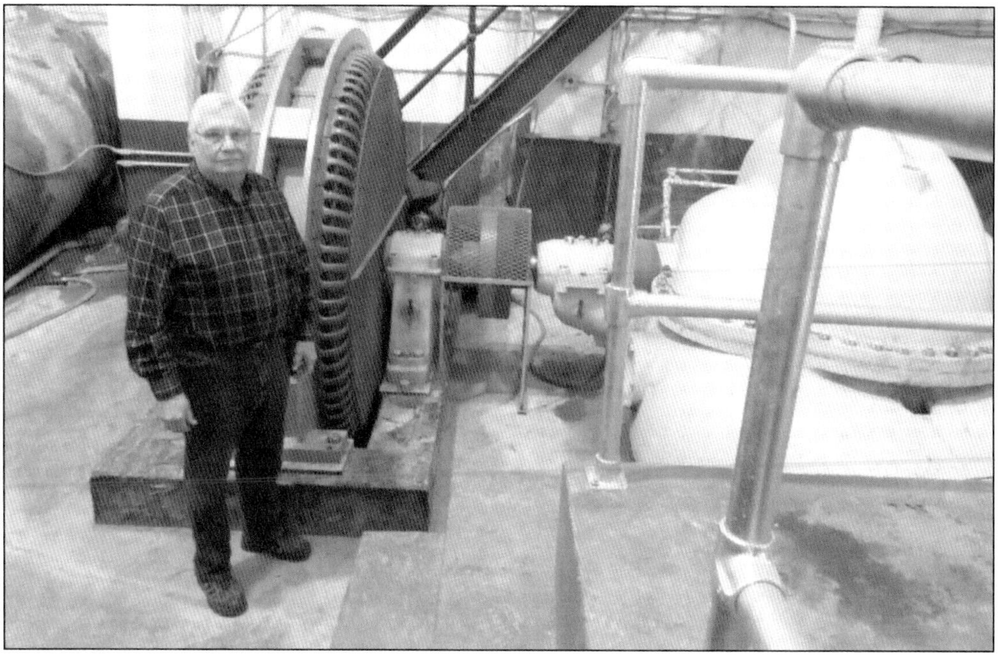

The Shannon Pump Station was built in 1908, and operates with three pumps that were installed in the 1920s. According to Herb Adickes, these pumps have operated for almost 100 years due to consistent maintenance and upkeep. Adickes (pictured here) became plant manager after Joe Crow retired in 1990, and retired himself in 2013. (Photograph by Lora-Marie Bernard.)

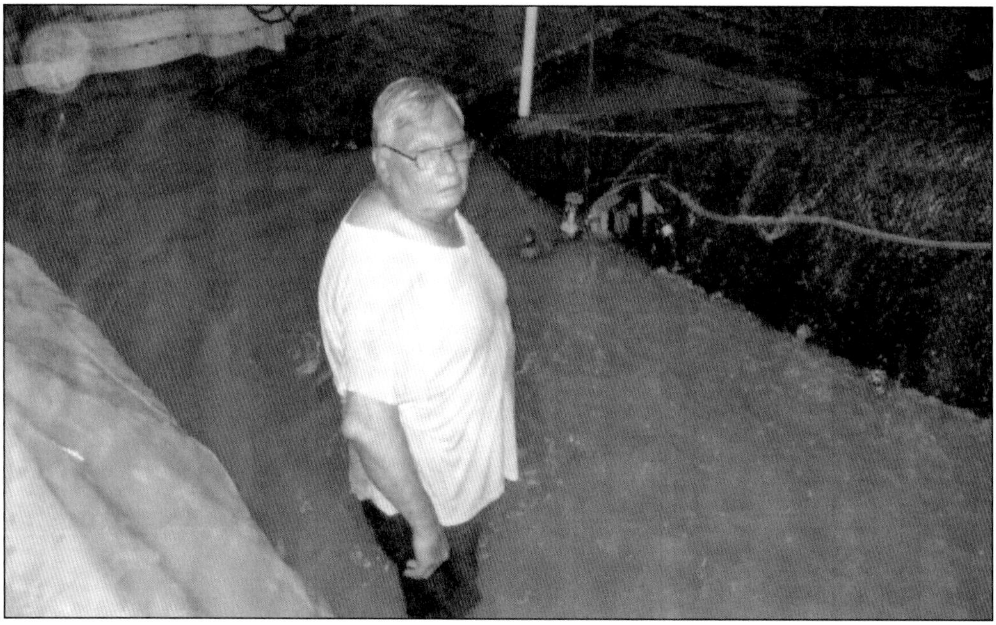

Mother Nature does not cause all the flooding on the Brazos. In 2012, Adickes found the pumps from Jones Creek to be inexplicably flooded. Two years later, while walking the grounds, the crew realized that a four-inch pipe that extended against the head wall and dam had broken. The pipe, which had once transferred steam from the station's outdoor boiler, had not been used in decades. Its purpose had been forgotten. (Photograph by Mack Chapman.)

In this photograph, Herb Adickes stands on the canal steps leading to the river pumps to show how high the river can rise. The picture was taken from about halfway down to the pumps. Before the millennium drought, pump managers had to understand the nature of the Brazos and be able to predict its flow up to three days ahead so that they could manage it. (Photograph by Lora-Marie Bernard.)

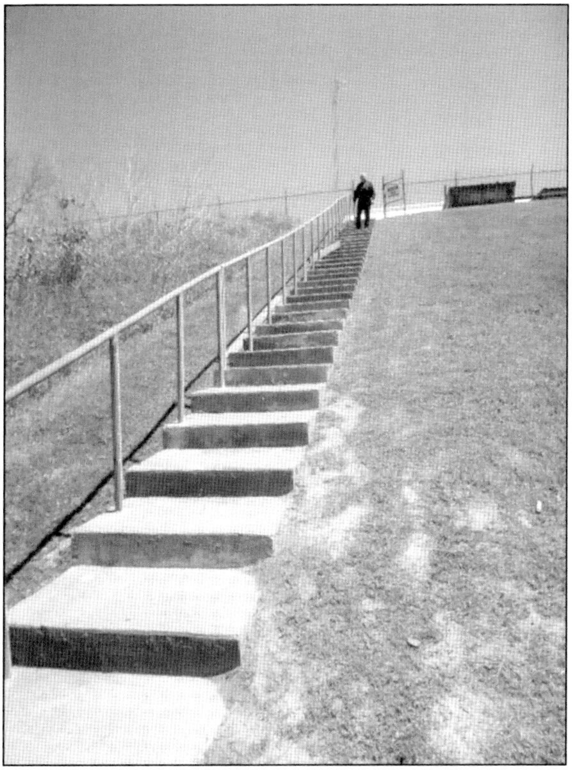

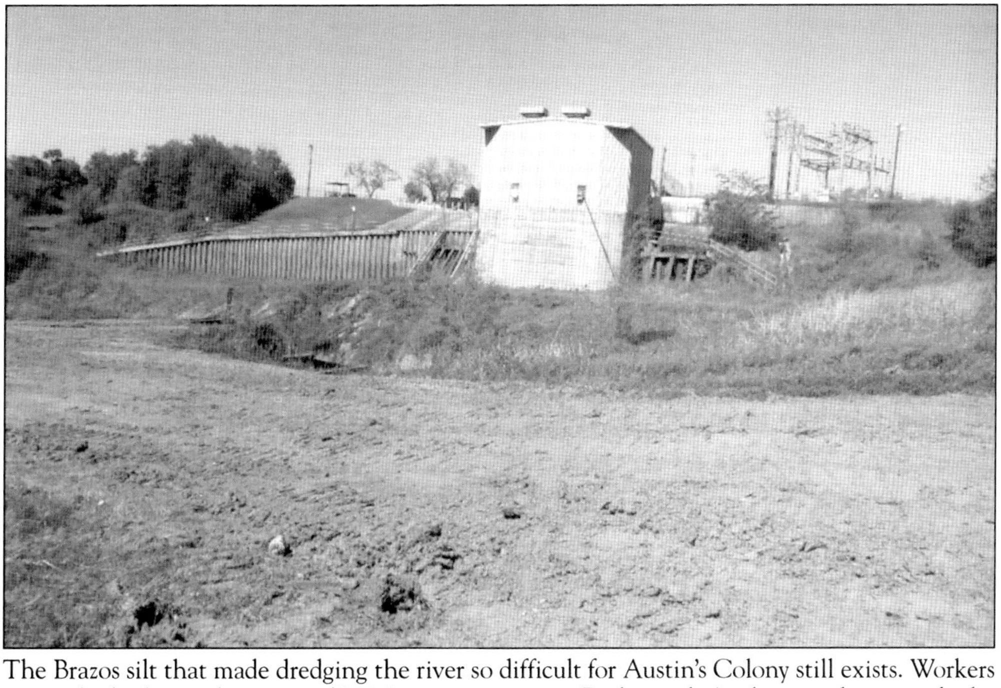

The Brazos silt that made dredging the river so difficult for Austin's Colony still exists. Workers routinely dredge at the pictured NRG pump station in Richmond. A silt mound surrounds the station, where workers pack it down to control its growth. After some time, weeds grow, and the workers mow the mound. (Photograph by Lora-Marie Bernard.)

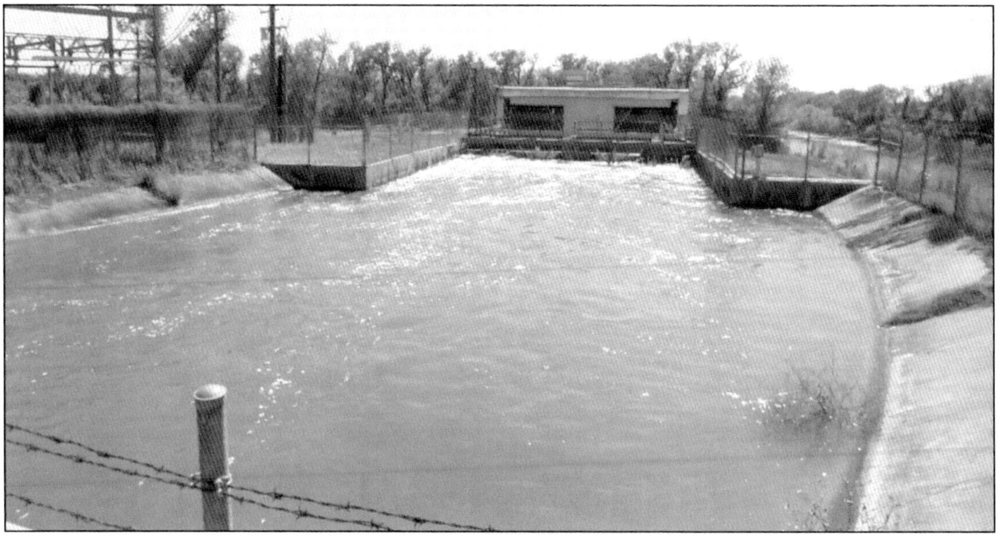

The water from the NRG pump station rises from the Brazos to Riverwood Drive in Richmond-Rosenberg. This pumping station may sit on the site of the turn-of-the-century station that was built on the river bend seen on pages 66 and 67. Water from this station travels to Smithers Lake, which is a reservoir for the local NRG energy plant. (Photograph by Lora-Marie Bernard.)

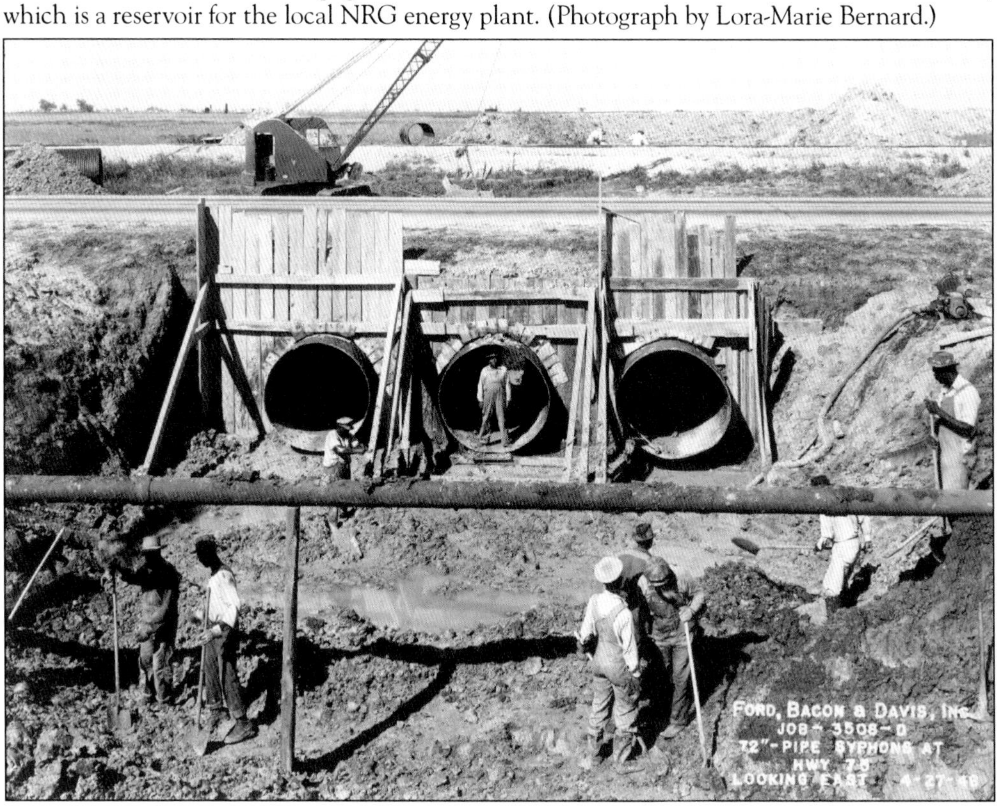


In this photograph, workers from Ford, Bacon & Davis Inc. of Houston build three 72-inch pipe siphons for a portion of the Briscoe Canal, which is now a part of Canal G. The job site was located on Highway 75, though this portion of the highway is now State Highway 3 in Galveston County. (Courtesy of Gulf Coast Water Authority.)

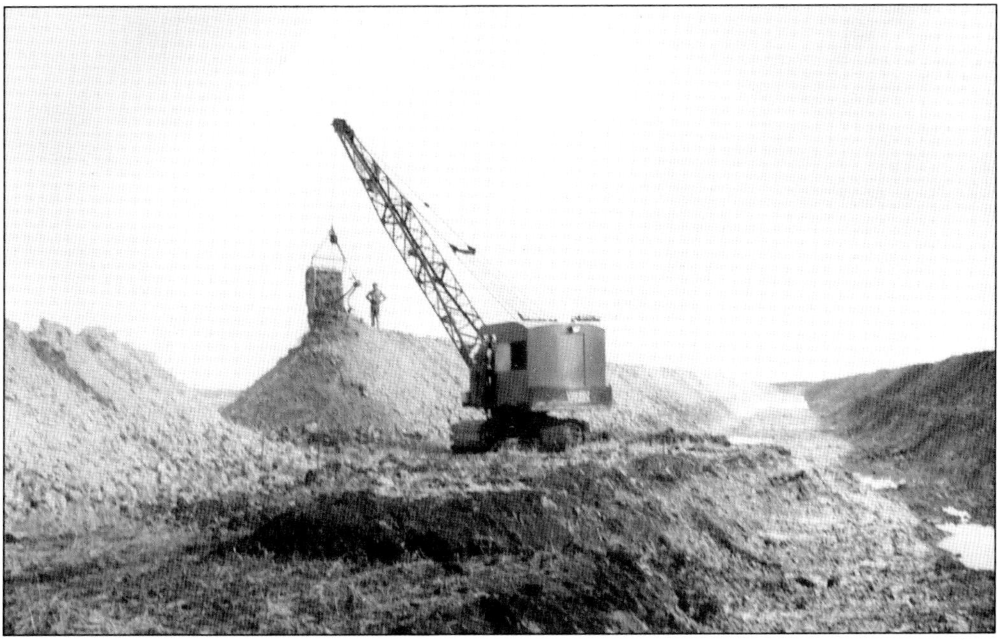

Here, a crane digs the inlet of a canal north of State Highway 3 and Humble Camp Road in Texas City. The canal parallels Attwater Road, where it travels into the Galveston reservoir to supply the Texas City petrochemical companies. The engineering firm of Ford, Bacon & Davis Inc. built this section in the 1940s. (Courtesy of Gulf Coast Water Authority.)

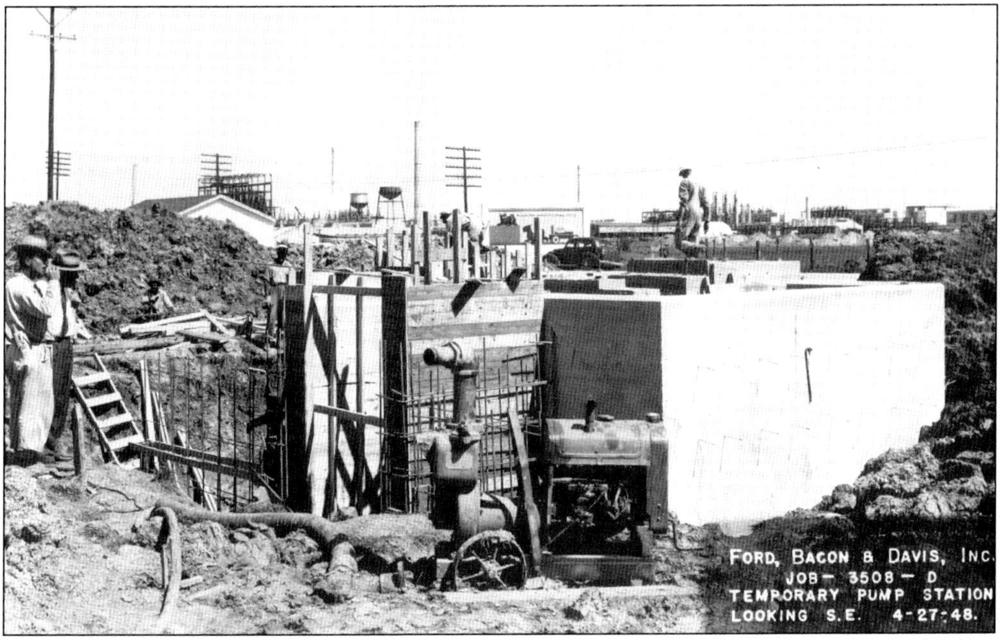


A temporary pump station was built in 1948 to support the building of the canal system leading to Texas City. Today, it is not clear where this station was built, or when it was removed. This photograph looks southeast at the construction site in April 1948, and water or industrial towers in the background reveal that the station may have been close to the reservoir. (Courtesy of Gulf Coast Water Authority.)

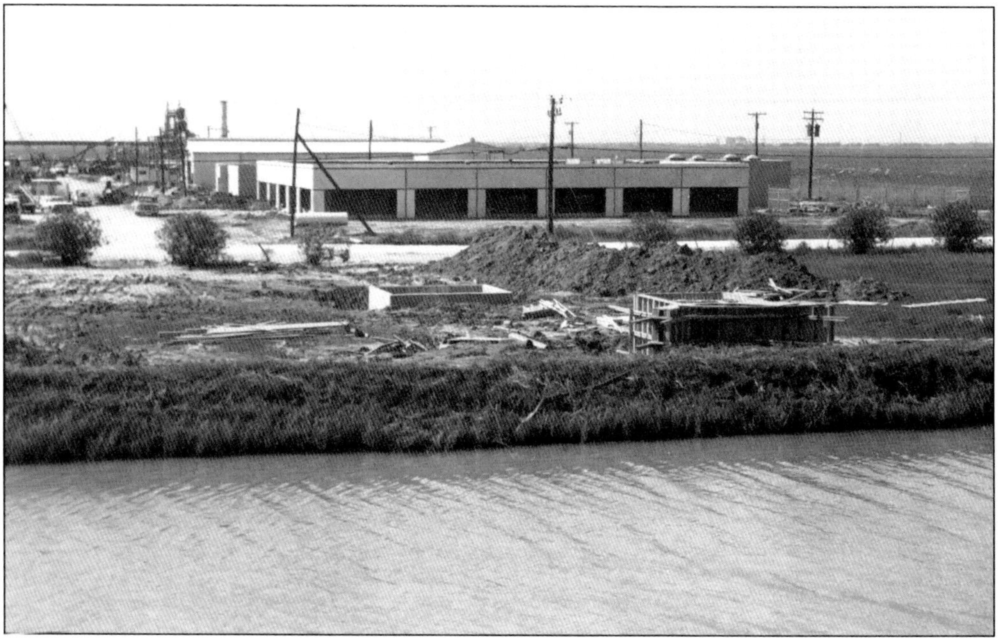

The 7,308-acre-foot channel reservoir in Texas City serves municipal and industrial needs, and maintains a 21-day supply of water. Levee roads break up the largest reservoir in the system, and its outer levee connects with the Galveston County hurricane protection levee system. Water enters this reservoir from the north. Other reservoirs include a combined 8,925-acre-foot reservoir comprised of impounded runoff, which the City of Sugar Land uses with the water authority. Texas City industrial customers also have a dedicated 65-acre-foot Terminal Reservoir. Three off-channel reservoirs in Brazoria County total 8,951 acre-feet of storage, and three additional off-channel reservoirs—with a total size of 864 acre-feet—in the Juliff and Chocolate Bayou Canal Systems are located in Fort Bend and Brazoria counties. (Both photographs by Lora-Marie Bernard.)

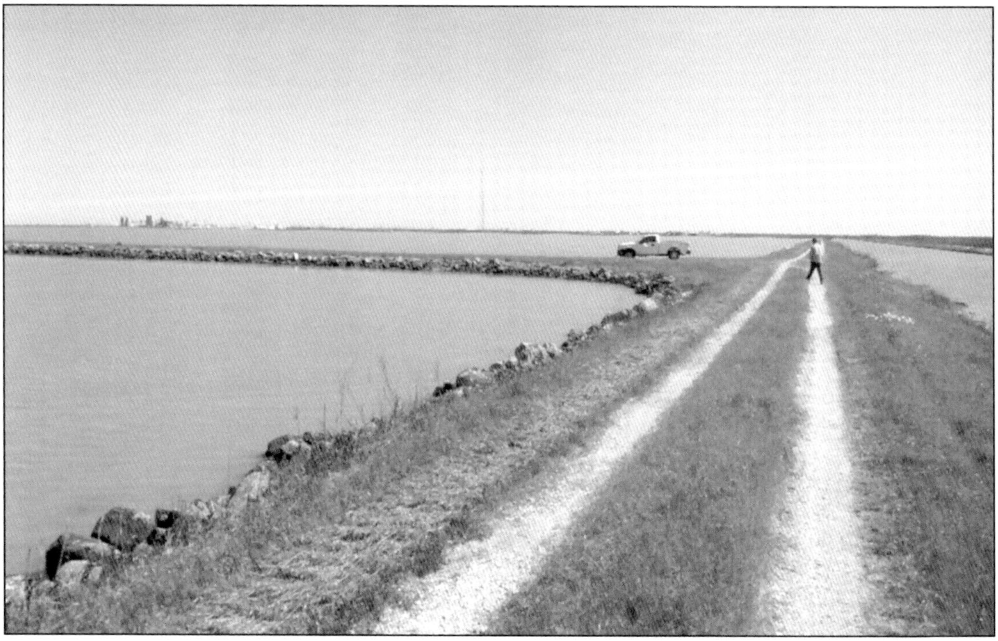

# *Six*

# The River with Two Mouths

In the late 1800s, the Army Corps of Engineers considered building converging palmetto jetties to control the mouth of the Brazos River. Instead, Congress authorized $400,000 to build concrete, brush, and stone jetties, but the project was abandoned six years later when construction could not reach over the sand bar to the necessary depth. Funding dried up, and discussion turned to old plans to dredge the neglected Brazos-Galveston canal.

Meanwhile, the Texas state legislature began letting private corporations build and operate deep-water channels. The Brazos River Channel and Dock Co. was organized around this time, and, in August 1888, Congress authorized it to improve the river's mouth.

Between 1889 and 1896, the company built two jetties and spur dikes. It also created a new port at Velasco, about five miles inland. When the company experienced money problems, the government took over the project in April 1899, and in 1908, dredged an 18-by-150-foot channel. The channel's depth fluctuated between 13 and 19 feet, which forced vessels to unload cargo in Galveston or Port Arthur before heading to the Brazos.

Throughout the 1910s, the Army built two locks on the river, but World War I interrupted future plans. By 1922, Congress abandoned a plan to dam the lower Brazos River, though it did dam the river farther upstream.

In the end, the Army Corps of Engineers decided to do what Mother Nature could not. It built a new mouth that acted the way the Army wanted it to, and in March 1925, Congress authorized funds to build a diversion dam seven miles upstream. It also funded a diversion channel west of the natural channel. The project was completed in September 1929.

This second mouth makes the Brazos River one of the most unique rivers in the country, and set it up as a successful industrial port. By the mid-1950s, chemical and petroleum companies settled into Freeport Harbor. Turning basins were dug in 1954, and Congress authorized the Corps to deepen the channel to 45 feet in 1970.

The river's old mouth remains today as a testament to how the Brazos's settlers and farmers conquered the river and built their communities. It took nearly 100 years, but man's wrestling match with the river had come to an end.

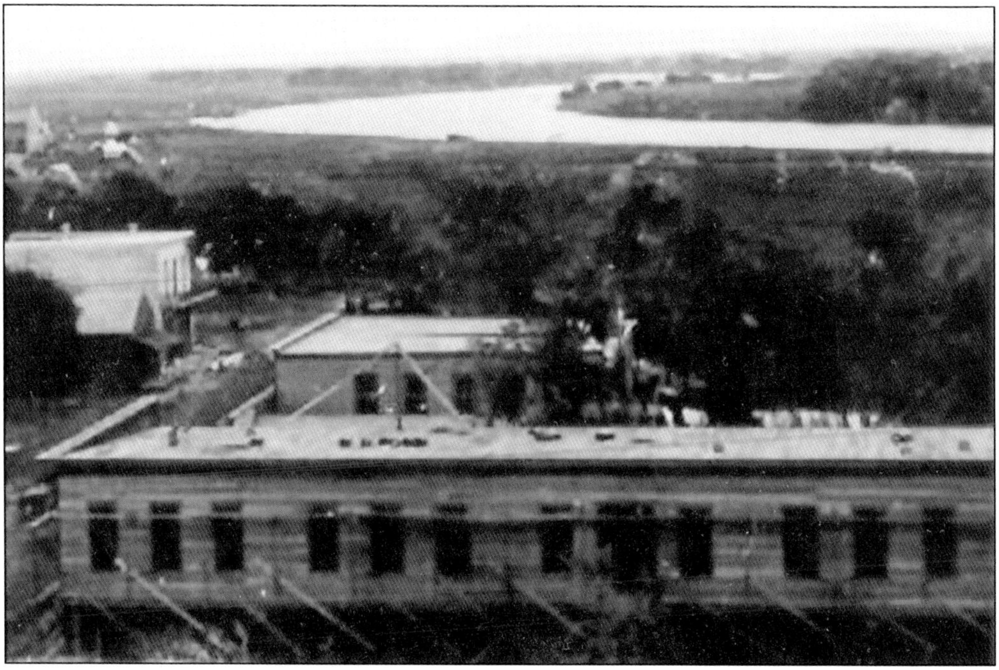

The above photograph shows the Brazos River from atop the Velasco Hotel. Vessels had smooth travels from the river onto the Brazos-Galveston Canal. During his presidency, Theodore Roosevelt was anxious to address national transportation concerns, which led to sweeping federal surveys of many waterways along the Gulf of Mexico. In 1917, the US Coast and Geodetic Survey documented navigation issues at the river mouth on the chart below. It shows the treacherous waters awaiting sailors. The sand bar is marked: "The Bar at the Brazos River Entrance is Subject to Changes." This shifting rise lurked beneath vessels immediately as they rounded into the gulf. At the time that this chart was made, the bar rose from 2 feet to almost 14 feet within a short distance. The survey notes that the bar was "hard," and in some places "sticky."

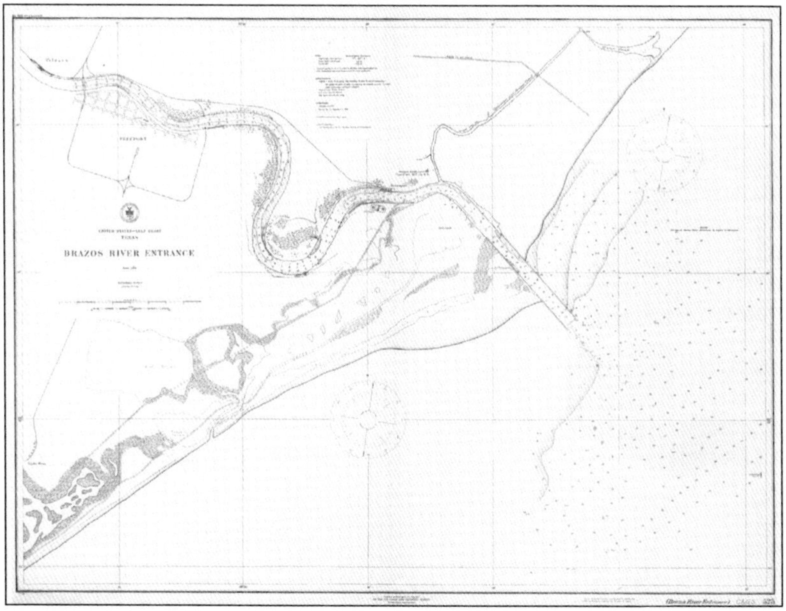

This geodetic survey from 1891 shows the channel with a light and a jetty. The federal government pushed for comprehensive national waterway planning and conducted this survey after local owners declined the government's offer to buy the canal. Meanwhile, local leaders met in 1902 and formed the Brazos River Impoundment Association to tame the river. This effort failed due to a lack of funding.

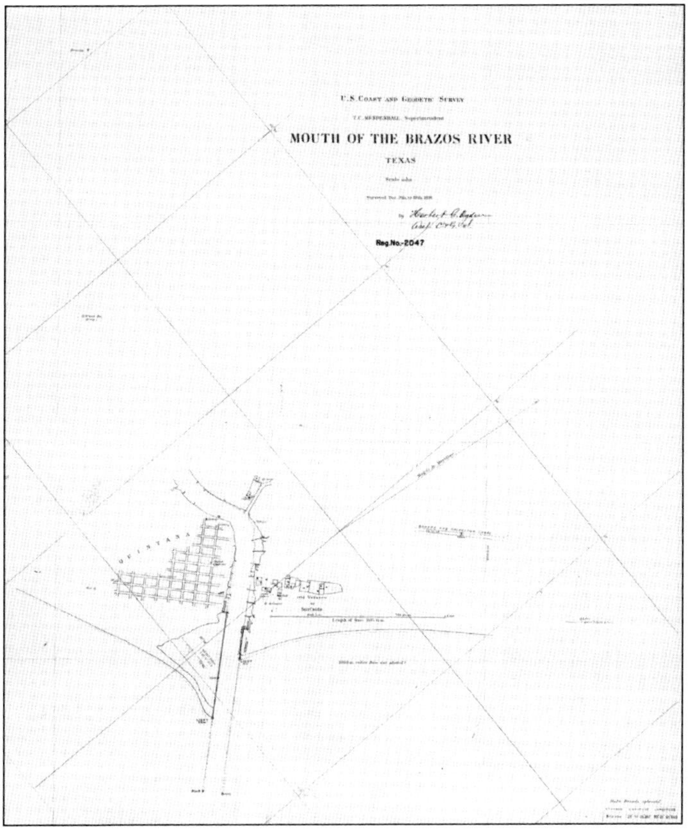


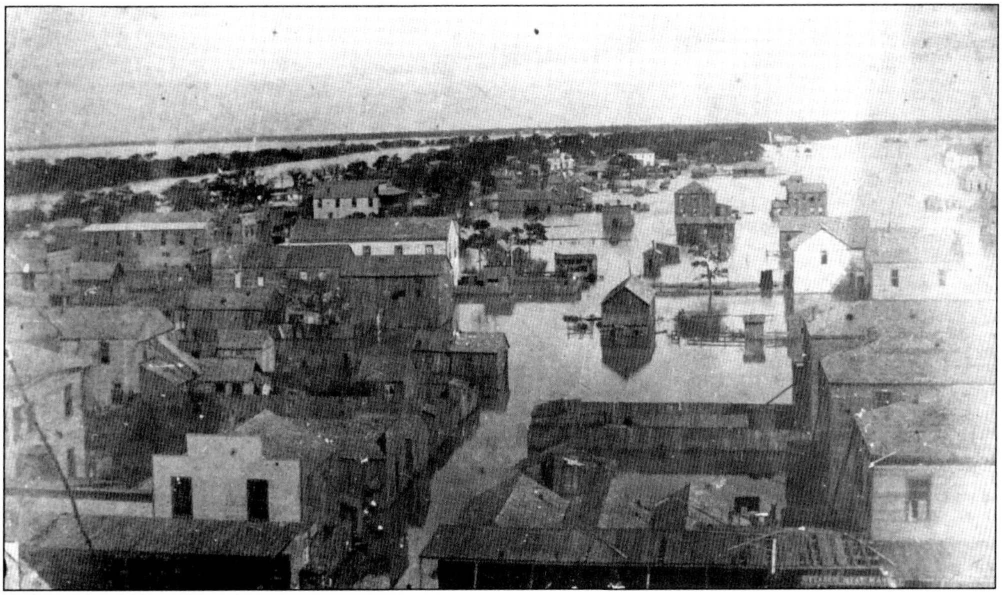

The 1905 Rivers and Harbors Act allowed the federal government to fund upstream locking and damming, but the 1913 flood destroyed the work and caused over $3.4 million in damage along the lower Brazos River. During the flooding, the Guadalupe, Trinity, Brazos, and Colorado Rivers left their banks and flooded 3,000 square miles of land.

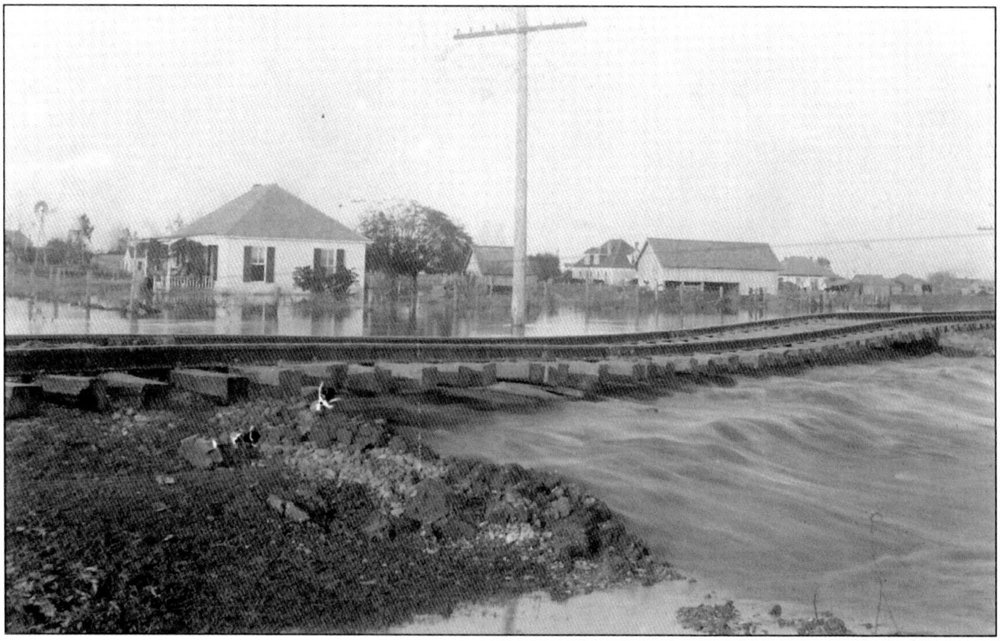

More than 170 people died in the 1913 flood, spurring local leaders' decision to move the mouth of the Brazos. Upstream, inhabitants tried to form the Brazos River and Valley Improvement Association, but it failed due to a lack of funding. In 1917, weary Texans approved the Conservation Amendment, granting the state control over the management of flood and storm waters. Funding quickly flowed to local flood control projects as a result.

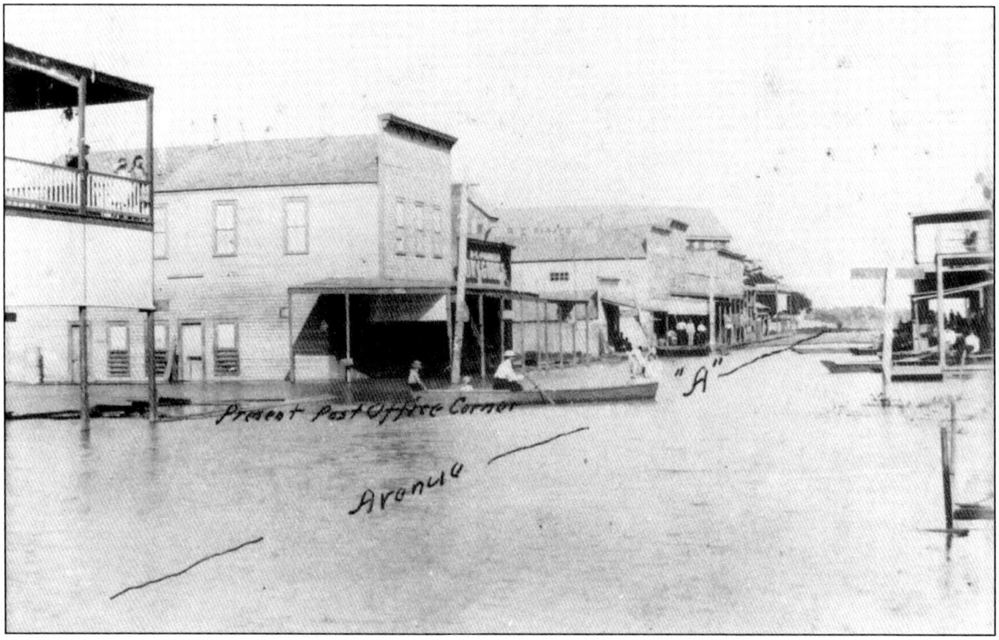


When flooding was routine, boats became a favored way to travel in Velasco. In this photograph, two women, two children, and a man navigate the town's streets in a canoe. Members of the community can be seen gathered on the dry porches and balconies of local businesses as they observe the devastation and wait for the water to subside.

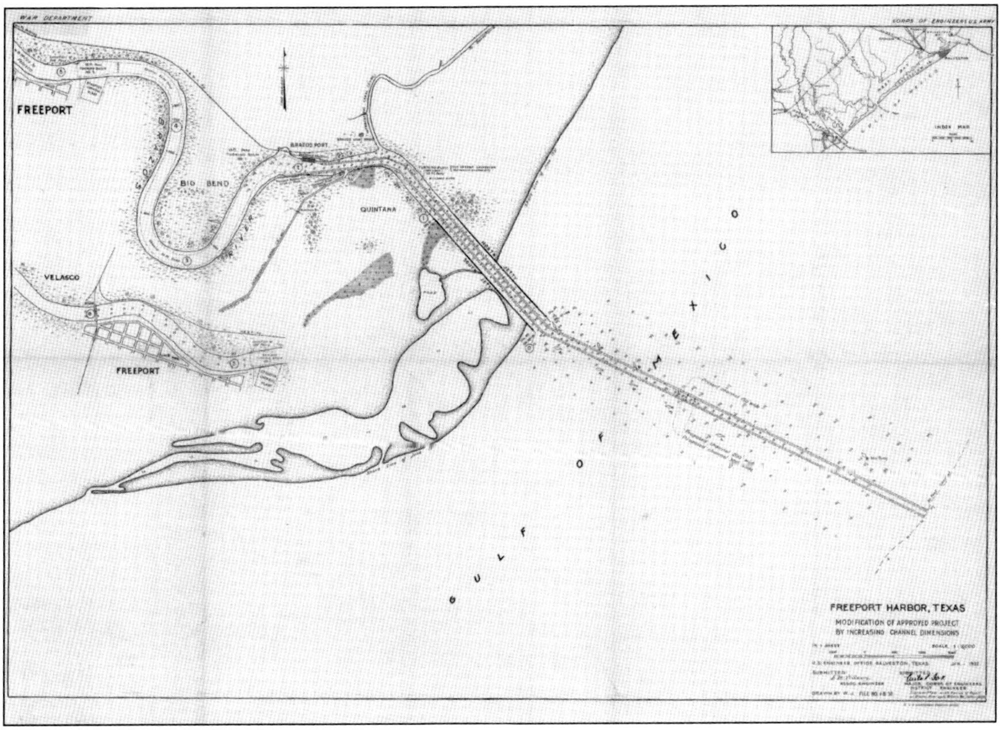


The 1930s brought several advancements. In the above survey from 1932, a lighthouse stands at the end of the channel, the Brazos Port is marked, and some river bends have transformed into turning basins. Additionally, the channel is a steady 25 feet deep. Regular dredge maintenance occurs, and the Stauffer Chemical Plant neighbors a 25-foot turning basin that was once the "Old Fery" [*sic*]. In the lower survey from 1935, dredge markers appear around the original mouth, railroads and trails have arrived, and a concrete jetty has been installed—complete with buoys and lights. The survey also shows a sand beach in the place of the treacherous moving sandbar.

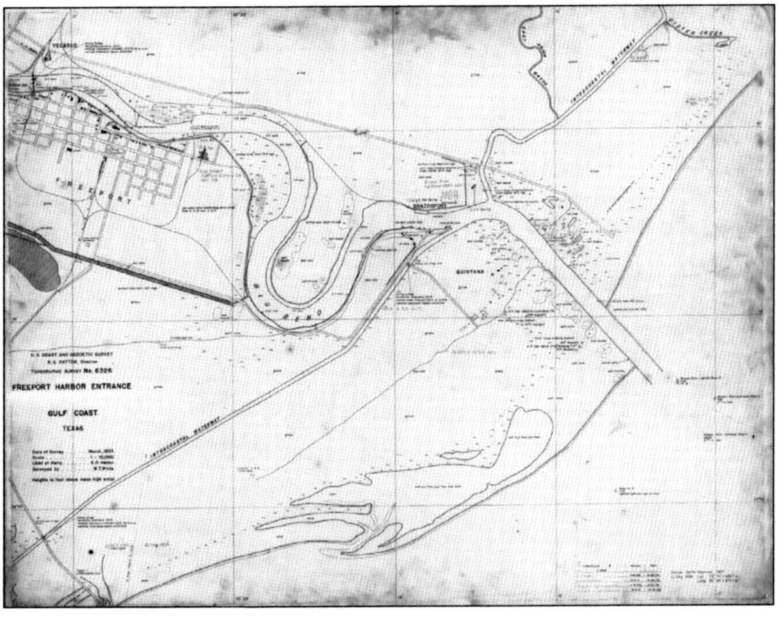

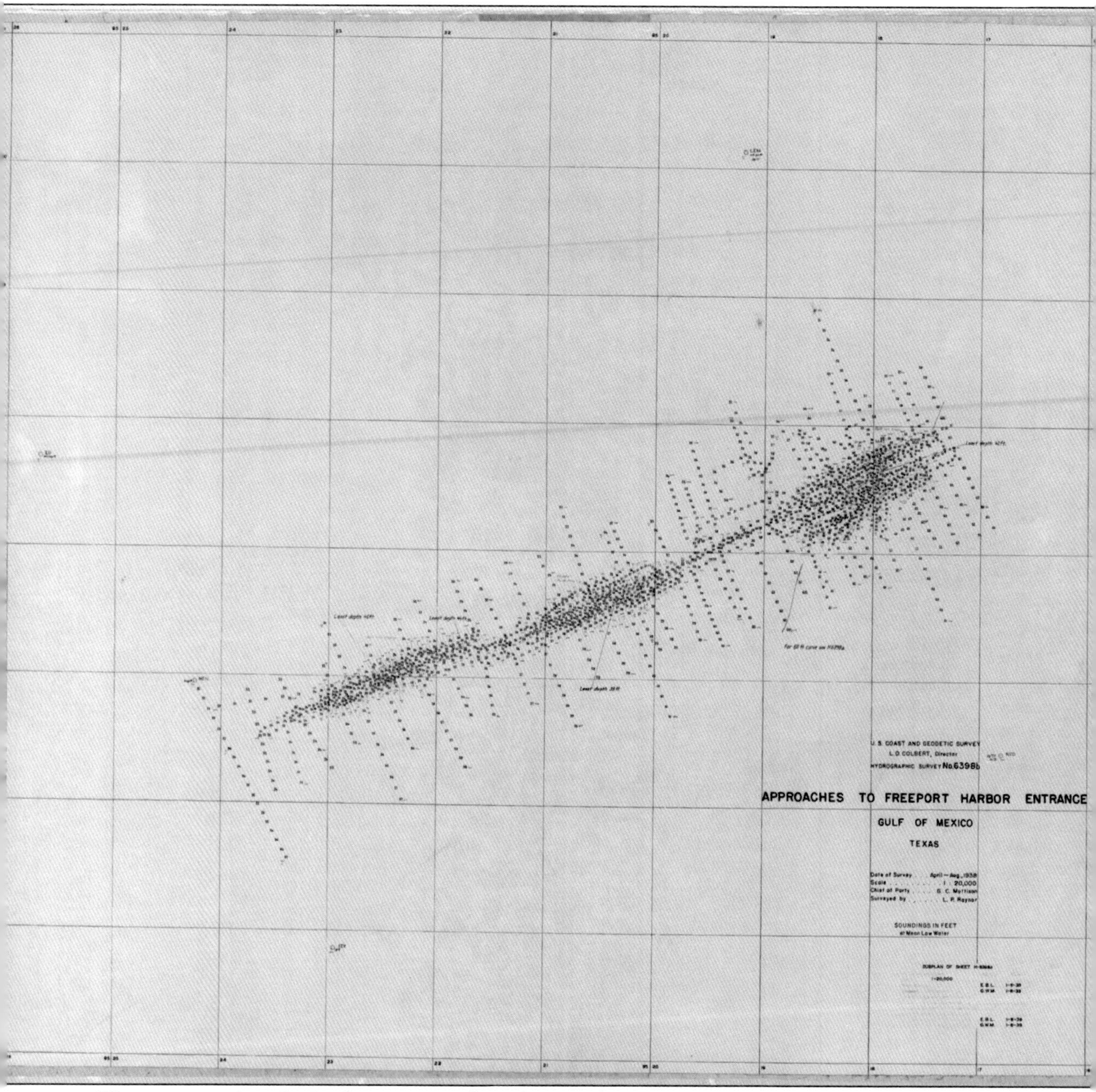


Three years after the harbor was reinforced, a geodetic study emerged on the depth of the gulf approaching the channel. It showed that water ranged from 42 feet to 60 feet in the gulf. This was the same year upstream river construction began on Possum Kingdom Dam. The state began steps to build 13 dams on the river and its tributaries. To manage this effort, the Brazos River Conservation and Reclamation District was created in 1929. Voters approved the district in Article XVI of the Texas Constitution.

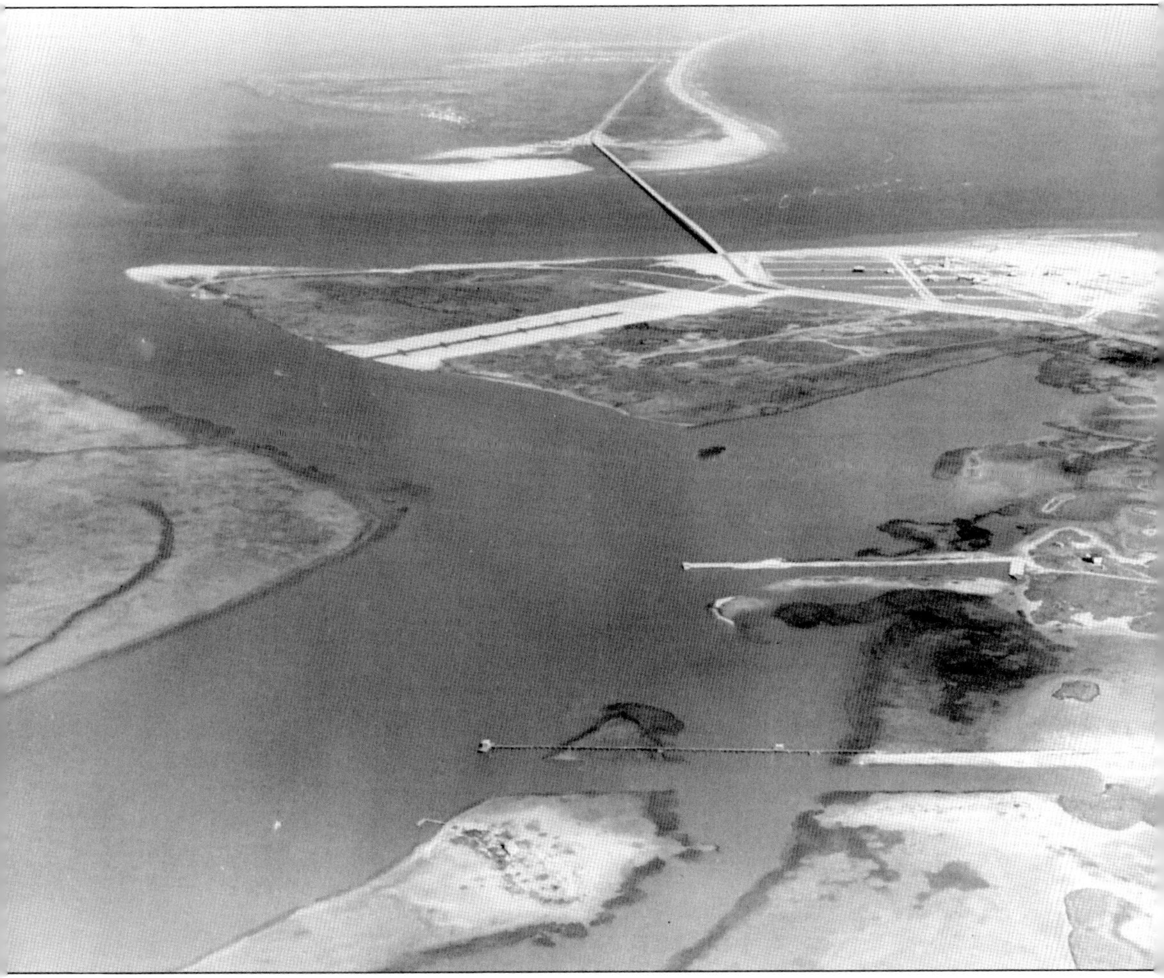

The federal government became involved in the development of the Brazos mouth because it wanted to expand the Intracoastal Waterway. Its chosen canal was active with steamboats, fishing schooners, small passenger craft, and other vessels, however, which meant that the government could not just begin improving it: it had to buy the canal. The Galveston and Brazos Navigation Company blocked these plans when the Army Corps of Engineers asked to buy the canal in 1887, and the company refused. Nine years later they reentered negotiations, and on February 11 1897, the company offered to sell the canal for $50,000. Congress authorized a payment of $30,000, which the company accepted in December 1902. In this photograph, the canal is shown at the San Luis Pass.

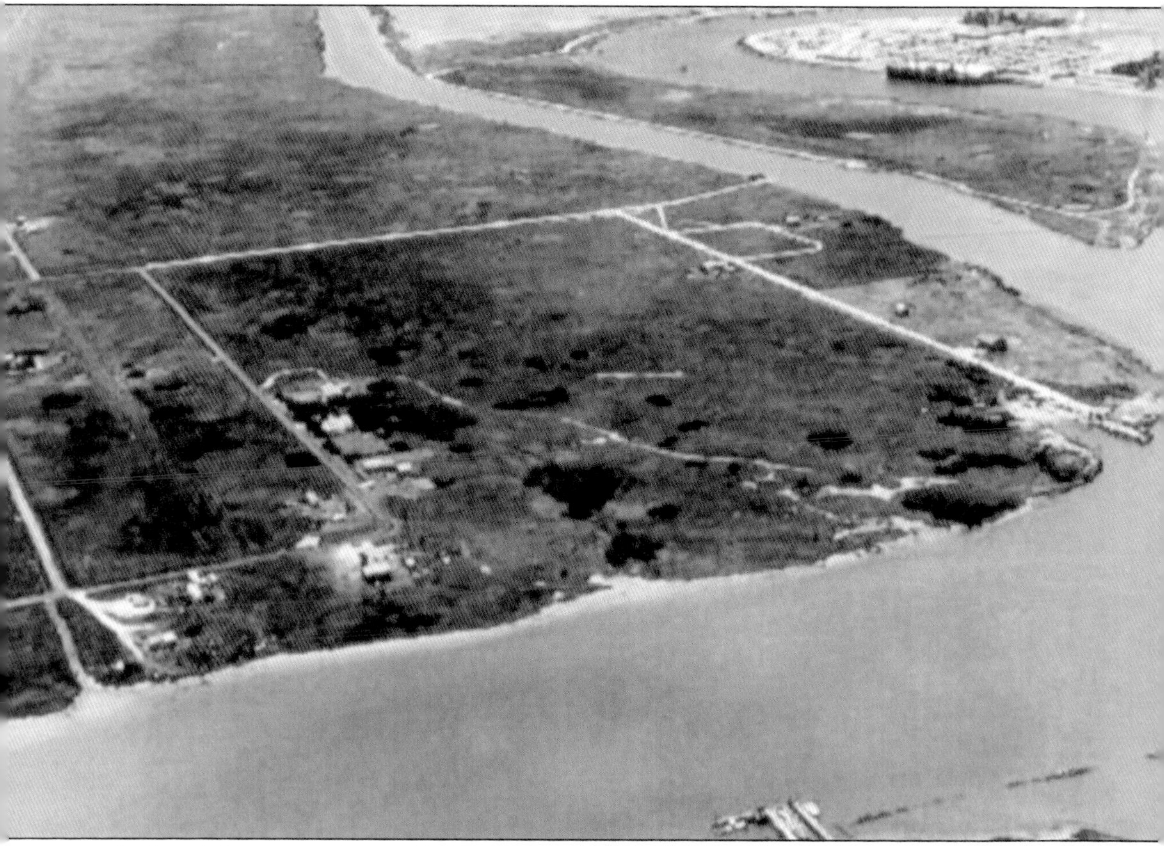

Within 100 years of the establishment of Austin's Colony, man had tamed the lower Brazos River. Local, regional, and national canals allowed man to manage its waters for economic and agricultural prosperity. The Brazos found a new outlet, and the original mouth became protected. All of this allowed for the development of a major coastal port. The Army Corps of Engineers gradually enlarged the channel, while the Gulf Coast Water Authority managed the major canal system, and the Brazos River Authority used a system of locks, lakes, and dams to control the areas upstream. The entire system would prove a marvel of civil engineering. The canal and both mouths of the Brazos River are visible in this image.

# BIBLIOGRAPHY

Alperin, Lynn M. *Custodians of the Coast—History of the United States Army Engineers at Galveston*. Galveston District: US Army Corps of Engineers, 1977.

Atchison, Topeka & Santa Fe Railway Co. *Rice Raising in Coast Country of Texas*. Chicago, IL: Rogers & Smith Co. Printers, 1902.

Block, William T. Jr. www.wtblock.com.

Gulf Coast Water Authority. www.gulfcoastwaterauthority.com.

Lumpkin, George E. "Economic Development of the Coastal Prairies." Thesis. North Texas State College, 1951.

Osborn, William S. "A History of the Cane Belt Branch of the Gulf, Colorado & Santa Fe Railway Company." *Southwestern Historical Quarterly 101*. (1998): 302–319.

*The Portal to Texas History*. The University of North Texas. www.texashistory.unt.edu.

*Principal Commodities Moving Through the Port of Texas City During Calendar Year 1921*. Texas City, TX: Texas City Terminal Railway Company, 1921.

Reagan, J.H., Z.T. Fulmore, C.W. Raines, George P. Garrison, and Mrs. Bride Neill Taylor. *The Quarterly of the Texas State Historical Association*. Austin TX: Texas State Historical Association, 1903.

Taylor, Thomas U. *Irrigation Systems of Texas*. Washington, DC: Government Printing Office, 1902.

*Texas Beyond History: The Virtual Museum of Texas' Cultural Heritage*. The University of Texas at Austin. www.texasbeyondhistory.net.

Texas State Historical Association. www.tshaonline.org.

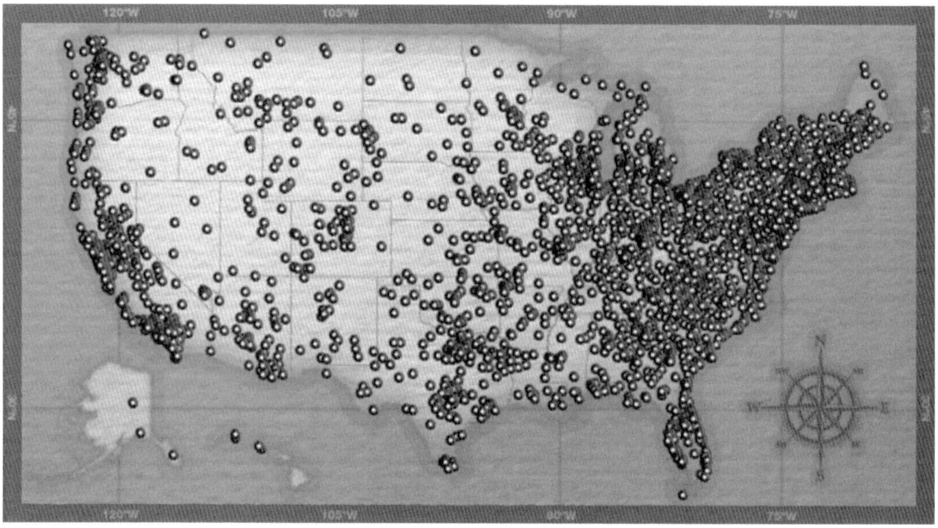